Surfacing

Yvette Abrahams . Gabeba Baderoon
Barbara Boswell . Panashe Chigumadzi
gertrude fester-wicomb . Pumla Dineo Gqola
Mary Hames . jackï job . Desiree Lewis
Ingrid Masondo . Zethu Matebeni
Patricia McFadden . Sisonke Msimang
Danai S. Mupotsa . Grace A. Musila
Leigh-Ann Naidoo . Yewande Omotoso
Fatima Meedat . Sa'diyya Shaikh
Zukiswa Wanner . Zoë Wicomb
Makhosazana Xaba

Surfacing

On Being Black and
Feminist in South Africa

EDITED BY
DESIREE LEWIS AND GABEBA BADEROON

WITS UNIVERSITY PRESS

Published in South Africa by:
Wits University Press
1 Jan Smuts Avenue
Johannesburg 2001

www.witspress.co.za

First published 2021

http://dx.doi.org.10.18772/22021046093

978-1-77614-609-3 (Paperback)
978-1-77614-613-0 (Hardback)
978-1-77614-610-9 (Web PDF)
978-1-77614-611-6 (EPUB)

The editors thank the College of Liberal Arts and the Department of Women's, Gender and Sexuality Studies at Pennsylvania State University for financial support of this book.

Project managers: Roshan Cader and Lisa Compton
Copyeditor: Efemia Chela
Editorial advisor: Helen Moffett
Proofreader: Lisa Compton
Indexer: Elaine Williams
Cover and page design: Hybrid Creative
Typeset in 11.5 point Crimson

To our teachers and our students,
and in memory of Elaine Salo

Contents

1. Unmaking

2. Positioning

3. Remaking

Editorial Note

Surfacing: On Being Black and Feminist in South Africa features the usage of Black, White and Coloured with upper-case initial letters in some chapters. This reflects the political choices of the authors in whose chapters they feature. In other chapters, black, white and coloured remain lower case, a style choice adopted by Wits University Press. Similarly, some chapters feature words and concepts from languages and histories outside of the English language. Translations and explanations appear for these words and phrases where absolutely necessary, with the respective authors' permission. In other chapters, we have respected authors' political preferences not to translate indigenous African language words and phrases.

Being Black and Feminist

Desiree Lewis and Gabeba Baderoon

surface (*n, v, adj*)
noun
outside, covering, skin, face
verb
rise, arise, come up, come to the surface, reappear, materialise, come
to light
adjective
outer, outside, apparent.[1]

Journeys through identities and knowledge-making

'Surfacing', especially in this book, has many meanings. In the most immediate sense, it may mean that those who have not spoken in public spaces now do. But black South African feminists have always spoken – through action, creativity and words. Many came to prominence during the anti-apartheid struggle in the 1970s, but others were visible before then. Several constellations of black feminist South African writing flourished in different regions and cultural forms. The significance of these constellations, as well as iconic figures such as Sara Baartman, Winnie Mandela and Miriam Tlali, has been severely neglected in the archiving of South African cultural and political traditions.

This book starts to address these omissions. It acknowledges the depth of a body of black feminist thought while also recognising the limitations of surveying the terrain. No collection is definitive. Nor can it be representative of a given topic or of a single group: there are always fractures, omissions and silences. Bringing together *this* group of black women writers conveys some of the key connections and dialogues among perspectives and voices that continue to be sidelined in publishing, scholarship and public debates in South Africa.

What *kind* of knowledge matters is linked to the question: *Whose* knowledge matters? The rapid rise of identity politics has been important to democratic struggles from the late twentieth century to the present. As the collection shows, the personal essay is well suited to the standpoint knowledge of subjects who have been silenced, stereotyped and politically subjugated. Globally, the essay form has been deftly crafted by black feminists including Audre Lorde, bell hooks, Michele Faith Wallace and, in Southern Africa, Zoë Wicomb, Bessie Head and Patricia McFadden. As storytellers, scholars and poets, these writers have demonstrated that big ideas need not be anchored in what are conventionally seen as 'big forms' – such as the academic article. Concision, wit, poetic force and autobiographical storytelling in the personal essay can carry enormous weight. As the poet and academic Danai S. Mupotsa illuminates, potent essay writing is the product of dense thought, autobiographical reflection and forms stretched to their creative limits.

The voices gathered specifically for this collection build on a literary legacy of feminist forerunners who have inspired their distinctive ideological and creative views. It is sometimes assumed that essays and writing from socially marginalised standpoints can generate only knowledge that speaks to the experiences of these groups. Black feminist writer Patricia Hill Collins contests this. She argues that 'seeing from below' can generate a new *non*-post-Enlightenment and post-colonial understanding of 'being human'.[2] Ideas derived from the European Age of Reason remain central to dominant notions of the 'human' even today. The explicit exclusion of Africans from such conceptions was used to rationalise slavery and colonialism, so the limitations of these ideas are particularly visible 'from below'. Those who are positioned at the margins see the world differently. They can intervene at distinct moments and from specific perspectives to offer understanding and insight that speak not only about and to – but beyond – their own locations.

Whether this knowledge is respected or taken up in the public domain is another matter. The crucial point is that this knowledge is generative and not only reactive. It does not only counter racist and patriarchal world views; it envisions new ways of being human and is therefore relevant to all. In other words, it produces future possible worlds. In one of her affirmations of commitment to imagining worlds beyond the realities of oppression, Bessie Head, whose contribution to black feminist literature was acknowledged only after her death in 1984, wrote:

> We learn bitterly, every day, the details of oppression and exploitation so that a writer automatically feels pressured into taking a political stand of some kind or identifying with a camp. It was important to my development to choose a broader platform for my work.[3]

During the 1980s, comments such as these made Head vulnerable to the charge of being apolitical. Yet her assertion constitutes a compelling call in the context of post-apartheid and post-millennial politics. At a time when political confidence in *primarily* classed, or *only* racial, or *pre-eminently* feminist transformation is being questioned by attention to complex identity politics and intersecting forms of subordination, Head's words remain powerful. They echo the themes of many essays in this volume by conveying a globally resonant desire for a vision of a just world.

Categories

Blackness in this anthology is conceptualised in line with Stuart Hall's emphasis on *identification*, rather than the state or condition of 'having identities': that is, a dynamic recognition of oneself in the range of possibilities called blackness.[4] The present continuous signalled in being black does not imply a fixed identity. Instead, it gestures towards the provisional standpoints and strategic locations that shape writers' perspectives on freedom, power and justice without essentialising, homogenising or hardening ways of seeing.

The need to avoid fixing black feminist ways of seeing becomes clear when we acknowledge the global and regional diversity of black feminisms. Black feminism has accrued meanings that are both wide-ranging and very particular. The histories and the breadth of the category, alongside its many applications, warrant an exploration of terms and the parameters of this anthology. As discussed in the next section, black feminism in the global imaginary is often synonymous with African-American feminist thought. Black and African diasporic writings are usually understood to be writings by those of African descent around the world, but not *within* Africa. In contrast, Carole Boyce-Davies's and Margaret Busby's anthologising work has been crucial in archiving legacies of writing across geographical borders that speak to connected experiences which are simultaneously raced and gendered, and also rooted in a sense of African ancestry. During the 1990s, Boyce-Davies's *Black Women's Diasporas* and Busby's *Daughters of Africa* offered crucial resources to a generation of South African literary critics who would shape the post-apartheid critical landscape.

In many contemporary cultural, political and academic contexts, however, globally resonant meanings of black and African diasporic feminism tend to marginalise South African and African traditions. This is not the result of deliberate exclusion by writers, editors or publishers, but an effect of the dominance of resources and networks at the metropolis. A strong case can therefore be made to foreground feminist knowledge produced on the continent *in conversation with, in response to, and as part of* a broader conceptualisation of black feminism than what is currently known. And since trends in Africa are so diverse, it is important to disaggregate the regional or national trends that constitute the varied body of scholarship and writing in and from Africa.

Apart from the subordination of black South African feminism to African-American and continental feminism, the meaning of blackness in South Africa is itself contested and fractured. Apartheid's compartmentalising of ethnic, religious and mixed-race groups has had a powerful impact on how groups continue to identify themselves. In earlier waves of anti-racist protest against apartheid in the 1960s and 1970s, many radical students, activists and writers refused this divisiveness and assertively embraced the label black as a unifying political identity. This was a response both to the racist designation of being 'non-white', and to the destructive partitions created by apartheid. Arguing in opposition to the nationalist ideology of the time, Steve Biko advocated for a philosophy of blackness constituted by consciousness – not skin colour. To *choose* to be black rather than non-white was an act of political resistance to the divisions of apartheid.

Paradoxically, post-apartheid preoccupations with recalling lost identities have led many younger coloured and Indian commentators to feel unheard, unseen and unrecognised in a transformative South Africa. In her work on race and specifically on coloured identity, sociologist Zimitri Erasmus holds the position that for some scholars, activists and academics, identifying as coloured in the post-apartheid period is integral to assertive self-naming. Amid this vigorous debate, the editors of *Surfacing* seek to reactivate the sense of political blackness associated with Black Consciousness. The return to political blackness gained currency with the rise of the #FeesMustFall and #RhodesMustFall movements since 2015, a period of concerted activism around identity politics and feminism. This period has seen calls to decolonise education, interrogate the trappings of post-apartheid democracy, and critique rainbow nation myth-making and its obsession with reclaiming cultural difference.

The embrace of political blackness, especially in younger feminist politics embedded in these movements, has also sparked an interest in African feminism: since 2015, many conferences, blog posts and book titles reveal a welcoming of this form of feminism. This has been driven by the need to connect racial politics to reclamations of canons and knowledge erased by hegemonic metropolitan traditions in South Africa. The work of the African Gender Institute at the University of Cape Town started some of this work in the early 1990s. But the widespread revival of African feminism in the country has been a response to recent educational, cultural and intellectual struggles: the call for decolonisation. The term's current broad appeal accommodates numerous meanings, some of which jostle uneasily against one another. An array of popular magazine pieces, digitally circulated information and images, and commercialised ideas that link African feminism to notions of glamour and success reveals how ambiguously the category has gained currency. We are alert to the impulse to revitalise the term, and the political and psycho-existential needs that drive it. But in our efforts here, we try to avoid the urge to simplify, essentialise, homogenise or limit the difference that the category African feminism offers to promote.

Contexts

Our methodology for sourcing contributions to this volume has been informed not by any narrow understanding of writers' formal citizenship or national origin, but by a more encompassing understanding of citizenship as participation: participation in dialogues about the confluence of power relations in South Africa's past, present and future. These include questions about how knowledges in South Africa have been hierarchically positioned in terms of gendered, colonial and global dynamics. By including both writers who embody biographical mobility and those whose work has been shaped by such mobility, *Surfacing* thus expands conceptions of what constitutes a national corpus of writing. These contributions involve the local context but also contain expansive and original responses to the challenge of crafting nationally resonant responses to racialised, gendered and authoritarian ways of seeing and being.

Such alertness to authority makes it clear that the collection's writers have attended to multiple and shifting relations of dominance. Intersectionality, a buzzword in recent debates about feminism, has fuelled an industry of research – often driven by white academics. This is because the term has been understood not so much as an attentiveness to power, but as engaging with a confluence of identities. A deeper understanding of intersectionality is at work in *Surfacing*. In the essays of many of its writers, the term is better conceptualised with reference to Jasbir Puar's explanation of assemblage. Assemblage provides a valuable strategy for understanding intersecting power relations and systems that constantly shift, proliferate and cohere, either to recuperate or contest varying forms of injustice and oppression.[5] Assemblage avoids this reification, yet responds to the need for theoretical alternatives. Anna Bogic contends: 'In an age of advanced capitalist globalization, the functioning logic of the world we live in today is more about folds than structures . . . In such a nondialectical and multilocal world, we are left with an increasingly difficult task of mapping sites of power.'[6]

The 'multivocality' and challenge of 'mapping sites of power' that Bogic identifies are traced in many of *Surfacing*'s essays. And the daring and resolve of forerunners who have sought justice by confronting interconnected power relations have inspired many of the book's contributors. Many black feminists transcended permitted political boundaries of resistance by insisting on the salience of gender and, by doing so, redefined radical politics.

Illustrating the multivocality in this volume, Makhosazana Xaba's chapter shows how a generation of women, born in the early 1900s, actively responded to the simultaneous operation of racial, colonial and gender discourses while working to educate young women to challenge oppressive discourses and power relations. Exploring enmeshed power relations in the second half of the twentieth century, Mary Hames uncovers the extent to which South African anti-apartheid feminists resisted interlinked forms of injustice. Reflecting on her development as a black feminist teacher in the 1970s, a time when the pre-eminence of race in anti-apartheid struggles drowned out attention to gendered ones, Hames recalls how women confronted violence against women within the anti-apartheid struggle perpetrated by certain male activists. This demonstrates that intersectionality, although not named as such, was being theorised by black South African women many years before the coining of this term by Kimberlé Crenshaw and its popularisation within a metropolitan black feminist tradition. Like other contributors, Hames reveals that the preoccupation with black women's perspectives and voices – within contexts of decolonisation and anti-racism – has a long history.

Black feminisms and South Africa

A Google Scholar survey of black feminism yields the names of numerous North Americans, including Michele Wallace, Patricia Hill Collins, bell hooks, Audre Lorde and many others.

Ironically, two iconic black South African women have been the focal point of black feminist commentary around the world: Sara Baartman and Winnie Mandela. They have been repeatedly invoked in North American–based black feminist artwork, scholarship and fiction, yet few black Southern African writers have achieved this status of universal visibility. It is as though black South African women are worthy of being invoked as icons by other black feminists, but rarely – even within post-colonial feminist canons – granted positions of centrality as intellectuals themselves. They often appear as material for other feminists' analyses but have not been recognised for their own feminist writing. The same is not true about black feminist work from, for example, West Africa, and especially Nigeria. Nigerian scholars such as Oyeronke Oyewumi and Amina Mama, and writers such as Ama Ata Aidoo and Chimamanda Ngozi Adichie are often canonised as exemplars of black African feminist thought in diasporic anthologies.

There are multiple explanations for this. They include hegemonised legacies of feminist thought in the US, since even though black feminists may be marginalised in the North American academy, their work is of great consequence globally. In addition, a significant number of African intellectuals, particularly from West Africa, have made their home in North America and attained prominent positions in the academy there. The migration of academics and academic knowledge between West Africa and North America is, of course, an uncanny echo of the North Atlantic slave trade. For various reasons, there are stronger solidarities and alliances among networks in the United States and West Africa than among African-American and South African feminists.

Whatever the reasons, and they are undoubtedly numerous and complex, South African traditions of black feminist thought – as opposed to North American, West African or diasporic black feminist ones – have been neglected in scholarly and literary networks. The absence of a deep engagement with such thought is also true *in* South Africa, where work from or close to metropolitan centres is far more visible (and therefore held as more important) than work from regional margins.

This collection is an intervention into the global and national circuits of knowledge-making, debate and pedagogy that, until now, have obscured the dynamic forms of black feminist thought and practice in South Africa. The book starts with Sisonke Msimang, and Zoë Wicomb and Desiree Lewis exploring Southern Africa's most hyper-visible black women icons. Both figures have been subject to numerous interpretations and reinterpretations, and yoked to racist and colonial fantasies as well as to twenty-first-century reclamations. What do these reclamations and retellings mean? And why is Sara Baartman, like Winnie Mandela, so often cast as a symbolic figure who, in the words of a key character in Wicomb's novel *David's Story*, 'belongs to all of us'?

Many of *Surfacing*'s contributors acknowledge the legacies which have moved and inspired them. For example, Barbara Boswell identifies Miriam Tlali's response to masculinist Black Consciousness literary traditions in the 1970s, and highlights a trajectory of fiction and autobiography – including work by Sindiwe Magona, Emma Mashinini and Ellen Kuzwayo – that boldly confronted gendered identities and relations at a time when many urged the importance of a unified black protest. In her excavation of intersectionality, gertrude fester-wicomb highlights her location as a lesbian, radical black woman who is also a practising Christian. Drawing attention to the intensely personal struggles of gender non-conforming public figures from the 1980s, she conveys their beleaguered battles for dignity and recognition at a time when neither legislation nor public discourse addressed entanglements of identity on the basis of sexual orientation, gender non-conformity and race.

Growing up as a Jehovah's Witness in a working-class Cape Town suburb, jackï job learns how to 'be a lady' from chastening biblical narratives, but eventually finds the beginning of an approach beyond ecclesiastical tales in the 'body's sensibilities'. Fascinated by the codes she learns by watching people move, job longs for a language that can contain her secrets and make her 'more than just this body'. She finds such a language in dance, an art that enables her to avoid being 'in the eyes' (simply pleasing to others) and instead makes space for a 'lady that is not ashamed of her body'. Employing a similarly capacious vision, two Muslim feminists, Sa'diyya Shaikh and Fatima Seedat, reflect on distinctly South African experiences of political protest to deliberate on the gendering of divinity. Shaikh traces her path to religious and political growth in which women like her mother and her female teachers offered a potent counterpoint to the patriarchal weight of both Islamic and secular education. Her resonant account of anti-racist and feminist activism in a Muslim group places us at the centre of events that helped shaped local and global debates on gender and Islam. In her essay, Seedat fascinatingly observes during a protest march in Cape Town that even radical feminists struggle to invoke a God who is not masculine. To her, the inability to reimagine the gender of divinity is a striking blind spot in feminist consciousness, exemplifying the cost of the feminist neglect of religion. As with fester-wicomb and job, the reader is alerted in these essays to the centrality of religious *and* broader spiritual concerns in many feminists' articulations of justice, freedom and existential good.

This book is concerned not only with the inclusion of marginalised voices; it also focuses on their power. In her incisive critique of both masculine and racist biases in the publishing world, Zukiswa Wanner references Maya Angelou when she poses the rhetorical question: 'Do I make you uncomfortable?' Her account of her journey in the South African publishing industry, its efforts to pigeonhole her, and her efforts to subvert its institutions, while ultimately offering an alternative, is a study in the disruptive and creative impact of black feminist practice. 'To surface' in this anthology therefore entails what Yewande Omotoso evocatively describes as 'the creative endeavour itself. The employment of imagination, using the act of making to unmake the ways of sensing and thinking that are often at the root of so much of what doesn't work in our lives and societies.' *Surfacing* consequently upends set ways of doing things, sedimented ideas, and tyrannical orthodoxies that haunt both the left and the right on the political spectrum in South Africa.

The perspectives in this book are politically black and feminist. They are positioned as intersectional or complicated by multiple and shifting identities, but they also caution against aspirations to be equivalent to our ascribed embodied identities. Many contributors acknowledge how entangled our experiences and subject positions are, inviting readers to speculate about discovered subjectivities that result not from reclaiming identities, but from envisioning new ways of being human. This is an invitation to understand that, beyond our need to be recognised, heard and seen in worlds that marginalise us on the basis of officially ascribed identities, we often strive to picture freedoms beyond these predetermined identities.

Freedom, as Makhosazana Xaba, Patricia McFadden and Yvette Abrahams show, is expansive and multi-faceted. It is not only linked to our liberation from material and ideological subordination, but also embedded in our richly erotic, sensual and existential desires. Xaba recalls her mother's forthright language about the body, alongside her own transcendent wording about discovering bodily pleasures through masturbation. McFadden and Abrahams, as intellectuals who deal with labouring with the earth in their writing, draw on women's knowledge of farming and healing practices to generate alternative economies of belonging and community. Their cultivation of food and herbs harnesses both old and new technologies, and fosters relations of reciprocity and abundance with their neighbours and the earth.

Such practices also gesture towards our struggle to create unexpected solidarities – such as those that might be built when feminists find themselves adrift on an ocean and under attack by patriarchal imperialist forces. In her essay describing a peace mission to Palestine by transnational activists, Leigh-Ann Naidoo's image of a boat steered by feminists with the potential to forge what Chandra Mohanty calls bridges of solidarity that transcend borders is a deeply inspirational one.[7]

Further rewriting the meanings of difference and dissension among black women, Zethu Matebeni and Panashe Chigumadzi unveil the affective and psychological complexities that often propel seemingly unreasonable political responses. Matebeni's engaging memoir refutes the familiar account of family rejection of queer people and instead reveals the protagonist's relatives to be a source of loving and expansive meanings for the word 'lesbian'. The speaker encounters a rich and complex view of sexuality through her aunt's personal library. Her understanding is further deepened by her grandmother's stories about her time at boarding school, which teaches the speaker a name for female intimacy that cannot be found in a dictionary. When she is attacked and almost raped at university, it is her family's immense emotional and spiritual resources that help the speaker to heal. Chigumadzi recounts the silences she 'heard' when speaking to women in her family about the many losses of Zimbabwean history. To write about a past marked by war, forced removals and fractured families, Chigumadzi learns to discern her elders' 'militant' refusal to speak and therefore to 'hear [their] silence'.

Ways of speaking, seeing and hearing

How we hear, recognise and see is often determined by the genres and art forms we use. A binary world where linear and unemotional knowledge is ascendant privileges the power of the written and not spoken word. The tyranny of the written word must, as many decolonial, post-colonial and black feminists have argued, be dislodged as part of the process of freeing knowledge-making. This would allow fiction, artwork and other artistic forms to encourage us to listen and feel in new ways. Wicomb's allusion, in her conversation with Desiree Lewis, to 'a mode of narration that none of us have dreamt of' invites an expansiveness of vision and of form.

But what does it really mean when we say that art *speaks* in ways that words don't? The reader is taken on a creative journey with photographer and South African National Gallery (SANG) curator Ingrid Masondo. Her visual essay explicitly defies the categories that situate other essays. Masondo encourages us to participate in her own tour of some lesser-known black women's photography as potent encodings of feminist ways of knowing. Her reflective comments therefore open up a space for us to respect the artworks on their own terms, rather than to bind them to a heavy-handed critical interpretation that reveals more about the interpreter than about the artist or art. And so we are given some space to breathe, think and imagine.

In her 'playful letter' to the artist Gabrielle Goliath, Pumla Dineo Gqola prompts a similar process of yielding space for the reader's active sensory engagement. Gqola enables us to experience works like *Bouquet III* and *This Song Is For . . .* through the emotions, insights and physical sensations the works arouse for her. Standing with her before *Ek is 'n Kimberley Coloured*, we feel ourselves 'stretched in [our] own skin'. Goliath's *Faces of War* sparks an epiphany about women's exclusion that leaves Gqola breathless: 'We created a country in which large-scale experiences of violence by women under apartheid were cast aside in the definition of past, memory and nation.' Gqola's journey through Goliath's art gives us an opportunity (rare in a world of knowledge-making where readers are expected to prioritise rational understanding) to sense, gasp and cry. Meanwhile, in Grace A. Musila's superbly crafted narrative 'My Two Husbands', the protagonist learns from her grandparents, both living and dead, how to navigate the unexpected consequences of her educational achievements. The important lesson that women's ambition should not be limited by masculine fragility is conveyed through humour, memorable characters and an exquisitely unfolding plot that brings the story to a piercing conclusion.

Such intricate work illuminates the unsuspected complexities of the world, often exposing readers to interpretations of human, social and political experiences that many publishers neglect. It therefore matters profoundly how writing becomes accessible to broad audiences. The South African publishing world has tended to welcome poetry and fiction by black feminists much more than their prose. During the '80s and '90s, several collections of feminist poetry were published by presses such as Ravan Press and Ad Donker, and in magazines such as *New Coin*, *New Contrast* and *Staffrider*, while the late 1990s and start of the millennium saw a surge of autobiographical writings. In contrast to this focus on poetic and testimonial expression, there has been a dearth of published intellectual, polemical and philosophical thought by black South African feminists. Correcting this absence, as the collection begins to do, is beneficial not only to South African feminists; in fact, it offers to audiences the richness of voices in whose work new understandings about human experiences, social subjectivities, society and culture in South Africa surface.

We believe that this collection will not only expand readers' knowledge and understanding, but also lead to a writerly pleasure that refuses the usual binaries between, for example, knowledge and creativity or creation and deconstruction. We hope that it will generate ongoing critical thought about South African politics and culture both among feminists and a wider audience. Such thought would focus not only on what it means to challenge racialism and heteropatriarchy, but on what sorts of political and communicative freedoms are truly emancipating and democratic, and what a visionary understanding of liberation can encompass.

CHAPTER 1

Winnie Mandela and the Archive: Reflections on Feminist Biography

Sisonke Msimang

When I was in primary school and living in Nairobi, we lived next door to a girl called Aida. Aida was not her real name, but all these years later I feel a feminist duty to protect her, given all that was said about her. This in many ways is the purpose of this story: to reflect on the duty of care feminists owe the women who populate the archive – and those who may yet enter.

Aida was older than I was. She was about 16 when I was eight. She lived with her father and that was it – just the two of them. I was in that phase of childhood in which certain older girls seemed impossibly glamorous. Aida was this sort of a half-grown girl who fascinated me – an almost-woman who still had the leisurely pursuits of a child.

Aida was Ethiopian, and she had large, exaggerated eyes that seemed exotic to me, but which are common on the streets of Addis Ababa. And she had a long and large and proud nose, which was always turned up. Her features were softened by her mouth, which was small and pouty, like that of a child. The thing about Aida was that everyone knew she had been pregnant, though no one was quite sure what had happened to the baby.

I didn't care, of course. The rumours didn't make a lot of sense to me, and what she gave me in time and attention far outweighed whatever it was that she had done to get pregnant and then unpregnant. So, I did what eight-year-olds do best. I followed her around without shame. After all, I was too young to be embarrassed by how much I longed to be like her.

Sometimes she would paint my nails and put lipstick on me. I always wiped it off before my mother got home from work, and if Bathsheba – the woman who looked after us – called me, I would move even more quickly. Bathsheba was under strict instructions to ensure Aida and I stayed apart. My mother hated me being in Aida's house. She hated the idea of me being in this girl's bedroom pretending to be older than I was, and 'getting influenced' by a girl whose father had so little control over her that she paraded the streets wearing make-up. My father hated lipstick, and my mother's instructions were a way of enforcing his will.

Every morning Aida would stand on the road and wait for the bus to take her to her school. It was a big pale-blue bus with the name of the college she went to written in large letters across its side. Everybody knew that the kids at that school were drug addicts and did nothing but talk back to their teachers and smoke cigarettes all day.

Aida would climb onto that bus (I once heard a neighbour call it a bus full of demons) in a short skirt or ripped jeans with her hair wild, and off the driver would go, taking them to some godforsaken place where learning was unlikely to happen. They had no uniform at that school because they were mimicking the American education system.

At the school I went to, the uniform was a dark-green dress that went just past the knee, matched with a blazer that was comically long. We also wore white socks and clunky black shoes better suited to England than to Nairobi, but they achieved the overall effect of making us look demure. Their ugliness reminded us that the purpose of our education was to teach us to read and write and obey. We were not in school to flaunt our personalities or to demonstrate our individuality. We were on a conveyor belt, part of the British education system, so none of us could reasonably expect to attend school with wild hair and kohl-lined eyes. That would throw off the system. No Aidas were allowed.

I grew up and we left Nairobi and I forgot all about Aida and her kindness and the baby she never had, and the distance my mother tried to put between us.

Much later, when I was in university, I dated a man – let's call him Deandre. Deandre and I broke up and made up a few times – in the way of dramatic university loves. In one of the periods when we were apart, one of his friends told Deandre that he and I had slept together. This was a lie. I had not slept with the friend. The accusation shocked me. Why would he lie? What had I done to make him think he could say something so profoundly untrue? So deep was my internalised misogyny that even in my outrage I blamed myself by asking what *I* had done to deserve the lie.

Deandre was not outraged on my behalf. He laughed it off and explained that sometimes men lied about women. He said that all men knew this, and their behaviour towards women took this into account. He explained that men 'never really knew the truth' about their partners and so his approach was, 'if you like her, ignore the stories; and if you don't, believe everything people say about her'.

Stories about women's fidelity, in other words, were designed as a test women could only win if men let them. The truth about the woman at the centre of a man's story was, in fact, incidental. What mattered were the objectives of the man telling the tale and his audience. If the tale was designed to pull down that woman, and it met a willing listenership, then she would be pulled down.

As I processed the fact that I had been lied about as part of a game I did not understand and had played no part in creating, I thought about Aida. It occurred to me that she might never have been pregnant. The innuendo about her supposed abortion was designed to signal the virtue of those who talked about her – in this case, the grown women who denounced her in order to demonstrate their own sexual restraint. My mother kept me away from her because of her own middle-class respectability. When they whispered about an aborted baby, they were really seeking to control Aida, to give weighty consequence to the wildness of her hair and the darkness of her eyes, the sexuality she refused to bridle. Aida was a prop, a mere backdrop against which they could project their own morality.

For weeks after Deandre told me about the lie, I fretted about Aida. Our stories suddenly felt intertwined. The more I thought about it, the more obvious it became that it didn't matter whether what had been whispered about Aida was true or not; what mattered was that it had stuck – that it had defined her. After all these years, I was still captivated by the story of Aida's unwanted, never-born baby.

The story about Aida's sins was so powerful that I could remember Aida's short skirts and skinny legs. What I had forgotten was how her hands felt holding mine as she painted my little fingernails. She was kind enough to let a little girl follow her around. She was generous enough to spray her perfume on the inside of my wrists and to giggle with me, but I had buried these acts of generosity and connection.

In my mind, Aida had stopped being a girl on the cusp of womanhood. Instead, she had become a story. She was a ghost figure who had slipped through my life. Even though I had adored her at the time, I had no proper memories of her. Over time I had become ashamed of her, and this shame had corroded my memories of her and turned her into a caricature. All I could remember now was a bad girl with wild hair and hollow eyes.

This is what women lose when we let sexist narratives strangle our real-life stories, and when we let ideas about who women should be take over the complex facts of who flesh-and-bone women really are.

By the time I wrote *The Resurrection of Winnie Mandela*, I had been thinking about this issue for some time. Aida had represented freedom to me. As a child I was drawn to her clear spirit of independence, but I was also taught to be suspicious of her. She had been an early warning, a portent of what happens to girls who are too much in the world.

The task I faced in writing about the incomparable Winnie Mandela was not unlike the task I faced in reframing Aida in my own memory. Just as I had to ask questions about why it mattered whether Aida had been pregnant, and what purpose that information served, I also knew that I had to ask questions about the political agendas that were served by the whispers that trailed Winnie Mandela. My role as a biographer would be to extract her truths from the racist and sexist narratives that had a stranglehold on her legacy.

Because sexism is so central to how the world is interpreted, the 'facts' about Winnie Mandela's life and times were often misrepresented or weaponised against her. I saw myself as part of a movement of people who wanted to ensure that Winnie Mandela could be understood on feminist terms. This did not necessarily mean celebrating her. As Shireen Hassim has demonstrated in her academic treatment of Winnie Mandela, it is entirely possible to examine the liberation fighter in feminist terms and not celebrate her actions or legacy.[1]

It is important then to understand that my interest in reframing Winnie Mandela was never about 'cleaning up' her image or revising facts. It was about recognising that the facts about her required contextualisation.

Having assumed the mantle not simply of biographer but feminist biographer, I knew that protecting Winnie Mandela's privacy would be paramount. It would be both an act of respect and a marker to those who will continue to study her in the future. I was too young to defend Aida – even though I knew she was being maligned. As a grown woman, who holds the power of the pen, I was perfectly positioned to do for Winnie Mandela what the anti-apartheid movement had done and continues to do for many of its male heroes. Indeed what they had done for Nelson Mandela himself, which was to protect his sexual privacy and uphold his personal dignity.

When Winnie Mandela died and the media began to replay the sexual insinuations of the past, those that had dogged her from the moment her famous husband was jailed, and her beautiful face began to appear in the media, my feminist instincts kicked in.

I was not in the least bit interested in determining whether or not she had sexual relationships while her husband was in jail, but I was deeply invested in ensuring that other people's ruminations about these matters did not constitute legitimate grounds for scholarship and writing about her. As an act of feminist historical retrieval, I wanted to protect her from this line of questioning, and also ensure that other women were not subjected to these sorts of discussions and debates.

Given the gendered double standard, it seemed both irrelevant and deeply damaging to subject her history and life to these questions. Politically prominent men simply aren't judged by their actions in the bedroom, and even when they are, they are seldom demonised in the way Winnie Mandela was and continues to be.

In the aftermath of her death, I read articles steeped in vitriol and innuendo. Mondli Makhanya, editor of *City Press*, recycled an old, mean and unsourced story in which Winnie was nowhere to be found the night it was announced that Nelson Mandela was to be released. She was apparently drunk and/or with a lover. The story had no sources, but Makhanya insisted on using it in an article he penned upon hearing of her death. The narrative is apocryphal – the errant wife out with her lover when the hero returns from battle.[2]

Meanwhile Thabo Mbeki did an interview on television on the very day she died. In it, the former South African president insisted that Winnie Mandela should not be singled out for celebration. He was eager to remind the public that she was 'part of a collective that fought against apartheid and not an individual'. He also reminded the nation that she had defied the leadership of the ANC in the 1980s when she refused to disband the Mandela Football Club.[3]

When Nelson Mandela died, no one spoke ill of the fact that he had defied the ANC by beginning the process of negotiating the end of white minority rule in secret. He did not have a mandate from his comrades. The man widely seen as the father of the modern ANC deliberately defied ANC policy and acted as an individual rather than as part of a collective.

In the wake of Winnie Mandela's death, the international press were no better than the South African media and key players within the ruling party. A widely shared headline published in the *Sydney Morning Herald* screamed, '"Mother" then "Mugger" of the nation'.[4]

In death, as in life, Winnie was gossiped about and derided. She could not escape the narrative that had dominated her life. The story that trailed her was simple and stark. It told of a young woman who had not existed before she met Nelson Mandela. In this story Winnie was invented as an adjunct to her husband. She was a sweet modest wife who was turned into an adulterous monster – either by the apartheid regime or by her own innate womanly weaknesses.

She had withstood these sorts of insults while she was alive, and had alternated between seeming either enraged by what was said about her or impervious to the slurs. Now that she was gone, many people seemed to take pleasure in her death. In some quarters on social media, there was a carnivalesque atmosphere in the weeks following her death. It had the feel of the scene in the film *The Wizard of Oz* where the Munchkins sing, 'Ding dong the witch is dead!'

Given all of this – the glee and the innuendo and the gossip and, of course, the very real ways in which Winnie Mandela was transgressive and participated in reckless violence – I regarded the project of writing about her with some trepidation. All biographers must reckon with the ghosts of their subjects. This ghost, I worried, might not let me rest.

In the end, the ghost of Winnie Mandela was not my biggest hurdle. I had to overcome my own ideas of what biography was in order to undertake the project of writing about her life in ways that were not typical of the genre. By its very nature, biography focuses on 'important people'. Feminism, on the other hand, is fundamentally concerned with challenging the notion of importance. Feminists examine the lives of those who have been overlooked and pushed aside and ignored – most often, women – and so feminists are often wary of claims of importance as a very principle. As Barbara Caine suggests, 'biography is . . . antithetical to some of the basic aims and approaches of women's history – and the avenue that seems most helpful for those seeking to understand the actual historical experiences of women in all their complexity'.[5]

In the 1970s, Gerda Lerner, whose work on feminist history gave birth to women's studies programmes across America, described the work of feminist biography as having several functions. On the one hand, she argued feminists needed to write 'compensatory history'. They had to undertake the work of writing about 'exceptional women, like queens, the wives of presidents, regents . . .' Feminist compensatory history would examine the lives of women who were powerful because of their proximity to male power.

Compensatory history was seen as a necessary corrective to the erasure of women because, in certain eras in all societies, the recorded histories of women were so scant. Lerner and other feminists writing in this era recognised that compensatory histories would do little to reshape how history as a discipline was written because the women centred in these histories were only important because of their access to certain kinds of elite men. Still, the work of writing wives, female lovers and relatives back into the historical record would prevent women from vanishing altogether, and so compensatory histories were seen as necessary first steps on the road to gendering history.

The next step was to fill the canon with 'contribution history'. This type of work focused on the stories of women who had managed to make significant strides in a man's world. In other words, they had been exceptional in their time by doing well in spheres considered to be feminine. For example, white women missionaries who arrived in South Africa in the mid-1800s excelled by *not* challenging the gender hierarchy. Rather, they did exceedingly well in areas where women were expected to thrive, and their stories are documented as a result. They contributed to male history.[6]

For Lerner – and for many feminist biographers who followed in her path in the 1970s and 1980s – writing about women's lives became especially interesting when it looked at how women lived *'on their own terms'* – what was soon termed 'recovery history'.[7]

On the spectrum of feminist life writing, the project I sought to undertake in respect of Winnie Mandela did not fall neatly into any of these categories. One cannot merely write about Winnie in terms of compensatory history, even though she was exceptional in many ways, and was of course linked to an important man.

It is also impossible to categorise Winnie Mandela as someone who contributed to history by playing by the rules and functioning on men's terms. Yet Winnie had never suffered historical neglect. She was not a personality whose memory needed to be recovered from the ruins of history and placed in the archives. Nor was Winnie ever written out of history or erased, and so in that sense there was little to be done by way of classic recovery – the way one might for a little-known figure.

Instead, she was demonised. She was not without fault, of course, but during her lifetime Winnie Mandela occupied the same position as a witch or a jezebel. She was present, but her story was hijacked. She was spoken about largely by men, often in ways that sought to diminish her power and impugn her character. Given all of this, the project I needed to undertake was clear, and I felt it was important to be explicit about my agenda. As I stated in the introduction of the book, 'I will not pretend otherwise, I am interested in redeeming Winnie Mandela.'

However, I was not interested in hagiography. Unmoderated adulation is unhealthy, undemocratic and anti-feminist. I did not want to suspend my critical faculties and rewrite history. It serves nobody to deny or downplay Winnie Mandela's violence. But I did not want to pretend that I had no agenda. Like most feminists, I am wary of claims of objectivity; and so I was undertaking the project of writing about Winnie Mandela because I could see how her story would be mangled by the historical archives.

Though no subject of examination is worthy of uncritical adulation, I was acutely aware that part of my task was to address the public vitriol to which Winnie Mandela had been subjected during her life and in the immediate aftermath of her death. In response, I adopted a deliberate and contrarian posture of admiration in my writing. This posture was not mere gesture – I certainly do admire her accomplishments. Still, the overall stance was a political signal designed to put across the message that the work of recovering Winnie's story required generosity and care. It required that her biographer acknowledge and respect her humanity.

Because I wanted to look at her gendered meaning – to see her in representative and symbolic terms rather than in standard or even strictly biographical terms – I resisted writing her story in a standard chronological manner. And yet it was apparent that providing a sense of the way her life unfolded, especially before she met Nelson Mandela, would be crucial to demonstrating that, while she was influenced by him, she was not made by him.

It was evident from the nature of the public debate that many people simply had no idea where she came from, and what had influenced her thinking and politics. In order to take her out from the shadow of her husband, to show that she had been a woman who lived on her own terms, it was critical to tell the story of her life in a way that indicated how she had come to choose Mandela as an ideological and intellectual companion; as a husband, as well as a comrade, on equal footing.

I wanted to understand how she had navigated power, even as she had operated within constraints determined by others. I wanted to return her to the terrain of the political – to insist she had not been mad or deranged or mentally unstable – that like men in the freedom struggle, she had operated on the basis of logical calculations about power.

Winnie Mandela needed to be recast as a rational being, as a woman who loved politics and fought for her country, rather than someone who had unravelled and became evil. Homing in on her political convictions, as well as her deep involvement in the anti-apartheid struggle, made it possible to view her violence in context.

As I wrote about her conduct in the 1980s, I wanted to make it clear that at a tactical level she made decisions that were brutal; that where others chose non-violence, Winnie Mandela embraced violence. Her targets were often children and young people. In this, she was not alone. This cannot be undone or diminished. Yet to take these actions and place them outside the context of the struggle for freedom, to say that she went rogue and was acting on her own, is to strip her of her sanity – to render her a madwoman. This depiction does Winnie Mandela a disservice, but it is also bad for the freedom struggle more broadly. I wanted to remind her detractors that she – and her comrades – were responding to and operating within a grand structure that was organised around the annihilation of the human spirit.

I made a deliberate choice, then, to write about her with an intimacy and a familiarity that is uncommon. Using the second person and speaking directly to her, I wanted to render her part of us, rather than to cast her out. I did not want to stand above her with a voice of authorial credibility. I wanted to sit with her, to look in her eyes, to adopt different stances in relation to her, as women do, as African women do, within the context of our relationships.

In the text, I deliberately address her as Mam' Winnie at times, while at other points she is Winnie. I do this by taking a leaf out of

Nelson Mandela's book. I was moved when I read his letter to her in which he pledged to stop addressing her as his darling wife, and instead to call her Comrade Nomzamo until she was released from jail. Naming matters.[8]

I also wanted to draw a curtain around her private life, to afford her the respect she was never given when she was alive. This is because women's sexual lives are nobody's business but their own. Those who decided to publicise her private sexual matters took something from her, and it is the work of those of us who defend women's rights to restore the privacy of women. The work of feminist recovery involves accepting that women belong to nobody but themselves, and do not have to account to society for their sexual lives – whatever these lives may look like.

The last task of recovery involved addressing Winnie Mandela's victims. Writing about her with care and respect did not mean ignoring or denying the suffering of her victims. On the contrary, it meant honouring them. It meant naming them all. It meant scouring the archives and recalling the pain of their families. It meant reinserting them into the historical record. Too often, Winnie Mandela's story has centred on Stompie Seipei. The others – not just boys, but young women too – who swirled around the edges of the movement in those dangerous and difficult times tend to be forgotten or have become mere footnotes in Stompie and Winnie's stories.

Writing about Winnie Mandela forced me to ask questions about her tactics. Having placed her actions firmly within the context of war, there were still important questions to ask about whether she made the right choices, and about whether her brutality could have been avoided. There are questions I still have about whether her righteous anger at having been used as a sacrificial lamb by the ANC was not misdirected. I believe she ought to have been sorrier about the havoc she wreaked. She never seemed to be. In other words, she was a victim, yes, and she was most certainly also a perpetrator. In this way, she challenges our ideas about heroism and about women's relationship with violence.

Because the Truth and Reconciliation Commission (TRC) process targeted her even as it refused to hold senior white officials at the helm of the regime culpable, it is easy to side with Winnie Mandela and to suggest that she was a scapegoat. Indeed, the TRC process burnished her status as the ultimate radical. She became an anti-hero – a people's saviour whose flaws were significant, but whose grit and determination were admirable.

Winnie Mandela was and is difficult to erase. Because her embrace of street justice took such a dramatic form, it was impossible to worship her without equivocation. Perhaps, in the end, this is why it is so important that feminists recover as much of her story as memory and records will allow. Although the term 'complexity' is used as a euphemism when it comes to Winnie Mandela, her legacy *was* complex. The flat villainous story that exists about her is not.

During her life, Winnie – like Aida, like me, like too many women – knew what it meant to be whispered about, and to be the subject of rumour and innuendo. In writing about her, I wanted to ensure, in some small way, that I contributed to an archival record which expanded the notion of who she was – and, by proxy, who black women of her generation were.

In her book *Wayward Lives, Beautiful Experiments*, Saidiya Hartman writes: 'The wild idea that animates this book is that young black women were radical thinkers who tirelessly imagined other ways to live and never failed to consider how the world might be otherwise.'[9] I have found no better articulation than this of the spirit that guided me as I wrote about the life and times of Winnie Mandela.

CHAPTER 2

Representing Sara Baartman in the New Millennium

Zoë Wicomb interviewed by Desiree Lewis

In late February 2018, controversy erupted around Willie Bester's sculpture of Sara Baartman, located in the main library of the University of Cape Town. The statue had been clothed in a kanga and headscarf, but a storm of debate and media attention arose when a university librarian, a white man originally from the United States, removed these garments. Globally, but especially in South Africa, the figure of Sara Baartman continues to surface morbidly in frenzied efforts by various groups to define themselves. These efforts are often emphatic about the project of defending Sara and telling her 'true' story. But what does this mean? In the following exchange, Zoë Wicomb and Desiree Lewis deal critically with the 2018 enrobing and disrobing, and explore what it means to represent Sara Baartman.

Desiree: Reading revisionist work on Sara Baartman since the start of the millennium, I've been struck by two main trajectories: one is evident in scholarly work by Pamela Scully and Rachel Holmes. Their projects aim to 'set the record straight' by inserting Sara as an agential human being. I can see that their work sets out to transcend traditions that focus only on Sara Baartman's violation, traditions that dominate critical, artistic and scholarly work from the second half of the twentieth century. So their revisionist turn seems to involve refuting the determinist model of Baartman (only) as a victim of history and demonstrating that she made choices: deciding for herself to go to England, for example.

These are respected historians and biographers. Yet I've been struck by the patent fictionalising in their studies, as well as the naivety of their projects as acts of representation. In Pamela Scully and Clifton Crais's *Sara Baartman and the Hottentot Venus: A Ghost Story and a Biography*, for example, the *Bildungsroman* form credits Baartman with the power of personal growth, mobility, choices in relationships, and so on. Baartman's story is also told using narrative conventions and styles reminiscent to me at times of Charles Dickens, or more contemporary potboiler mysteries.

The other trend, often followed by those who claim a marginality similar to Baartman's, also fixates on telling her true story – yet refuses to acknowledge how pasts are always shaped by presents, how writers' and activists' retrospective sense-making inevitably colours storytelling about figures in the past.

To me, your novel *David's Story* refuses blunt post-millennial position-taking – both in avoiding the victim/agent binary *and* in not laying claim to 'the real story'. Yet the novel does seek to imagine Baartman. Zoë, what does this act of imagining mean for you as a novelist and as a critic of the kind of representation that assumes that this icon's life can and should be correctly told? Maybe another, blunter way of asking this is: what motivated you to write about Sara Baartman in a novel focusing on nationalist struggles? And were you conscious of what you definitely did not want to do, or of what forms of storytelling you wanted to avoid or challenge?

Zoë: Indecent to comment on one's work but let me see what I can do. Firstly, I don't think there's a 'correct' way of telling the Baartman story. When historians fictionalise, is it not because there are few reliable historical documents available to piece together a full, true story? It wouldn't surprise me if someone came up with an artefact or mode of narration that none of us have dreamt of, although it would be objectionable if the story and its events were perverted; in other words, there are elements of the story that are incontrovertibly true, and it would be unethical to tamper with those. I too am concerned about the idea of a woman who is poor, uneducated and living under the oppressive conditions of the Eastern Cape in the nineteenth century making *informed* choices for herself, hence my own cautious approach.

My David uses Baartman as a subterfuge. He resists telling the story of the woman activist Dulcie, and so covers up by telling the story of Baartman (I call her Saartjie, the affectionate name still commonly used in rural communities). In other words, Baartman can be seen as a ready-made cipher: her history – situated as it is in oppressive colonial history – lends itself to all kinds of meanings and manipulations, always available for metonymic displacement. It is more palatable for David to cite Baartman than to admit that a talented, black woman revolutionary like Dulcie is persecuted within her own misogynistic liberation struggle; besides, he can't be sure about the truth of Dulcie's situation – another parallel with Baartman. But Baartman's story in my text is deliberately not told in terms of narrative conventions, because I have no desire to add to the plethora of narratives; for me, there is nothing new to be said. Instead, David's account is *reported* by the narrator, without the novelistic detail that, according to her, he has deployed. Instead, she *lists* key elements, all in one sentence, using the deictic 'the' (a direct reference to that which is already known), as in 'the treachery . . . the cage . . . the turning of buttocks . . . the cold'. My narrator refuses to produce yet another Baartman narrative. And David's page of writing about Baartman itself peters out into scribbles, marked by the word TRURT, a form of 'truth' that the narrator claims to be a coloured Cape Flats phonetic transcription of the word, whose meaning can't be pinned down. In other words, the novel also makes a point about Baartman and miscegenation, in line with my account of Griqua identity (with all its false claims about Khoe purity) being blurred.

Nevertheless, for all my narrator's refusal to tell yet another story, it is also the case that by the very inclusion of Baartman as a topic in my narrative about race and nationalist struggle, I, the author, acknowledge her iconic status, her position as a cipher in colonial history. What I trust my narrative does not suggest is equivalence between Dulcie, a relatively privileged woman who has chosen a course of action, and the powerless Baartman.

But to return to miscegenation: I understand that one of the assumptions made about Willie Bester, and one that fuelled the outrage, was that by dint of his name he was believed to be a white Afrikaner; a strange assumption because Baartman too, like very many coloured names, is European in origin. Of course, this is no excuse. Any thinking critic would have done her homework about the artist if she had never heard of him before. This assumption patently overlooks the history of sexual violence and miscegenation visibly borne by a significant number of South Africans.

Desiree: Your statement that 'Baartman can be seen as a ready-made cipher: her history – situated as it is in oppressive colonial history – lends itself to all kinds of meanings and manipulations, always available for metonymic displacement' explains a great deal about the controversy surrounding Willie Bester's statue. UCT's Black Academic Caucus had the following to say in defence of their covering of the statue and its subsequent uncovering by a white librarian:

The label 'Hottentot Venus' continues to haunt our memory of Sara Baartman. This moniker . . . may have been repudiated by renowned scholars . . . but it has persisted as the lens through which Sara's story is seen . . . The impatient and impetuous action of removing the kanga and head-wrap has not only disrobed us but has robbed us of that much-needed space for multi-faceted debate and discussion

> . . . Taking the robes off so unceremoniously is to shame all of us, reminding us once again how black women's bodies easily become the repository for violent histories.[1]

An argument that you've repeatedly made, Zoë, is that 'shame' and 'pride' are two sides of the same coin. My understanding of this is that speaking with pride by telling ennobling stories about a group or an individual always stems from and reinscribes a psychosocial position of lack, deficiency and desire. I'm often surprised that many people refuse to see the logic of this argument, and continue to insist that pride is not necessarily linked to shame. Could you explain what you mean by the connectedness of shame and pride in the case of the clothing of Willie Bester's statue by black feminist activists at UCT in 2018?

Zoë: Yes, I've spoken about shame and pride in relation to coloured identity, and elsewhere have cited Kwame Anthony Appiah, who insists that identity ought to be related to the ethical. Cultural membership, he says, quoting John Tomasi, 'is a primary good only in the same uninteresting sense as, say, oxygen'. For Appiah, identity is 'like form: you can't not have it'.[2] So I am suspicious of statements of shame or pride. If you are comfortable with your identity, you simply are X and wouldn't need to make declarations of pride, which, as you say, is transparently about lack and desire, hence the flip side of shame. Instead of exorbitant identification then, the ethical course of action would be to converse with Others, across national, religious, racial, sexual and other boundaries.

Of course, this can't be universal. I am, for instance, sympathetic to defiant and strategic movements such as Gay or LGBT Pride that seek to overthrow the unethical violence, discrimination and contempt of the dominant culture. Gay Pride marches open up conversations through their visibility. Such a political movement ultimately aims to enable an individual to say: I am X, rather than I am proud to be X. Similarly, Biko's Black Consciousness Movement of the 1970s aimed at turning the black consciousness of inferiority inflicted by apartheid into black pride and power. Following a dialectical process then, the false thesis of inferiority and powerlessness is exposed, but the exposure does not amount to the truth of its antithesis; instead, the strength produced by assertions of black power/pride provides the basis for further considered thought about identity that could then become as comfortable and unremarkable as oxygen.

But back to the Baartman/Bester case: the women understandably feel empathy with Baartman, but to claim that they themselves have been disrobed is puzzling, since this undermines empathy, which allows one to enter the feelings of another, rather than to foreground the self. Baartman would have, among an array of feelings, suffered shame (that rightly should have belonged to the perpetrators of her abuse), but there is no basis for privileged people claiming equivalence with a poor, abused woman on display in nineteenth-century colonial Europe.

The unilateral decision to cover up the figure presumably asserts pride in claiming her (which ought to wipe out shame), but would a conversation across the political–aesthetic divide not have been a more productive course of action? If the claim that 'removing the kanga and head-wrap . . . has robbed us of that much-needed space for multi-faceted debate and discussion' sounds reasonable, it is, in fact, disinguous. The sculpture itself did precisely that: it provided, through its mode of construction, a space for dialogue that the one-sided act of enrobing has disregarded. Bester is a respected anti-apartheid artist with a track record of dissidence, deserving, I think, of discussion and consultation, especially given the complex and polysemous nature of art. In fact, does common courtesy not demand this?

Desiree: One of the assumptions made in the Caucus's explanation of this action is the 'fact' of a shared narrative, a collective story that black people, by virtue of their situated experience of violent racist representation, can tell others and themselves. Yet the iconographic figure of Baartman doesn't have a singular meaning in articulations of black experience in South Africa. One obvious indication (implicit in the Caucus's response) is black women's enlisting of Baartman to signal *gendered* black experience; in other words, the extent to which 'black pain' is usually masculinised. This is a dynamic that South African feminist Fallists have powerfully exposed, and one that the collective flags. Even more noteworthy (and far less obvious) is Baartman's varied signification in black women's recent narratives.

For example, South African visual artist Senzeni Marasela's *Covering the Hottentot Venus* positions Baartman in a story of her own and her mother's existential displacement in apartheid and post-apartheid South Africa.[3] Her artwork dramatises the continuity of pasts in presents by drawing parallels between the dislocation of three different black women (herself, her mother and Sara). Yvette Abrahams's biomythographic writing corrects the colonial record and creates a conceptual space for Sara Baartman's voice.[4] Diana Ferrus's poem foregrounds Baartman's displacement in relation to the poet's responsibility to 'take her home' and, in so doing, creates a sense of restored subjectivity and newfound political agency.[5]

These varied symbolic uses show how the apparent 'collectivity' of black women's situated knowledge splinters into particularised narratives with varying themes and discursive functions – one focusing on autobiographical testimony of colonial and post-colonial violence, the second emphasising the restoration of voice, and the last foregrounding political agency and a form of 'closure'. It seems to me that this wide-ranging narrative use of the figure of Baartman is what is conveyed in the words of the central character of *David's Story*. When David says, 'Baartman belongs to all of us', he is not confirming her singular meaning in a shared narrative (which he seems to believe), but attesting to her heterogeneous role in stories with different sense-making functions in the present.[6] To me, your argument does *not* imply that we cannot or should not represent Baartman in progressive or critical ways, that, in a sense, all representations of Baartman are 'politically suspect' and 'wrong'. I sometimes think that some interpret analysis of the politics of the representation of Sara Baartman (especially by black women) to mean that no one should presume to write about her at all! Rather, we should think very self-consciously and self-reflexively about the discursive and autobiographical complexes that underpin this. Willie Bester's artwork, as a work that conveys political and aesthetic meanings about Sara Baartman, is often left out of the discussion of how and why his sculpture was enrobed. Can you say something about this?

Zoë: The Caucus's idea of a shared narrative, a collective story that black people can tell because of their experience of representation, is one that I sympathise with. But the notion of something that cannot be represented is surely dangerous; it harks to the *Bilderverbot* of Mosaic law, the second commandment that ensures that the single meaning of God must not be challenged by representations or graven images in which other meanings will invariably surface. (But then the enrobing does have a strong whiff of the postlapsarian: a stooped, head-hanging Eve fleeing from Eden with her fig leaf, ashamed of her nakedness.) The question of art and meaning arises: for the enrobers, a single meaning of Bester's Baartman-in-shame is asserted, but what on earth does the figure of a covered-up Baartman mean? Anything but pride. I understand that the entire figure, including the head, was enrobed, which would confirm your suspicion that some believe her very representation to be unacceptable.

Your reading of 'Baartman belongs to all of us' is insightful, but it occurs to me that it also carries the simple sense that no one can or should forget what was done to her and what she endured. Really, in that didactic sense, Baartman belongs to all of South Africa. It is as well to think through her trials: the spectacle was not simply about laughing at a woman's naked body; gendered, yes, but it was specific denigration of the steatopygic other. Here, then, a reading: Bester's sculpture, by resituating and recontextualising that naked body in the legitimating space and dignity of a library, gives her a new, defiant meaning that frees her from mockery and normalises her steatopygia. The phrase 'bringing Baartman home' thus achieves yet another meaning as the library becomes the place of her recovery, a place where she is dignified and can be remembered as such. Notably, the artist does not invest her with that overused and often misdirected notion of agency.

One of the objections, according to the Caucus's statement, is that Bester's work is based on the caricatured image of Baartman, so that viewing the sculpture becomes a problematic 'looking at that humiliation'. I would argue that by using the well-known image, he *references* her abuse and instils in his sculpture the history of that violence; in other words, that history becomes indelible, but at the same time his unique construction, by *transforming* the original image, deletes the old humiliation. Bester makes no attempt to give his Baartman the appearance of human flesh, so the constructed figure has nothing in common with art history's female nude. The sculpture manifestly does not meet the Black Academic Caucus's claim that it sets up the same scopic relations as the 'canon of Venus . . . the fantasy object of male desire'. Shame, on the part of the viewer, thus seems to be a wholly inappropriate response.

Covering the work up may be a response to a feeling of shame on behalf of that naked body, but that is to accept the dominant culture's view of what has been categorised (and scientifically pathologised) as steatopygia and thus as abnormal and ugly. There is, of course, a curious double paradox to shame, a complex reflexive process. Firstly, the shame rightly belongs to those who trafficked and exhibited Baartman, the perpetrators of evil who ought to feel ashamed of themselves; instead, the shame is deflected to and absorbed by the victim. Secondly, shame is an intense feeling experienced by the self, which is experienced at the same time as if in the presence of or by another's derisory gaze. For me, the success of Bester's sculpture lies in drawing the viewer's attention to these paradoxes.

My reading of Bester is, of course, in relation to his entire oeuvre, his reputation as a dissident artist, for meaning is not separate from origin. I see the enrobing, then, as a profoundly disrespectful act, in relation to both Bester and Baartman, and if the enrobers did not know the artist's work, it was surely incumbent on them to find out. Ignorance among academics can never be excused.

Desiree: Yes. When I first learned about the enrobing, I immediately thought of what you are now raising about Willie's statue . . . simply and straightforwardly, that it is an artwork involving meaning-making. And that choosing to cover it signals a refusal to engage with a particular (as you say, well-known dissident) artist's vision and creative representation. The representational aspect that has always struck me most – about all Bester's work, but this one in particular – is his use of recycled materials. And it seems to me that with this, the sculptor prompts us to think a great deal about *how* Sara Baartman's body has been represented, what meanings have been attached to her body, the palpable violence to which her body has been subjected – both materially and in acts of representation. This is what one critic has to say about this:

> Bester's patchwork can be taken as a significant sign, by means of which the specific image of Sarah Bartmann [*sic*] simultaneously represents many different bodies and histories . . . The recycled matter . . . calls to mind the many contexts in which her body was circulated . . . Her head is adorned with a diadem, fabricated by a bike chain from which coins are hung. There is a dog collar around her neck with a lock, and her feet are chained. The most important connotation of all this recycled scrap iron is that there is absolutely nothing natural about this woman's body.[7]

Zoë: Oh absolutely, I agree. And it is unbelievable that this aspect of the work, the history of abuse and mockery implied by the materials, is overlooked. In fact, the diadem of chain and coins, so reminiscent of the crown of thorns placed on the head of Jesus, who, as Christians believe, died for all, shows that Bester does not need to be told by the Caucus that Baartman is a symbol. His construction implies that the name of 'Hottentot Venus' is a cruel mockery, just as the crown of thorns mocked Jesus as 'Saviour' or 'King'.

Now I do not for one minute suggest that the critics of Bester's Sara believe the sculpture actually to be Sara (and therefore further insulted by being yet again on display); however, there is a fundamental sense in which the criticism fails to understand the nature of representation. It brings to mind the simplistic, thoughtless criterion of a work of art being good or bad because it is so very like the thing in the world, or not like the thing that it represents, without any thought given to *how* it is represented, the use and handling of materials, of intertext, or aspect, etc. It brings to mind René Magritte's artwork in which the drawing of a pipe that floats in space has a handwritten text beneath it: *Ceci n'est pas une pipe* (This is not a pipe). So Magritte asserts that the work is its own model rather than an affirmation of resemblance, that it has a material existence independent of the thing in the world. As Foucault points out in his study of this work, the reference is to the relation between discourse and the image. The direct reference ('this') points to the common discourse where one would, according to the convention of language, say of the drawing, 'this is a pipe'. But no, of course it's not. When we say, 'this is Sara Baartman', we bring to the statement and to our apprehension of the work also a body of discourse (largely insulting) that has been generated about Baartman, the abused woman. But the sculpture is NOT Baartman; rather, it is a representation of her that invites us to think about what we are actually looking at. The thinking viewer, having thought at first about resemblance, would now surely shift to note similitude, note that in spite of looking *like* Baartman, the surface does not attempt to resemble flesh (as do paintings or sculptures of nudes): instead, Baartman's history is referenced; her abused 'body', made of scrap metal, bolts and chains, etc., is, as Rosemarie Buikema points out, conspicuously constructed. In fact, Baartman cannot escape construction.

Desiree: Interestingly, Buikema also draws attention to an earlier controversy, and the fact that the protest in 2018 had a precedent in 2009. When the statue was first unveiled at UCT more than a decade ago, some black staff and students were outraged about what they saw as Sarah Baartman becoming again, well into democracy, an 'othered' body on display.

But it astounds me too how this assumption (that the statue perpetuates colonial 'othering') can be made *without* considering the artist's treatment of his subject. I sometimes wonder whether there is not something about trauma and pain that makes a 'rational' reading of certain acts of protest limited in some way. Maybe the response indicates that the identity politics that drove the enrobing as a kind of public ritual involves a baffling combination of psychology, affect, memory and cognition, rather than 'rational' politics.

It also occurs to me, when you speak about over-identification, that very individualised memories, traumas and incidents for black academics and students at UCT propelled the enrobing as a performative act of protest. The public ritual might create the impression of a rational collective political response, yet the emotions anchored by this ritual were and are in some ways always in excess of it. So the clothing of the statue of Sara Baartman at UCT conveys meaning, creates provisional closure and constitutes political agency for a group of black women. Maybe the ritual ends up functioning (in a necessarily non- or anti-rational way) as many narratives in identity politics do: a story told to give coherence to a story about different selves who try to speak collectively, as 'one'.

What are your general thoughts about how Sara Baartman has served as an icon in identity politics – whether in South Africa or elsewhere? You spoke earlier about understanding the protest of minority groups demanding recognition and dignity, so where, for you, do things somehow go awry? I'm also curious to hear more of what you think about the Caucus's claim about nakedness 'shaming us all' in relation to this . . .

Zoë: Your attempt at understanding the enrobing of Bester's sculpture at UCT as constituting political agency for a group of black women, and as a possible way of creating closure, makes sense, even if the protest does appear to be performative outrage. If only there were not the futile quest for a coherent narrative. Besides, if Baartman ought to be remembered, closure, which would amount to silence and historical effacement, is surely not desirable.

I imagine that the cool, fashionable young things flaunting their blackness in skimpy clothes and elaborately aesthetic hairdos, strutting their stuff in the streets of Cape Town, would laugh out loud at the missionary position of diagnosing shame in the state of undress. But back to us old, overdressed academic folks and the question of where things go awry. My guess would be in language, in the rhetorical that so readily invades it – and rhetoric is about excess and display. Now, if trauma and pain undoubtedly characterised life under apartheid, I am also acutely aware of the banalisation of the word pain, the hyperbolic trope that it nowadays constitutes. We do, of course, routinely speak of being pained, a rhetorical device to speak of feelings of discomfort, but to refer to existential pain begs investigation. No matter how we choose to theorise existential discomfort, angst (bourgeois or otherwise) or even the real somatisation of feeling, we surely must distinguish between these and actual physical pain as in assault on the body. Think of Winnie Mandela, who never presented herself as a victim in pain. Her unspeakable torture suffered at the hands of the security police was divulged only with the publication of her prison diaries and letters in 2013. Or take women like gertrude fester-wicomb, who were incarcerated during the anti-apartheid struggle and suffered surveillance, physical indignity, humiliation and gendered torture; they still live with the indelible memory that fuses physical and mental pain, a gendered torture that can't be spoken of. It took unimaginable courage to resist this torture; fester-wicomb (unlike her male counterparts) did not buckle under pain, did not betray her comrades and deliver names to the security police.

In her book *African Americans and the Culture of Pain*, Debra Walker King offers a persuasive take on the question of black pain. She reminds us that the 'Enlightenment' view of the natural savage supported the belief that slaves did not feel pain as whites do, which I imagine goes some way towards black people wanting to assert or even flaunt their pain. But Walker King points out that 'popular perceptions linking black bodies to a legacy of pain compromise and sometimes diminish the power of the human voice and will to support and encourage soul survival'.[8] (Njabulo Ndebele holds a similar position as articulated in his Helen Joseph Lecture, 'They Are Burning Memory'.)[9] If pain, Walker King argues, is employed as a tool of resistance against racism, it also functions as a sign of racism's insidious ability to exert power and maintain control over those claims. Winnie Mandela knew this only too well.

In the light of actual experiences of torture and pain, the black pain activated by viewing an unclad Sara Baartman is, of course, prosthetic. Subjectivity may render prosthetic pain as real as actual physical pain, but it would be foolish to ignore the difference: the materiality of an amputated arm, say, renders you actually disabled and leaves you with the memory of severance and loss. Which is not to deny the force of prosthetic pain, but it is as well to consider the practical distinction. Now, empathy with Sara Baartman should also admit the singularity of her experience, the unspeakability of a more or less unclad, black woman's body in icy, racist, misogynistic Europe, stared at and mocked as a steatopygic freak. Thus, the statement that Baartman's nakedness in the gallery 'shames us all' – well, not only does it erase her singularity, but it also seems to me an affront for privileged women to claim equivalence with a powerless, abused Baartman; in fact, the excess of over-identification wipes out empathy as it ricochets to focus on the self. Really, it tells us of the ease and emptiness of such rhetorical utterances versus the unspeakability of Baartman's actual torture, and the impossibility of knowing what that actually felt like. For all the legitimate gains we've made in terms of subjectivity, I do believe there are limits to its value, since subjectivity exists on a spectrum that could dwindle into solipsism – clearly an unhealthy state for the body politic.

Desiree: Your point about subjectivity existing on a spectrum makes me think about how different stories, artworks and performances draw their inspiration. I'm intrigued by how differently subjectivity is manifested in various stories or acts invoking Baartman. To take the case of the stories told around Willie Bester's sculpture: the librarian removes the cover from the statue and tells a story to an implied audience: 'I am an enlightened believer in freedom of speech and reject this irrational "censoring" of "artistic freedom"'. The subjectivity defined here assumes the idea of a rational self acting without being 'burdened' by political partisanship . . . a liberal humanist idea that speaks volumes about entitlement. I imagine the Caucus tells their story through ceremony: 'We are covering the statue and in so doing as black women we reclaim our denied dignity.' The act seems to be justified on the basis of claiming intimacy. And this seems to be different from Willie Bester's subject-positioning, in which he speaks about his empathy:

I heard about the experience of Sarah [sic] Baartman and I found some parallels with her story . . . While listening to a poem written by Diana Ferrus, it already came up to me as a sculpture . . . [Her proprietors] fled to France with her and they continued in France until her death. And if that was also not enough, they then dissected her body and put it in glass bottles. It seems that this deep-rooted racism went beyond your death. It never stopped. I identified with what she went through.[10]

Claiming intimacy or empathy seems to undergird the various implicit or explicit self-inventions or representations in the public responses to Baartman in the new millennium. Would you agree? And if so, what ethical issues are raised by this? You spoke earlier about definitely *not* wanting to contribute to existing narratives. Yet there *are* political and ethical imperatives for you. I am thinking about how, generally, your critical writing critiques victim narratives and images in South African literature and culture. Therefore ethically and aesthetically addressing many issues linked to the representation or invocation of Baartman in South African literature and culture. Or how fiction, as captured in your short story 'Another Story', provokes the reader to think carefully about what storytelling means in relation to identity or identification. Who tells stories, and to whom? And how do they come to 'matter' politically? You mention 'the singularity of [Baartman's] experience, the unspeakability of . . . [an] unclad body in icy . . . Europe, stared at . . . as a steatopygic freak' that can generate 'empathy'. Can you say something more about this? What sorts of narratives, politics or representation of Sara Baartman do you believe to be culturally and politically important or inevitable in our post-millennial, post-apartheid present? And why does the figure of Baartman continue to resonate so strongly?

Zoë: Yes, an interesting codification of responses to the sculpture, although I imagine that Bester's account comes retrospectively, in defence of his work. As for the librarian, I agree that his position is foolishly high-handed, and sympathise with the idea that his action enraged the Caucus into digging in their heels. In both cases, dialogue, discussion and consultation – the courteous route and the challenge of crossing political and aesthetic boundaries – would have also been the ethical route that could have brought more positive understandings of the work for both parties.

Although Baartman was by no means the only African displayed in Europe, I refer to her singularity because of the well-documented history of her abuse, starting with slavery and including the comparative anatomist Georges Cuvier's study that pronounced the Khoe as the lowest of the human species. She encapsulates so much of the history of colonisation and exploitation in South Africa, also the extermination of Khoe peoples, as well as the history of representation itself. Baartman, then, is woven into our history and will be remembered as an icon. At the risk of sounding pious: perhaps the UCT debacle teaches us that we need not decree on kinds of representations, their importance or legitimacy; that, instead, we ought to initiate conversations around representations, especially contested ones. As it happens, I believe Willie Bester's sculpture to be an important work, and part of its importance is also the aftermath, which includes the fact that we are discussing it here. So the Baartman story endures (just as the grotesque history of slavery in the USA endures and generates artworks), and there will always be responses to representations of that story.

You mention my 'Another Story', which I can barely remember, except that it relates to Sarah Gertrude Millin's shocking representation of mixed-race people in her novel *God's Stepchildren*; it suggests through the names that the central character's family history was appropriated by Millin. The story is also self-reflexive: when the central character returns and tells her neighbours of her experiences in Cape Town (including her disgust at seeing representations of steatopygic Khoe figures in a museum diorama), she acknowledges that the story she tells varies according to whom she tells it. The title – I could have called it '(Yet) Another Story' – indicates that the telling of stories generates other stories, and that the original events are invariably transformed in the telling. Such transformation is, of course, central to the politics and ethics of representation, and perhaps as a South African I am unduly exercised by its implications.

Desiree: I really do find what your story raises fascinating in thinking about Baartman's representation recently. You fictionalise the descendants of a subject stereotyped by a writer whose obsession with coding race and gender led her to produce imaginings very much in sync with nineteenth-century colonial views of Baartman. And you create imaginative space for the telling of different stories. To me, then, the story reveals not only the inevitability of retellings and 'yet another story', but also the possibility of quite *another* marginalised or silenced story*telling* (involving both the story and the community in which it can be created and heard).

This makes me think about the recent upsurge of creativity invoking Baartman among radical young women artists and students in South Africa. I mentioned Senzeni Marasela's artwork earlier, and there is also *Exhibit S, Ode to Sara Baartman*, a poetic performance by Thola Antamu in 2016; Lady Skollie's series of connected paintings, 'Hottentot Venus'; *Saartjie vs Venus* written and performed by the poet Lebo Mashile and workshopped last year; and many more I suspect I don't know. You are, of course, not living, writing or teaching in South Africa, and haven't for a while. But having done so for many years, what do you think might explain the renewed upsurge of storytelling and artistic work by young black South African women writers and artists in recent years?

Zoë: You are right about Millin's representation chiming with colonial views of Baartman, and in my story, the central character is outraged that her niece, Sarah, should repeat Millin's insulting words about their people. The older woman is shamed; she silences her niece, claims there is no such book in which their lives are written about, advises her not to think about such stories of old times and, in fact, brings closure by slumping into a faint. As for the upsurge of works that invoke Baartman: I am not surprised that the iconic figure continues to exercise young artists and writers, who hopefully approach their subject with greater confidence and self-belief than my generation. No doubt they are still fuelled by outrage and the desire to re-present disparaged representations. There are, after all, in South Africa still plenty of reasons for wanting to confront colonial injustice and set the record straight. That, of course, is also what the UCT enrobing set out to do, even if I disagree with their interpretation of the work they wished to 'correct'. We have all in the processes of re-presentation and reclaiming relied on the value of subjectivity. What UCT's Baartman debacle has shown is the limitation of subjectivity, which in itself is subject to intersubjectivity; that it is valid only in relation to the subjectivities of others, and that such civil relations cannot be achieved without open-minded discussion and consultation.

1.
Unmaking

a playful but also very serious love letter to gabrielle goliath

Pumla Dineo Gqola

Dear Gabi,

I am not very happy with you.

> Words become me
> They are the flowers in my hair,
> Jewels at my neck and ears[1]

On 13 February 2014, I went to pick up *Bouquet III* from the Goodman Gallery in Parkwood, Johannesburg. I was thrilled. Of all the things I had lost or had had to give up, the triptych had been what I longed for the most. Things. Except art is always more than a thing. I was getting used to living in a house whose main passage no longer had another one of your triptychs, *Ek is 'n Kimberley Coloured*.[i] I was no longer pausing to inhale its rich deep reds, allowing myself to be stretched in my own skin as a Blackwoman from this place. I had made my peace with its absence. But it is only once *Bouquet III* is up in

---

i   The direct translation of this from Afrikaans is 'I'm a Kimberley coloured'. Kimberley is the capital city of South Africa's Northern Cape province.

my favourite part of my house that I allow it to feel like home. When I moved to a new house I lived in too briefly, I felt the same way. Even now, several years later, in a new city, I stare at the triptych, mesmerised as I drink my morning coffee, and also when I am just too lazy to move off the couch to drive, write or cook.

> Some bits falling off
> Other parts sprouting.
> Inside of this cocoon
> I dream of flight[2]

I stumbled into your *Faces of War* installation, and I was ready to be provoked, taught and enchanted. I was in too good a mood to expect simple engagement. Quite frankly, your art had spoiled me. As I walked about that Valentine's Day eve at the Goodman Gallery, very pleased with myself, I saw my face reflected on the glass frames of the various digitally manipulated faces below which I read: 'Faces of people who may or may not be victims or perpetrators of domestic violence'. The combination of monochrome photographs, the light and glass created a mirror effect. You knew this would happen. Each audience member would be trying to spot cues about whether the digitally manipulated face was that of a perpetrator or victim. Some of us would pay very late full attention to the 'may or may not be', and realise that it was impossible to tell. There were no signs. The person may be neither. On each attempt to let the eyes provide answers: two faces.

I think it is you and another artist, and old friend, Ingrid Masondo, who helped me think of survivors of gender-based violence as the walking wounded, and not a minority. Yes, after all the work. Still. Even after all the work Ingrid and I and other feminists did as Rape Crisis counsellors in our early twenties, I did not fully grasp this. There are no obvious signs. I knew this in one sense, but in another, it did not register. What would it mean if we took the statistics to signify that those we encounter are more likely to be survivors than not? Yet how was I able to think about our country as one in which women lived under siege, and not make the connection? Of course, some have deliberately misunderstood and mocked my phrase 'walking wounded', but I choose not to care.

But back to *Faces of War.* I was thinking of Ingrid's question about what happens to all the Blackgirls and Blackwomen who were publicly abducted and raped by jackrollers and Ntsaras and other gangsters. She asked about where that trauma goes, and I have never been able to forget that question. I remember how much fear the names of these gangs struck in my own heart as a teenager at a boarding school in Inanda. I only knew of them from second-hand stories of schoolmates who came from townships in the Transvaal and Cape Town, where such gangs were a terror. I was never in any danger of crossing their paths; I came from a very different part of the country. Yet, what did my peers say that communicated their fear – and shared it – so effectively? We were becoming Blackwomen, and mixed in with all the other lessons, good and bad, was this communication that apartheid South Africa did not belong to Blackgirls.

Maybe it is not a coincidence that Barbara Boswell and I were born in the same year, and she says we might both still be suffering from PTSD from the 1980s. Two Blackwomen who were 21 in 1994, fully grown under apartheid, in very different manners, yet in ways whose similarities are still revealing themselves. In her work, Barbara also points out that the fact that gender-based violence was left out of the definition of apartheid human rights abuses laid the groundwork for a very specific form of sanctified disremembering of Blackwomen's life experiences. We created a country in which large-scale experiences of violence by women under apartheid were cast aside in the definition of the past, memory and nation. When I read this, I gasped.

When I read it again, recently, I gasped. Here, the same teaching as *Faces of War*. And so, I started to carve out a piece of my brain to house this installation the day before Valentine's Day in 2014. It was not just the photographs. Your video offered the same combination of discomfort and illumination. I have not been able to stop thinking about the footage featuring the audibly human sounds that are simultaneously familiar and indecipherable.

I chuckled as your point hit home.

I fetched a notebook from my car and took notes because I was going to write an essay on your installation. It sat patiently with me as I edited and rewrote the harder parts of my book on rape. It probably leaked into parts of that book, given how much it continues to teach me. I thought the essay would be written soon, and I kept planning to write it. I referenced *Faces of War* as offering a conceptual vocabulary for thinking about how to proceed against violence, in conference papers and in lecture series given to students in foreign lands. Yet, the years rolled on and the essay remained unfinishable.

Then one day in June 2019, Rozena Maart knew just how to phrase an email to make me write my essay. What she requested was a paper for a special issue of a journal she was editing. She knew nothing of this long story I am now burdening you with. And so, in between my job that requires very different kinds of writing to the forms I dream about, I wrote, reread and plotted the essay, at last.

But then, in the week I aim to finally finish my essay, my son, Danielle Bowler and I walk into *This Song Is For . . .* at the Monument Gallery as part of the National Arts Festival. There are so many women whose work I love present. It makes perfect sense that we all encounter one another in the room you made possible, in this space Ernestine White-Mifetu has curated. Sometimes, we have wet eyes and lips tightly pressed together in a failed attempt to smile; at other times, there is joyful discovery as we hug for a long time. All these women are devoted to ending patriarchal violence. Each one of us is obsessed with imagination and interiority. Ernestine talks us through the exhibition and implores us to sit through the full two-and-a-half-hour duration. We read every word in each rape narrative on the purple wall. We sit on the cushions and listen to each song with increasing discomfort at the sonic disruptions.

A woman comes up to me as I read Flow's words and recites my words back to me. They have nothing to do with rape. They are about writing and not asking for permission, I think, from my second book. I do not recognise them as she mouths them, but mistake them for a shared experience. I am trying to understand what she is telling me. I search her face. However, she smiles, thanks me for saving her life, and rushes out of the room. I am confused and dazed, and take a few minutes to understand. Then I sit back on the floor and watch the songs on the giant screen with all the others of different genders. We are trying to do what Ernestine has instructed us to do. But none of us hear all the songs that day; the gallery shuts down for the day and we stream out.

That night, on social media, I post about how life-changing this exhibition is. The next morning I drive back from the neighbouring seaside town my son and I are holidaying in to see the rest of it.

This second time, I bring my thinking self, notepad in hand, walking and sitting through *This Song Is For . . .* again. I see the parts I missed in yesterday's hour. A woman leaning against the same pole as me volunteers that she cannot concentrate and will return when 'they have fixed the audio'. She is visibly shaken when I tell her 'it's not broken; it's deliberate'. Belatedly, I think I should have let her find out for herself. I return to my notepad and my thinking brain, move around the space again.

> she was riding my story like she
> had been there
> like she had held my storm
> speaking like she was my voice itself[3]

Something inside unbuckles, but I don't understand because I am rereading the words from yesterday and am therefore prepared. The scratch is on 'because everybody hurts' and I continue to read something, a feeling I recognise but had not ever wanted to articulate. It is a strange connection; unwanted, but I cannot overcome it.

A relief at being found out is not as pleasant as one might think.

'when did i lose my virginity?'
at 13 when i first made that choice
no! it was at 6 when the choice was made for me
just before my body was fully formed[4]

Thinking brain notwithstanding, my eyes had been wet all along. Now, however, my watery eyes become a flood. I have no idea what is happening. I cannot tell you exactly why I am crying. Every bit of liquid is flushing out of my body. It seems I am not peri-menopausal either. But I am standing in the middle of the room like this. And I already did all the work of healing from this. Yesterday's tears were empathy.

Why the hell am I crying today?

When it rains
let it rain hard,
so that I can hide in the midst of clouds
travel with the storm[5]

I have already, finally, healed from all of this, so the flood takes me off guard. Wonderful Hilda realised that although I walked into her therapy room with one set of crises, my six-year-old self was finally demanding attention. She said, 'The recent set of events is upsetting, yes, but whenever the response is the appropriate kind but magnified, something else is at play.' And she was right. And I finally looked my helplessness and anger and determination to survive and excel and flourish in the eye. And, slowly, I am healing. So why am I standing in the middle of the room crying quietly but uncontrollably? And how can I cry so hard and not know what I am crying about?

And, perhaps now you understand why I am not very happy with you. I brought my analytical brain-self, already knew what the soundtrack, the video and the walls said. I did not come here to be unbuckled. Yes, I know what I wrote in the essay I did for Danielle, which she had commissioned on the spot the day before. You are quite the alchemist, unmatched in your capacity to make us feel too much when we had really just planned to keep our spectacles and lipstick on, and think. This terrain is my work too. I already feel too much when I am writing about the rape epidemic in our country, on our planet. And I know there is nothing wrong with it, but I am not the kind of person who weeps uncontrollably in public.

But the real reason I am not very happy with you is not the tears. Already obsessed with your existing work, I do not have the time to be obsessed with yet another thing. I have deadlines to chase in the evenings, after my day job. Instead, I am now knee-deep in the foolishness of writing you this letter.

So, thank you for messing with my head constantly, and for changing my life.

Sisterly,
Pumla

PS I am so glad you are not going to make another artwork for a few years because I actually have an overdue book manuscript too.

CHAPTER 4

Teaching Black, Teaching Gender, Teaching Feminism

Mary Hames

As a schoolchild and then later as a university student, my experiences inside and outside the classroom influenced my approach to teaching and learning in profound ways. As a University of the Western Cape student in the mid-1970s, I received all my political education outside the formal university classroom. Many intellectual exchanges took place among my peers and did not revolve around a conventional teacher–learner relationship. Before and during the early 1990s, outside classroom learning was central to creating a milieu of exposure to and engagement with radical political ideas and fiction. At a time when much radical Black intellectual written work, by figures such as Stephen Bantu Biko, Alex La Guma and the poet James Matthews, was banned, liberatory education took place mainly on shop floors, in private houses and, in my case, in the bush around the campfire on the margins of campus. The Black Consciousness Movement (BCM) played a major role in my education, especially during 1976, a time when the South African Student Organisation (SASO) was active on all historically Black campuses.

My late teens and early twenties were marked by the struggle against apartheid and the sharing of banned reading material. At that point, suspect books were not readily available as reading material in the university library or classroom. You had to trek all the way to the centre of the city, where banned material was kept under lock and key in the National Library of South Africa in Gardens in Cape Town. Researching there meant that your name was entered in a register so that the state could perpetuate its surveillance of political dissidents. Strict records were kept of users. Academic libraries were supposedly granted the right to possess banned material for bona fide research purposes, but the white university librarians were, not surprisingly, agents of the state.

As a library science student, I became adept at searching for material that could not be found anywhere else. The BCM network on campus also distributed so-called questionable material for discussion. While we were subjected to apolitical and often conservative rote learning in lectures, we became knowledgeable – through our workshops, reading groups and camping trips, with material written for Black people by Black people. The names of Frantz Fanon, Amílcar Cabral and Stephen Bantu Biko, amongst others, slipped easily off our tongues. The debates among us helped us develop tools of critical and often outraged questioning of the material we were taught in the classroom. We debated what it meant to be Black in an apartheid university taught by mostly white academics originating from historically white Afrikaner universities.

But our political education was focused on race and class, and we were learning in a context in which 'the Struggle' was primarily against racial oppression and economic injustice. At that historical juncture, our awareness did not include a consciousness of feminism, sexual orientation, sexual identity, gender and gender identity. In retrospect, it was clear to many of us that our world was embedded in heteropatriarchy and sexism. For all of us on the left, this was an era where compulsory heterosexuality was the norm. The slogan 'Each one, teach one' was popularised and we taught each other about the kinds of racism we had experienced. At the same time, I recall how many women (friends and colleagues) were subjected to abuse by their male partners; but at that time, we had nowhere to go, and no language in which to articulate our experiences. Sexism was rife, and while women students had to leave university for a variety of reasons connected to their gender roles and statuses, the men always stayed enrolled.

This deep way of knowing the wrong done to women, based on lived and embodied experience, subconsciously taught and prepared me to explore different ways of learning in the twenty-first-century neo-liberal education environment. I also think that in my subconscious mind, I prepared myself to unpack my approach to teaching about violence against women, and how we could develop strategies of action. Today we have the language, the awareness, the legal and policy framework, and the technology to publicly organise and demand gender justice. Yet I, like many others, have the powerful legacy of experience, what many feminists would call standpoint knowledge.

Looking back, race and racial oppression loomed large in my mind. I remember how we stood in front of the bulldozers deployed by the apartheid state against those working-class Black people it deemed 'surplus' non-citizens. We helped to rebuild flattened shacks on grounds that now belong to the university, and generally struggled in spaces that even today carry for me the memory of both violent repression and determined resistance. Yet that history for many is now long forgotten, erased by new high-rise buildings proudly pronouncing the era of post-apartheid modernity. During my student years, we often had to negotiate our lives in a hostile world in which apartheid forced us to live, learn, work and play in specifically created racially designated spaces. This artificial racialised world fostered the formation of coloured identity, which at the time was marked by contestation. At a time when senior administrators and academics were white, the university became a 'colouredstan' after normal academic hours. It was as if a big sign reading 'No whites allowed' emerged when class ended and darkness set in.

There were very few Black lecturers at the university when I started as a student in the early 1970s. The rector was a caretaker rector appointed by the apartheid government shortly after the student protests in 1973, and we awaited with anticipation the arrival of Richard van der Ross, the first Black rector of the university. Petty apartheid manifested itself in separate toilets, staff rooms and even staff organisations. White staff also received special allowances or what was commonly called danger pay as compensation for working and teaching at a Black institution.

Since the inception of the university until 1975, the rector's position was occupied by white men. For years, Adam Small was the only Black lecturer. The university council, senate, professoriate, senior administration, and secretaries were made up of white people only. There is anecdotal evidence that when Van der Ross was appointed as rector, his white secretary asked to be transferred to a lower position as secretary to one of the deans 'because she could not work under a coloured boss'. These racist attitudes and forms of othering prevailed both inside and outside the classroom, with the opposition to this institutionalised racism reflected in the student protests of 1973, one year before I entered the university. I would become an active protester in 1976. The memorandum of the 1973 student protest highlighted at length how colonial the university curriculum was, and how the white academic and administrative staff had exceptional power to exercise punitive measures. Students were, for instance, advised not to consult Adam Small's work because it was too 'offensive'.

In addition to the institutionalisation of petty apartheid, there was the socio-geographical location of the university on the periphery of the city of Cape Town, far from amenities usually associated with a city university. This isolation made it easy to cordon off the university in times of protest. The South African Defence Force (SADF) was at all times stationed opposite the main university gate and would enter the university at short notice as soon as they suspected trouble. Mental and physical threats were always close at hand.

It was extremely liberating both socially and politically when Black Consciousness entered our world. Through conversations, songs, arts and culture, we became a reflection of our true selves. We embraced our Blackness with pride. This was reflected in our social activities; Hillary van den Heever taught his peers photography, and Andries Oliphant made provocative films about race in the middle of Voortrekker Road in whites-only Bellville. A cycling club was started, and our leisure activities were increasingly linked to our determination to reinvent ourselves as political beings. As individuals and a group, we were excluded from all these activities in the white world because of the colour of our skins. A hiking club was formed, but even in nature there was separateness, as Black and white people could not sleep in the same overnight facilities.

The Black Consciousness student leadership in the 1970s made it clear that we should boycott all events that took place in white Cape Town, or at any historically white higher education institutions. Our independent student leadership proved that as students we could carve out our own political and social paths without interference from the white-led administration. In effect, we created our own spaces of politicised learning, leisure and entertainment. And in many ways, we lived happily in our own world; we did not pine for the white cultural world – exemplified, for example, by the Nico Malan or Baxter theatres. Nor did we want to partake in racially segregated activities such as the white intervarsity rugby matches. In any case, the operative popular slogan of the time was 'No normal sport in an abnormal society'.

The year 1976 was a watershed one for me. We hosted the first ever Black intervarsity match at the university. At night various cultural performances took place, from poetry to drama. A group of us camped in the bush bordering the sports fields and the 'squatter camp' between the university and the Peninsula Technical College (PenTech), which also included the Bellville Teachers Training College (Bellville Onderwys Kollege or BOK). This was in fact the hub of coloured further education; for the first time, everyone identified as politically Black.

During the intervarsity tournament, we made friends with students from other Black campuses such as the universities of Turfloop,

Zululand (Ngoye) and Fort Hare. We had intense political discussions around the campfire and consumed copious amounts of beer. The iconic James Matthews (we called him Brother James) spent many a night with us around the campfire, and we would share poetry and songs and powerful debates. These events were forerunners of the most effective countrywide student protests ever experienced. Just reminiscing about those days makes me delirious. We were most creative in a time that was most oppressive.

By the time the Soweto uprising came in June that year, we were ready and well connected across Black campuses. UWC students played a major role in organising protests in the Western Cape. The slogan 'When UWC sneezes, the whole country coughs' became popular. We protested, and sang freedom songs such as 'We Shall Overcome' and struggle songs dedicated to Oliver Tambo and Umkhonto we Sizwe (MK). We became addicted to Timmy Thomas's 'Why Can't We Live Together' and Pink Floyd's 'Another Brick in the Wall'. We formed solidarity with both the support workers and academics on campus. At this point we were ambivalent about our rector, and some of the graffiti on the walls and roofs of buildings declared him a 'sell-out' and 'traitor'. I still remember one that said 'Tricky Dicky has done it again!' Yet he was always at the front of the protest marches in his academic dress, leading staff and students against the apartheid onslaught. This tradition was continued by his successor, Jakes Gerwel.

Throughout the 1970s and 1980s, countrywide student and worker protests became the catalyst for change in the education landscape. We believed that 'People's Education' was the key to liberation. Workers' and alternative colleges such as the South African Committee for Higher Education (SACHED) became important sites of learning for people who would otherwise not have had access to education. Magazines such as *Work in Progress*, *Speak* and *Agenda* were at the forefront of teaching Marxist feminism, and helped raise awareness of the rights of women workers. Books like Paolo

Freire's *Pedagogy of the Oppressed*, shared outside the classroom, were the antithesis to the oppressive Christian National Education curriculum taught at the university.

I became increasingly aware of the inequities that patriarchy enforced, and, during the late 1980s, women like Jean Benjamin started to play a major role in my becoming a feminist. She was our very own Joan Baez with her guitar and her presence at struggle gatherings. She taught us through song, dance and performance about the oppressive roles imposed on women, and, once again, this was a next step in teaching me that there were different ways of learning when formal education was so inadequate.

Transforming the education landscape was one of the primary goals of a post-apartheid South Africa. The apartheid engineers were adamant about subjecting Black people to a type of education that would keep them in subservient roles as manual labourers, and perpetuating the master, servant and maid relationships. Laws and policies were crafted and separate educational institutions were created to keep Black and white people from studying together. Amenities in the institutions were carefully designed so that staff and workers from different race groups could not use the same toilets or recreational facilities. It was therefore necessary to implement a different kind of social re-engineering of the post-1994 education and training environment.

The new legal and policy framework was geared towards transforming the higher education environment, and merging institutions or some of their academic departments and faculties was high on the agenda. Legislation such as the South African Qualifications Authority Act 58 of 1995 set out to standardise qualifications, while the objective of the Skills Development Act 97 of 1998 was to skill and reskill previously disadvantaged groups of people so that they could obtain and retain gainful employment. The workplace was supposed to become a learning centre. The Education White Paper 3 of 1997 was an important departure from apartheid Christian National Education, with the intention to redress institutional cultures and mission statements, and address imbalances in race and gender profiles.

But almost thirty years after South Africa's first democratic election, we are still struggling with the process of redress, and the curricula within institutions continue to focus narrowly on the mechanical training of professionals. In my opinion, the present-day curricula have not fundamentally transformed the social and political consciousness of students.

As a small contribution to the challenges of the bigger education picture, I decided to participate in the official curricula, as well as continuing to teach outside the formal classroom. Over time, I realised that the teaching methodologies for volunteer students at the Gender Equity Unit (GEU) and in two faculties – the Department of Women's and Gender Studies (WGS) in the Arts Faculty, and pre-service teacher students in the Education Faculty – differed. Each teaching situation came with its own challenges. The volunteer students came from different disciplines and faculties and were drawn to the programmatic work of the GEU because they were looking for a place to belong. I found that some of the students in the WGS department were students who had originally volunteered at the GEU and had made the connection between feminist activism and theory. I volunteered to teach in the pre-service teachers' course because of the necessity for teachers to have a better understanding of the needs of the learners. This is particularly true because of ever-changing social and legal frameworks, especially concerning sexual and gender identity.

My goal was to find ways to teach feminism, gender, gender identity and sex, sexuality, and sexual orientation in different settings. To teach differently, it is important to understand the past. The mid-1990s marked the thriving of WGS programmes at South African higher education institutions. These programmes were mainly responsible for teaching theories of feminisms, gender and sexuality, and sexual orientation. By the early 2000s, these programmes usually became fully fledged academic departments. However, the drift of donor interests, self-inflicted austerity measures, mergers, and the rationalisation of academic departments at some institutions led to the constant threat of closure, and in some cases, actual closure, of WGS departments. The 'disciplining' of women's and gender studies as programmes formally set up as intellectual orthodoxy challenged the transgressive nature of feminist activist thought, and this kind of mainstreaming into the academic project slowly killed liberatory practices and activism.

New categories of teaching and learning involved a new layer of professionals, and positions such as deputy dean, director and pedagogical specialists mushroomed in the various universities. Despite these developments, students increasingly searched for answers about themselves: what it meant to be Black, questions about their abled or (dis)abled bodies, their communities, and how their multiple sexual and gender identities fitted into the broader patriarchal and heteronormative academic world and society. Each body experienced violation and discrimination differently, and we desperately needed the courage and space, both physically and metaphorically, to talk, to write and to research about the self.

Questions such as 'how do students learn?' and 'why do they learn?' became even more pertinent in a world where education has become increasingly commodified, and where institutions use terminology such as 'throughput', focus on skills training for professions, and regard entrepreneurship as one of the most important attributes of a graduate. Universities now train students to be effective within capitalist structures, the market and the workplace. Do we teach students how to become effective and dependent modern-day wage slaves? Or do we want them to become independent critical thinkers? How can we teach differently and learn from past activist experiences in teaching for liberation so that students come to know more than just what is in their textbooks? The underlying question here is: what did liberation mean for the building of a post-apartheid South Africa?

Spaces for lateral thinking have been compromised by reward systems that are dependent on competition, neo-liberal market research projects, profits, donor funding and pathologies. Studies increasingly focused on the diseased, violated, indigent Black populations. Specialised research chairs on food security and HIV/AIDS have been established at institutions of higher learning, and Black women have become the subjects of research. This research often pathologises Black women's bodies, with some studies increasingly making them spectacles of hypersexuality. Education, according to Paolo Freire, is never neutral. I believe that research proposals to donors and funders are capitalising on the (prurient) interest in these pathologies, with the result that student researchers are steered towards research that supports the main interest of the principal academic researcher. This subjectivity brings even more pathologies.

My primary objective was to ensure that students did not see themselves as perpetually indigent, violated and diseased, based on my firm belief in providing a supportive environment where Black women could find their own voices. I regard 2006 as the defining year for me starting formal programmatic work and teaching beyond the classroom. The outside classroom teaching started at a time when South Africa was supposed to celebrate various achievements with an impact on women's lives. It was the fortieth anniversary of the Women's March; the thirtieth anniversary of the 1976 Soweto uprising; and the tenth anniversary of the birth of the 1996 South African Constitution. But these celebratory experiences were overshadowed by the continuous violence against women and girls. Several leading political figures were also implicated in incidents of rape, assault and sexual harassment.

I decided to raise awareness and conscientise the campus community about the violence against women on and off campus. The idea was to create a space where women would feel free to speak and share their respective experiences of violence, whether personal or not. Our aim was to perform a skit or play that spoke out against the endemic violence against women. The university did not have a dedicated theatre or drama department, nor did it teach drama as a subject. However, I remembered how effectively we had raised awareness about violence against women during the apartheid era, when Jean Benjamin taught us how to raise awareness through performance at political events. Although she was a lecturer in psychology, her political teaching took place outside the classroom in her home and at political rallies and fundraising events. Back then we got together to create a play, and she taught us how to sing the Afrikaans song 'My naam is Jan, Jan, Jan. Ek is 'n man, man, man'. She accompanied us on her guitar. Our play depicted triple oppression experienced by Black women, for whom violence, race and gender intersect at home and in the workplace. I realised then that with a few committed people, you can start to change opinions.

I approached the English department on campus, as well as performers in the arts and culture world to assist me with writing and directing a performance piece. However, nobody was available. I was eventually referred to a Norwegian exchange student, Elizabeth Stokland, from Stavanger University, who was based at the Centre for the Performing Arts at UWC. She was willing to help us put a performance together. We advertised all over campus for women students who might be interested in such a venture. Several students from the university, one lecturer from the WGS department, and two women from the broader community were interested in taking part. Over a few months, Saturday mornings were dedicated to teaching, sharing experiences and writing various pieces.

There were several challenges to overcome, and during the talking and writing sessions we grappled with identity, sexism, racism and ableism, and dealt with the fact that primary, secondary and higher education failed to teach students holistically. Religious fundamentalism became evident a couple of weeks into our Saturday sessions, when one of the participants told us that she was going to withdraw because there were too many swear words in the pieces, as well as too many sexual references. She informed us that she had joined a charismatic religious student organisation and gotten married to Jesus. She subsequently dropped out of the sessions.

The sessions were fun-filled and creative, and we usually shared a healthy soup that the students called *poespas*, which in Afrikaans means 'mishmash', because it was filled with all kinds of vegetables and chicken pieces. But the name was also a play on the name that was eventually given to the production: *Reclaiming the P . . . Word*. Nonetheless, the sessions could also be sad and traumatic when the participants shared more about themselves as time went by, and we got to know each other better. The women opened up about their experiences, sometimes for the first time in their lives. During the sessions, the participants explored their pain, their silence, their shame and ultimately searched for healing. The written pieces reflected their traumatic experiences.

This group learning allowed the participants to make friends across social, political and language lines. The longer the participants stayed in the volunteer programme and shared their lived experience, the more they realised how common their experiences were, and they became each other's support systems. They usually continued this support and friendship long after they completed their studies.

The intention was to have a once-off performance, but after the first one, there was a huge demand for more from both the performers and the members of the audience. The audience identified with the different pieces, and we would have post-performance conversations about the play in the old-fashioned feminist manner. We started to perform all over the Cape Peninsula: in theatres, community halls, holiday resorts and psychiatric hospitals, as well as other institutions of higher learning. While the performances were the products of months of work, it was the pedagogical process that we developed – an activist pedagogy – that had a lasting impact.

Important to the process was the safe environment in which the conversations could take place. There was no judgement, and women could share without fear or prejudice. Intimate, safe learning spaces contributed to feminist teaching and learning. They offered the opportunity for reciprocity, or a dialogic learning environment where the roles of teacher and student were constantly interchanged. Because it was not based on modular learning with a fixed curriculum, the pedagogy methodology was flexible; participants could enter, exit and return at their own pace. The criteria that formed the foundation were that everyone should respect each other, and that all personal information shared should remain confidential within the group.

The first session usually covered 'Getting to Know Each Other', where participants were introduced to each other. There was always the consciousness that everyone's experience and background differed. Here are a few of the expectations that were shared at one such session:

'I want to debrief my emotional stories. I want peace.'
'I want a change in perspective, thoughts, and different opinions. Growth. Writing deep. People should become confident.'
'Hopes. No expectations. Everyone can take a piece of the space because it's a beautiful journey.'
'Change in myself. Speak more of my own language. Embrace African history and culture.'
'To find closure. Usually fear the unknown. Find me/ourselves.'
'Expect to be wiser. Illuminated. To become a stronger person. Better woman. Unconventional thinking. Change. Add on to what I am.'

This session highlighted that the current discourse on Black women fed into the new kind of PhD research which described them as Poor, Hungry and Diseased. This pathologising strengthened the resolve to act, and to dispel the myth that Black women are incapable of looking after themselves. The students would reflect, discuss and write short pieces or poetry on these 'perceptions' and their experiences.

It was the writing process that was the most educative. There were no academic or writing rules. The participants were not bound to a genre, and the collective writing process proved to be particularly healing. They became new cultural writers who realised that apartheid and violence had not only affected us mentally but left their scripts on our bodies. We were claiming a place in Black women's cultural theorisation. Besides writing a collective script, following a process of feminist awareness-raising, where we discussed and reflected on readings, videos and personal experiences, we also used the design of a poster as part of the teaching and learning process. The poster for the performance piece, *Words4Women*, was a collage we made of the words that women are called in local languages. We wrote these words, which dehumanise and infantilise women, and which we often carry on our bodies and in our demeanour throughout our lives, all over the image of a naked woman's body.

Figure 4.1. Poster by Carol Burmeister.

However, this methodology could not be applied in the formal classroom, where curricula had to be submitted to academic and senate committees for approval. The classroom represented structural learning, with a formal syllabus and limited time for deconstruction and transgression. Knowledge gained was subject to testing by examination. Formal assignments had to be written and presented in a set academic style, and there was little freedom for creativity. At the end of this learning process, students were rewarded with a degree or diploma. The contact period with them was limited, and one could not really give quality time to exploring their feelings and determining their in-depth understanding of the readings.

In the WGS sessions, there was some degree of exploration and understanding because they were a smaller group of students. In addition, one could assume that those present had chosen to study this field because they were interested in and had some background knowledge of feminist theory, or they were pursuing gender studies in line with their own sex and/or gender identities. However, the fact remained that they could not explore as much in their own time or at their own pace. Neither could they take time out and then return the way the volunteer individuals could, because they were bound to an academic time frame. They were also busy with other modules, and some of them worked full-time.

The third group I taught consisted of the pre-service teachers in the Education Faculty. Here the challenges and pedagogical distance were even greater, as these students came from different disciplines and faculties. The classes were huge (over 200 students) and were the most diverse in terms of gender, sex, discipline and language. This placed a heavy burden on the teacher because we were unaware of what the students' deeply existing prejudices and biases were. The different pedagogical practices in each student's disciplinary background offered additional challenges.

The pre-service teacher students also did school visits and practice teaching and were often away from class for weeks.

This made consistent in-depth teaching and follow-up difficult. In big classes, very few students actively took part in discussions, and it was easy to hide prejudices. It was always the same students that questioned theories and perceptions. Those with strong opinions often dominated, and the students that had always been marginalised because of their gender identity, sexual orientation or disability continued to be sidelined. I had to make special efforts to draw students in to participate but could never really build the same kind of intimate teaching space as in the case of the volunteers and smaller WGS classes.

I elected to teach about gender and sexuality, as well as the different forms of violence affecting learners and teachers. We asked students to observe the attitudes and behaviours at the schools they visited, and then write reflective assignments on their experiences. This methodology proved to be enlightening and liberating, but some students experienced it as hostile and disruptive. The students in these classes came from a variety of socio-religious backgrounds, and the teacher had to disrupt the conformist and assimilated learning that most of them had been exposed to. Learning about spectrums and non-binary, non-conformist gender and sexuality allowed for risk-taking, but also made the classroom a place that exposed the vulnerabilities of both student and teacher. Rogério Junqueira, a well-known queer theorist and pedagogue, reminds us of the dangers of 'the pedagogy of silence', 'the pedagogy of the closet' and 'the pedagogy of insult' that create opportunities for both teacher and learner to make insulting and hurtful jokes or remarks.[1] In these classes, I often had to turn to authoritative measures to curb the hate and misogyny I sometimes heard expressed.

Upon reflection, it is obvious that applying a feminist pedagogy when teaching students with whom you are more familiar makes it easier to ask questions about the self. In these instances, we were able to talk and analyse the trauma and the happiness that we experienced without any judgement. We were able to trust and to interrogate our feelings, and for the educational drama group, the reward was a performance piece that gave life to the process. In the WGS class, the satisfaction came from continuous feedback and reflection, and ultimately the completion of the students' degrees. We knew that these students understood what they had learned, and we felt confident that they would apply some of that knowledge in their lives and careers. However, although there were some success stories from the big pre-service teaching classes, I could never be sure whether these students would ever be able to teach differently in their future professions, given that the school system remained hostile to those perceived as different from the heteronormative. For as long as feminist learning was and continues to be regarded as a threat, challenging the status quo will be hard work.

CHAPTER 5

Querying the Queer

gertrude fester-wicomb

Introduction

Today, sexual orientation, queer struggles, locations (particularly the urban–rural divide) and LGBTIQ identities are foregrounded in most South African discourses on freedom, justice and democracy. This was not always the case. Simon Nkoli, the anti-apartheid and gay rights activist, once addressed his comrades on the matter, saying, '*I am black and I am gay.* I cannot separate the two parts of me into secondary or primary struggle. They will all be one struggle . . .'[1] As activists in the 1980s, we were strangely situated: we were progressive educators in political movements and struggles that offered little or no space for us to grapple with central aspects of our personal and political identities. The lives of three queer South Africans who have been fairly prominent public figures by virtue of their activist, educational and political work – Richard Rive, Sally Gross and myself – exemplify this contradiction. By looking at their lives and mine in this chapter, i[2] trace the ways in which queer struggles under apartheid were embedded in lived intersectional experience, even though this experience has been explicitly theorised and written about only fairly recently.

Fragmentation was typical of the identities of South Africans who, in their personal or public lives, resisted gender binaries and dominant heterosexual scripts. We deviated from prescribed gender scripts and homonormativity in complicated and often messy ways. As has been the case elsewhere, South African feminist politics and discourses provide conceptual tools for understanding the politics of difference based on gender, as well as on race, class and other aspects of social identities. I draw on my lived experience and learned knowledge of feminism to unpack these lives and my own.

Radical struggles to live and find freedoms from prejudice and authoritarian violence – at different levels – have been central to the lives of many who resisted apartheid. Multiple struggles against patriarchy were enmeshed with responses to religious chauvinism, and colourism, even among Black South Africans, as well as classism, elitism and prejudices about language. These multiple dynamics have long been a feature of the politics of Black South Africans, with such intersections of oppression being contextually specific. They reveal the ways in which a particular national context, and, more specifically in the cases i discuss, the context of Cape Town in South Africa during the 1960s–1990s, shaped distinctive senses of belonging and exclusion in the intersectional[3] struggles of public figures in the anti-apartheid struggle.

Richard Rive

To me, Richard Rive, born in District Six, a writer and teacher who lived on the Cape Flats[4] for his entire adult life, personifies the complexities and contradictions of power, homophobia and internalised patriarchy. He was well known as a progressive writer, educator and political persona, yet he was plagued by his inability to accept his sexuality, as well as deep prejudices about gender and skin colour. He was an internationally renowned writer, eloquent academic, educator and leading member of the New Unity Movement (NUM). His academic excellence led to scholarships, culminating in his doctorate at Oxford University. Rive's biographer, Shaun Viljoen, emphasises Rive's silence about his family in his autobiography *Writing Black*, but nevertheless points out the significance that Rive attached to the portrait of his 'obviously white' grandfather on the mantelpiece and the glaring absence of his dark-skinned grandmother's photo.[5] Rive acquired immense public power, yet he seemed plagued by his very dark skin throughout his life. This obsessive colour-consciousness illustrates the racial violence often perpetuated within communities and families in race-obsessed apartheid South Africa, especially in the Western Cape. It can be seen in apartheid planning and separate development: the presentation of the rightful home of those of mixed race, or Coloured, being the Cape Flats.

It is my conviction that Rive's torturous experiences of discrimination were even more strongly manifested in relation to his sexual orientation. I suspect his homophobia stemmed from his deep-seated investment in patriarchy and, to a certain extent, misogynistic conditioning. As was the case with all who lived under apartheid, Rive was deeply affected by the power relations that both oppressed us and also shaped our personal senses of 'self' – as men, as Black, as Coloured, as 'properly' gendered, 'respectable' Coloured women, 'normal' Black men, or entitled White men. To resist dominant scripts was difficult – a struggle often achieved at the cost of losing family members, the respect of work colleagues, friends, and even allies within the political struggle. Few of us had the courage to risk such extreme isolation.

The first time i encountered Rive was as a student at Harold Cressy High School. Our school participated in sporting events with South Peninsula High School, where Rive taught and was a sports administrator. He was definitely in charge and treated with deference by fellow sports administrators and teachers. Yet at one moment, as he walked towards the stands, some South Peninsula students started chanting, '*Chocca, Chocca!*'[i] Soon the wooden stands reverberated as students from different schools joined in the chanting. I recollect feeling immense sympathy for this dignified man, singled out for such virulent attack by those whom he taught and to whom he devoted his working life. It must have been excruciating for Rive to have thousands of students jeering at him because of his dark skin. I have no doubt that this taunting about his Blackness, a pattern that must have started in his early childhood, instilled in Rive a deep solidarity with the oppressed, and may well have been an important catalyst for his political activism.

He was the outsider in many ways in his Coloured family: the darkest, with an unknown father, and a bookworm. His sister, Georgina, was 12 years his senior, and he did not have much of a relationship with his siblings. His self-consciousness about his dark skin, along with his loneliness, could also have been a driving force in his athletic and academic successes, both as a scholar and writer. Rive was determined to use his craft, putting pen to paper, in his anti-apartheid struggles. His dedication was evident early on when, in a short story he wrote as a teenager, 'The Bench', he portrayed a Black South African who dared to sit on a 'Whites only' bench. He won an award for this story.

In his biography of Rive, Viljoen comments on how proud Rive felt that he was able to secure a post at the highly respected South Peninsula High School. It was set aside for mainly upper-class and English-speaking Coloured students, rather than Afrikaans-speaking and working-class Coloured people, in the Western Cape. Rive remained at this school for nearly 20 years, convinced that education and sport could lead to transformation. He coached students and was central in the Western Province Senior School Sports Union until 1975, when he became head of English at Hewat,

---

i *Chocca/Chokka* is the black secretion/ink of the squid, but the word could also be a reference to chocolate. In a conversation with Viljoen on 21 June 2020, he explained to me that in his research into *chocca* he found that both meanings were relevant. He also expressed that *chocca* was used as a form of endearment as well and was never maliciously intended.

a teacher training college where those destined to teach at Coloured schools were taught. An eminent academic, and the only teacher with a PhD at Hewat, Rive chose to teach there in spite of offers from local universities, because it was strategic for good education. He told me that he rejected a post at the White University of Cape Town, for example, because they did not include any African literature in their English curriculum. He believed he was making a crucial political intervention by teaching future teachers.

I eventually became a colleague of Rive's in 1982 in the Hewat English department, which he headed. My experience of teaching there was characterised by boycotts continuing into the post-1994 period. Rive and i were on a staff and student liaison committee to address student grievances, and we often disagreed. I believed he did not always respect the students' concerns. He spent more time correcting students' language than paying attention to the content of their complaints. This may partly have been ideological intolerance: students supported the ANC, whereas Rive was affiliated to the Trotskyist NUM. However, his insistence on 'quality' language and his inability to identify with the needs of the young students highlight the contradictions of the man who consistently supported (including financially) and encouraged students.

An animated and jovial entertainer, raconteur par excellence, he was the central attraction of any party/discussion with his Oxford English accent and booming voice. His was a larger-than-life personality, and his murder at the age of 58 was a tragedy. Keenly interested in his community, he was scathingly anti-apartheid. He often adopted young students (although boys only, according to my research) to assist with their schooling.

Rive's writings prominently featured 'moffies'.[ii] They were depicted as colourful characters and, perhaps because of Rive's

---

ii *Moffie* was originally a term of ridicule for gay men until it was appropriated as a term of pride by LGBTIQ people themselves (similar to how the word 'dyke' has been reclaimed by some lesbians).

own ambivalent sexuality, he painted them as compassionate, lively people. He was often invited to international conferences, and on his return home after a conference in Japan, he was clearly upset with me. Later he shared that he had been attacked by feminists about the lack of strong women characters in his texts. So this local feminist had to bear the brunt of his anger! Yet what i find puzzling is that Rive did his thesis on Olive Schreiner and was a great admirer of what he saw as her liberal ideas about gender and race. But, rather perplexingly, the many feminist questions Schreiner raised did not seem to have influenced him at all. Virago Press, a renowned British feminist publisher, invited Rive to publish his work with them, and he later blamed me ('you feminists') when they reneged on their offer on learning that he was a man.

Rive was an oxymoron: a patriarch with enormous contradictory public powers and skills which he used unashamedly; but privately a person with deep pain and loneliness and someone who was never publicly reconciled with his homosexuality. He never had any public intimate relationship in South Africa that we knew of. What seems to have been a pattern of picking up young men ultimately led to his tragic murder in 1989.

Within the political context of constant protests and police repression, there were few occasions when we discussed personal lives; instead, politics and education dominated. We spoke of human rights, but not LGBTIQ rights. With my women teacher colleagues, i sometimes did, as a few of them were feminists and some in same-sex relationships, but discussion was limited to our clique. There was another gay male lecturer, Peter Voges, at Hewat, but Rive seemed to have little respect for Voges's work and creative art. For educational staff members involved in the mass democratic movement, there were minimal spaces for intersectional issues: apartheid was the problem; race and occasionally class issues were core problems as well, and this Rive embraced. We in women's movements were often accused of dividing the struggle.

I remember two occasions that might have offered opportunities for some personal discussion. One was at Rive's home. The atmosphere was affable, and he commented that i had a very exciting life. Because of my ambivalence towards him, i did not take the opportunity to venture into a personal conversation. On another occasion, a lesbian staff member, Colette, invited us to lunch. He was not the boisterous animated rowdy Rive of the staffroom, but a gentle soul, sharing stories of his experiences. There was none of the anger or insulting banter that usually characterised his exchanges; instead, a quiet, engaging and admirable person emerged – a warm, open and friendly man. It is with regret that i recall his constant requests that i invite him for Sunday lunch. I always retorted, 'Later, when i have time.' In retrospect, the quiet, engaging Rive that i had glimpses of at Colette's lunch may have been the complex and compassionate person i would have come to know had i invited him to my home.

Sally Gross

Unlike Rive, Sally Gross, assigned male at birth and given the name Selwyn, was open about her sexuality and mis-gendering. An outspoken and brave advocate of rights for intersex people in South Africa, Sally's pioneering spirit is not forgotten. She died relying on the charity of others. Her death shows the neglect that intersex people endure in a society that does not accommodate or understand.

Historically, if a baby was born with ambivalent genitalia, it was customary for doctors to decide which genitalia was more prominent and perform medical 'adjustments' to make the baby conform to the ideal presentation of one sex. With the rise of the intersex movement, intersex people have demanded that such infants be left as they are and be able to decide at a later stage what they prefer, or to choose to remain as they are – a fairly recent development.

Gross was one such intersex baby, born on 22 August 1953. Her family was Jewish. According to tradition, because she was designated a boy, a circumcision ritual took place that was 'botched up'. In her remarks about resisting binaries, she often credited her secure sense of self to feeling accepted by her parents:

> I am profoundly grateful I was spared surgery and was brought up in a way which left me pretty unneurotic about my body, all things considered, and that, believe me, is quite an extraordinary achievement. And the one thing which I certainly never had any reason to doubt was my parents' love.[6]

But the love of her parents could not shield her from the harshness and alienation of this world.

Gross's activism was wide-ranging. As a White South African man, she could have enjoyed a life of privilege, yet she chose to work for the oppressed. She was a member of the ANC in exile, worked in Palestine, read philosophy and theology, was fluent in Hebrew, and later converted to Catholicism. As Father Selwyn, she taught at St Joseph's Theological Institute in Cedara, outside Pietermaritzburg, and later at Blackfriars, Oxford, and elsewhere. In similar ways to Rive, she might have been prompted towards solidarity with others who were oppressed because she herself knew the pain of being seen as 'abnormal', 'inferior' and in need of 'correction'.

After 40 years, Selwyn decided to resolve her gender identity. She asked for a one-year sabbatical from her monastery in order to meditate on her concerns. This was allowed under strict conditions: she had to go where nobody knew her and was not allowed to meet with persons from the priory. If she wanted to attend Mass, she had to ask local archbishops, who consulted her superior. This she found challenging. Her superior was unsympathetic. The fact that she was then a woman and ordained, considering that Catholicism does not allow women to be ordained, further compounded her problems.

During her transitioning, she chose the name Sally. But the very church that Sally was first attracted to and that led to her conversion to Catholicism was also one to repudiate her:

I had expected that the attitude of the church would have been loving; I thought there would have been support. I did not believe that at a time when I needed friendship and contact more than any other time in my life, these, specifically, were denied me.[7]

In one of our days of sharing experiences, Sally and i discussed our ambivalence about our religions, faith and the institutionalised religions and the inherent patriarchy in them. As much as we enjoyed being part of the church, we also felt angry and hurt by many aspects of it.

Unlike Rive, Gross openly articulated her personal dilemmas: '[As] a very young child I had sense of something being awry in the area of gender, about my own bodiliness. I didn't know exactly what it was, but there was a sense of things being awry . . . of being different.'[8] But Gross was born into secular and faithful worlds that only understood two sexes, male and female.

When Gross returned to South Africa, she had many problems with the Department of Home Affairs. She had left as a man and returned a woman. She approached a gender equality commissioner, Sheila Meintjes, and myself to enquire how we could assist her and other trans and intersex people. When i met her, i was deeply impressed by the amount of research she had done on intersex people globally. However, she was not able to do much research on their position in South Africa. I questioned whether we could not do more local research, since this would be needed if we wanted to facilitate any change in laws, and she met with Meintjes and me to share her ideas about researching the South African situation.

It is ironic that the Commission for Gender Equality, a Chapter 9 institution whose main mandate is to promote and support constitutional democracy, functioned in an autocratic manner.

There was opposition to our working with Gross, even though hers was clearly a key gender issue. We had meetings with her to strategise about best approaches. What subsequently happened spoke volumes about the ignorance about gender justice in circles that should have been promoting democracy and showed up the open hostility towards gender non-conformity. There was some confusion about correspondence sent to the Department of Home Affairs regarding the issue of trans and intersex people. The then chair of the commission thought that, as commissioners, Meintjes and i had undermined her by communicating directly with the minister of home affairs. Although the Commission for Gender Equality Act 39 of 1996 does not grant the chair more power than other commissioners, the chair proceeded to act as if she had. This was challenged by commissioners Rashida Manjoo, Sheila Meintjes and me. Ultimately, the chair instructed us to discontinue the project. The acrimonious atmosphere at the time was such that we were compelled to stop. This i still see as my betrayal of the cause. Through my intensive discussions with Gross, i was convinced that the Constitution comprehensively covers the rights of all persons in Chapter 2, clause 9 (sub-section 3): 'The state may not unfairly discriminate directly or indirectly against anyone on one or more grounds, including race, gender, sex, pregnancy, marital status, ethnic or social origin, colour, sexual orientation, age, disability, religion conscience, belief culture, language and birth.'

Sub-section 4 stresses that no person shall discriminate on the above grounds. The fact that no discrimination should take place on the basis of one's birth (whether intersex or not) implies LGBTIQ people are protected. Furthermore, clause 10 stresses: 'Everyone has inherent dignity and the right to have their dignity respected and protected.' I believe that, as commissioners, we failed Gross and all trans/intersex South Africans. This is especially the case given that research has shown that South Africa has a high incidence of intersex babies: it is estimated that around one in 50 is born with some degree of non-typical sexual differentiation.

In 2010 Gross established Intersex South Africa, an independent intersex community organisation affiliated with the global organisation Intersex International. She resigned from her secure government position at the Land Commission, and used her own money to set up this structure; such was her commitment to supporting and educating others. She was a pioneer in drafting national legislation and including the term 'intersex' for the first time within the definition of sex in South Africa's anti-discrimination law of 2000. Subsequently she also worked on legislation related to the Alteration of Sex Discrimination and Sex Status Act 49 of 2003.

The organisation Intersex South Africa was demanding in terms of energy and finances. Towards the end of her life, Sally was compelled to request financial aid from friends for rent and medical bills. As her health worsened, she became nearly paralysed before her death. It is ironic and tragic that this valiant fighter for marginalised people died alone.

My experience

Now to pick up the thread of my own story. I grew up in a Coloured family as classified by apartheid. My sisters and i disliked the idea of greeting in our family. It was socially expected to kiss relatives on the mouth. I would be defiant and kiss their cheeks instead. This was seen as disrespectful, and i recall people sternly saying, *'Groet reg!'*[iii] This was the opportunity that older men would seize to touch my breasts. I felt helpless until i worked out that i could hold my arms to form a barrier in front of my breasts.

My parents believed in education, including ballet and piano lessons. I loved playing the piano but disliked my teacher because he would touch me inappropriately. I was rapidly learning that being a girl child meant vulnerability. I did not have the courage to say

---

iii Afrikaans greeting translated as 'Greet properly!'

anything to my parents – they made such a fuss of him. But i killed him off in a short story, 'Epitaph for a Piano Teacher', published in a school anthology about children's rights.

Our maternal grandparents had a smallholding at the foot of the Swartberge with the Vinknesrivier (which translates as 'Weavers' Nest River') flowing through it. Weeping willow trees on the banks made it idyllic. Most of the family visited during December, and we grandchildren performed concerts displaying our talents. Some 'White' cousins would play guitar. After a while, these cousins no longer came to the farm, nor did they visit us at our home. We assumed that, as these cousins were growing older, they were no longer willing to mix with Black people. Instead, they had all the privileges and opportunities available to Whites in South Africa at the time. It was with interest that we saw their photographs in local newspapers for achievements in gymnastics. The childhood guitarist became a professional singer and was regularly featured in the local media. We were shocked at the pride some of our family took in these achievements.

But even though i was categorised as Coloured under apartheid legislation and therefore considered inferior to Whites, i too had some privileges. I was keenly aware of the opportunities living in the city gave me compared to family members who remained in the rural areas. I spoke English, and this opened many doors for me.

I was always very close to my cousin Mary Jane, a wheelchair-user the same age as me. I regularly visit her at the Cheshire Home for the Disabled, where she has lived for most of her life. Once i asked her if i should bring her books, and she said she preferred TV. Education was not a priority at these institutions. Meanwhile, i was travelling the world as a 'gender diva', able-bodied and having had a range of educational and other opportunities.

Our home in the Cape Town suburb of Maitland bordered on Windermere, which was then a colourful and peaceful area of diverse people, who lived mainly in brick homes and some made of corrugated iron. Among its fascinating characters were Kewpie and the hairdressers. They mesmerised me; they had beautiful hairstyles and wore make-up – Kewpie's eyebrows were two arched lines dramatically drawn above the eyes. Kewpie and the team (Patsy and Mitsy) were the best hairstylists in the neighbourhood, and very popular. They wore exotic clothes – neither solely men's nor women's apparel, but unique combinations of the two. They were a happy lot. One day on the bus, Kewpie and Patsy sat in front of me. They spoke loudly – they did not have a care in the world; the world belonged to them. Then Patsy said to Kewpie: *'Toe sê hy nogal vi 'n cheek vi my SY! Wat dink djy davan?'*[iv] As i grew older, i learned that the community called them *'moffies'* – with admiration but also ridicule. They chose to be defined as gender non-binary and dressed and lived as they desired. I admired them but was puzzled by this new element in my six-year-old world.

Church played a big role in our lives. Ours was in the city centre, and most of the congregation lived in District Six. We never missed church. But it was a strange set-up – we were a church of freed slaves, but we belonged to the same synod as the White *Moederkerk*.[v] Many asked why we did not join the Coloured *Sendingkerk*.[vi] I heard that we had to have a White minister, otherwise they would insist we go to what seemingly was the inferior *Sendingkerk*. I could not really understand the full implications of this church of God for whom all were equal, and yet apartheid reigned.

---

iv 'What a cheek – addressing me as he! What do you think of that?' [Afrikaans].

v Mother Church. The Dutch Reformed Church, to which our church belongs, took a decision at the Synod of October 1857 that it was 'God's wish' that the separate races not take Communion together. Subsequently it was divided into separate racially exclusive churches. Our church, St Stephen's, was one of the first churches for freed slaves, formed in April 1843. This 1857 Synod decision i see as the start of apartheid and justified by the Synod as 'God's Word'.

vi Mission Church. It was for Coloureds but was formed after our church had joined the Mother Church. The other race-exclusive church was the Dutch Reformed Church in Africa, which was for Black Africans only.

Although we were members of the only Black branch of the *Moederkerk*, my parents believed that Catholic schools were best, and so i was enrolled at St John's School next to the church. Every Friday at school we had to go to Holy Mass. On the other side was the Whites-only Holy Cross Convent. There we were, every Friday, sitting across from one another in church, us on the right side and them on the left. They did not look at us, nor we at them. There was an unspoken antagonism between us. We also were a bit of a motley bunch – some of us did not have uniforms, others were barefoot. We felt so inferior to them, all neat and smart with panama hats. We were in the church of a God who symbolised equal love for all, yet there was polarisation and hostility between the two groups of Jesus' children. The contradictions puzzled me. Was this Christianity in practice?

Church was mostly a lovely place to be and as a choir member i loved singing. There were friends and annual picnics at Boulders Beach in Simonstown. Church council members were stern men who wore black suits. In fact, i was scared of them – but not of my father, who was kind and loving. He was the *kassier-skriba*, secretary and treasurer, of the church, and principal of the church school (which was a slave school started in the 1840s) for 45 years. The men were the leaders at all levels, but it was the women who brought in the money with their hard work at church bazaars and other functions. This division of labour puzzled me.

I was about nine when i overheard that church elder A.B.'s wife complained to the council that he had beaten her. Things like these were usually kept secret or just ignored. What happened to Mrs Benjamin made me sad and mad. I did not know the words patriarchy and power then, but i knew that i had a problem with men's socially sanctioned power to rule and abuse women.

Then my beloved Boulders Beach was declared 'Whites-only'. I do not remember picnics after this. District Six was declared White. De Nova Hats in Hanover Street, our annual shopping destination for

Christmas hats, was no more. In the past, we often visited Aunt Mary Hendricks at the top of Hanover Street. What i remember most about her home was the enormous fig tree in the yard. She and her family had to move to the Cape Flats, as did the majority of our congregation. Similarly, the entire Maitland/Windermere area changed. Forced removals took away the colourful characters and our friends.

Many things changed in the church over the decades. I was the first woman chairperson of the church council in 1994 and worked very closely with our young minister. Some congregants were concerned that he was unmarried. In 2005 i travelled to the UK to complete my studies. While there i received the news that our minister's male partner had outed him (i knew about his relationship as we had discussed it in the past), and then committed suicide. On my return, i learned that the church council had suspended the minister's service. I was interviewed by the media about the suspension, and stressed human rights, freedom of choice and the Constitution. Church council members openly challenged me. I was not allowed to counter what the church council had decided, but i insisted that i could and would. As a commissioner for gender equality at that time, my mandate was to uphold the Constitution. Of course i would do so now too, irrespective of being a commissioner or not.

Aspects of my childhood made me question South Africa as a 'Christian' country, marked as it was by so much inhumanity, and i steadily gravitated towards organised political activism and involvement. For a teenager, there were no political structures through which to voice grievances. With the help of a teacher at Harold Cressy High School, Anne Harries, we formed mixed drama groups through which we raised community issues. In 1971, when I was a student at the University of the Western Cape (UWC), designated for Coloureds only, the Black Consciousness Movement gained momentum. We continued using guerrilla theatre. At UWC, we then formed the South African Student Organisation (SASO). As an active member, i was deeply shocked by the patriarchy of the male-only SASO leadership, which sometimes treated women members as personal fiefdoms. Thereafter i moved to the University of Cape Town, which was for White students only. As i wanted to study drama, which was not offered at UWC, i had to apply for a special permit to attend UCT as a Coloured woman. There we questioned the content of our courses: we were Africans, but there was not a single African author in our entire English curriculum, so we staged protests.

These formative early-life experiences – apartheid, inhumanity, violence against girls and women, the marginalisation of Kewpie and the LGBTIQ community, the disability of my cousin and others who were treated as burdens – all contributed to forming my political consciousness. Ultimately, this became expansive, and was never confined to awareness of racism only. I joined the United Women's Organisation (formed in 1981), an overtly political organisation which, despite apartheid, had about 6 000 members from all race groups, fighting apartheid and women's oppression. It was shocking how many so-called progressive men challenged us for dividing the struggle.

I also reflected on my own privileges as an English-speaking, urban descendant of enslaved and First Nation women. The aforementioned afforded me entitlements that many South Africans could only dream of. Not long ago, my only living aunt, Una Munnik, started counting at a family gathering. I realised she was counting in Khoekhoegowab. On my questioning her about this, she explained that they spoke Khoekhoegowab as children. I regretted not ever having spoken about this to my mother while she was alive. I realised we were robbed of language and culture through colonialism, and that echoes of this were rapidly disappearing with the passing of my aunt's generation. This was another layer of loss, one i had not even explored.

Conclusions

What Rive, Gross and i had in common was that we did not fit comfortably into nuclear families. We did not have conventional heterosexual partners or marriages (except for my brief violent one). All three of us had a commitment to social justice, and actively tried to counter injustice. The ways in which we dealt with personal and identity politics depended on the contexts and challenges of our lives. Gross and i came from loving homes. Gross was the courageous pioneer, confronting the prejudice against the marginalised intersex community. In my case, i do not believe in labelling myself, as i believe sexuality is fluid. Most of my life i challenged injustice and especially focused on marginalisation and intersectionality. Rive, in contrast to us both, never publicly spoke out about his sexual identity. When he wrote about sexuality, he seemed to perform an ostentatious homophobia.

The idea of queerness as a defining feature of identity is in many ways misleading in the light of the vastly different social experiences that Rive, Gross and i had. As a woman, i spent much of my life being haunted by violence or the threat of patriarchal violence. Neither Rive nor Gross experienced this – that i know of – although it could be argued that in the ways both of them died was an element of patriarchal violence. Yet i never experienced the horrible taunts that Rive had to hear about his dark skin colour. I never felt the terror of being outed as a gay man in a country where heterosexuality was a central marker of 'proper' masculinity – even among those who considered themselves to be on the left. Nor did i ever experience Gross's no doubt frightening experience of being seen as a man when she experienced herself as a woman.

Life-story writing, even when briefly done as in this chapter, can tease out the nuances of complex intersections of identity. While the growing industry of scholarly work in this field is important, it may be the case that more stories and personal reflections about worlds that we know intimately will help us to understand what intersectionality really means.

CHAPTER 6

South African Feminists in Search of the Sacred

Fatima Seedat

August in South Africa is Women's Month, remembering the 20 000 women who marched to Parliament in 1956 to protest apartheid pass laws. In 2018, as commemoration, an independent group of feminist activists called for a #TotalShutdown, marked by, among other things, nationally coordinated marches in various cities to present the president with a series of demands addressing the high rates of domestic violence in the country. I attended the Cape Town march, where people began gathering at 9 am and finally began walking around 11 am. The march itself, many remarked, felt like a relatively safe space; men had been asked to stay away and only women-identifying and gender non-conforming people were welcome to attend. Personally, I enjoyed being in a space where I could walk easily, unencumbered by the discomfort of bumping into or making contact with male bodies. Here, I was unafraid to smile freely wherever my eyes moved across the crowd. As a friend explained, the male-free space provided a sense of security.

By 1 pm we had finally reached the gates of the Parliament, where the formalities began with, to our surprise, a call to a Christian cleric to begin the proceedings. I will leave it to you to imagine the outrage when the first words from the woman officiant were 'In the name of God the Father'. Regardless of the booing and heckling, she continued her prayer almost unaffected. Later, as she passed near me through the crowd, I listened in as another marcher asked her why she could not speak of God the Mother. In the officiant's failure to respond adequately, my sister-marcher shared her view that clerics are 'brainwashed' such that the possibilities of a female God evade them. There was another prayer by a lay Muslim woman volunteer from the crowd. While there was no reference to God the Father in her prayer, there was also no special attention to the alternative gendered possibilities of the Divine.

This situation will not be news to many of us, and it represents an important issue I come up against regularly as someone who takes both gender and religion as areas of critical academic study and activism. In this case, even as the organisers worked within a feminist politics, they had not been able to manage the masculine representation of the divine at a march designed for women-identifying and gender non-conforming individuals. This is one way in which gender work responds to religion: namely, to add women and stir so that in this case a female cleric offered us an unreconstructed male God. Feminist work more often, though, finds it easier to ignore or simply dismiss religion, preferring instead a secular orientation. Despite the increasing feminist readings of religion, the broader feminist and women's movement frequently overlooks religion or excludes it. The result is often an uncritical or unwitting inclusion and acceptance of a male-gendered divinity. While we had deliberately and intentionally asked men to stay away from the march, we had not found a way to make similar deliberate and intentional demands to exclude a male God; as a result, we had not thought to include an idea of divinity in a way that spoke directly to the concerns of women marching against domestic violence.

Theorising our gods

In Mary Daly's iconic work, she invites us to make an 'essential leap beyond God the Father' and its associated 'patriarchal fixations'.[1] This requires replacing divinity as a noun which renders God as Supreme Being, with divinity as an 'intransitive verb that does not require an object', where divinity is God as Being. But in doing so, Daly also cautions against a feminist movement that adopts 'a mere semantic shift', changing vocabulary without 'a profound alteration of consciousness or behaviour' and context.[2] In this profound change, divinity as Being is possible not only for our concepts of the sacred or supreme, but for all individuals. It is through this process that people who do not identify as men may come to see themselves present in the divine and challenge God the Father, 'an idealized projection of masculine identity'.[3] Evident in both Daly and the woman officiant's opening statement, the challenge of the divine Father lies in how women and gender non-conforming people become present in the face of a divinity framed in masculine ways. How do people who do not identify as men come into divine and sacred Being when God is a man? It is not sufficient that a woman should lead the prayer. What is required is an intentional recognition and engagement with masculinist constructions of divinity and religiosity, and a deep, intentional feminist response based on radical engagements with spiritual subjectivity.

Women at the march could not have expected the contradiction they were drawn into. For many, gender-based violence is a direct result of the correlation of masculinity with divine authority. So the rejection of male authority leads, in an almost natural and necessary progression, to the dismissal of a masculine God. It is a response to the constraints of a masculine God for women's spiritual subjectivity. Relapsed Muslim academic Qabila, the protagonist of Kharnita Mohamed's 2018 debut novel *Called to Song*, illustrates the difficulties presented by the masculinity of the divine: Qabila is only able to regain her relationship with divinity once Allah becomes feminine; in becoming female, God returns to relevance for women's ways of Being.

Yet feminist thought has characteristically ignored religion, and not because it does not find religion relevant to women's lives. Ironically, the distance may be precisely because feminism reads religion as overly inscribed in women's lives. In drawing distance from it, feminist thought hopes also to reduce or eliminate the relevance of religion for women's lives. Unfortunately, this hasn't been and is also not likely to be the case; the millennial return to religion or the anti-secular turn we are witnessing at present has made certain of this. As a scholar of French political history, Joan Scott draws on experiences in the Global North to illustrate the false equivalence of secularism and equality, which analysis also gestures towards the roots of this difficult history between feminism and religion. The result in feminist discourses is evident in two aspects. First, discourses on equality have characteristically excluded religious women or women who also associate with religion; and second, women's equality discourses exclude a literacy of religious discourses which might otherwise allow for deep and necessary feminist critique. Religious literacy beyond the politics of devotion and worship are mostly absent in feminist activism too. A combination of these erasures allowed for a march against gender-based violence that began 'in the name of the Father'.

While women's voices articulated the Christian and Muslim prayers that began the formalities, women's ways of Being were not reflected in the divinity that was brought to the march by the Muslim volunteer either. Among Muslims, the common response to associations of masculinity and divinity are that God in Islamic thought is not a father in the Christian sense of God the Father and God the Son. And so, while divinity in Muslim thought sits easily and necessarily with the universal Creator, fatherhood in the familial sense does not. Notwithstanding the absence of a notion of divine fatherhood in Islamic thought, the masculinity of the divine does not dissipate through an ungendered Muslim notion of God.

On the contrary, even with an ungendered God, Muslim tradition speaks of God in the grammatical masculine. And as the masculine linguistic form translates into an existential one, the grammar of God brings masculinity to godliness and aligns divine authority with masculinity, from which is produced a template for the structure of human gender relations. Feminist readings of Islamic thought either challenge the associations of masculinity with authority or reframe the traditional grammar of divinity. Egyptian feminist Muslim scholar Omaima Abou-Bakr and theologian amina wadud examine the twin concepts of male responsibility in the form of financial maintenance (*qiwamah*) and male guardianship in the form of marital authority (*wilayah*) as the primary means through which male–female relationships have been conceptualised. wadud highlights how this construct 'deliver(s) subservience of the female to the male in every kind of relationship'.[4] She proposes an alternative in the form of the *tawhidic* paradigm, which consists of a triangular relationship in which men and women believers associate in a horizontal relationship characterised by equality and reciprocity, and are each connected by a separate line that converges in a transcendent God. In wadud's triangle of *tawhid* or divine oneness, the Divine is located outside of masculinity and femininity, and neither precedes the other in their relationship with the Divine.[5]

Abou-Bakr explores the conflation of the language of masculinity and divinity with male authority over women through verse 4:34 of the Qur'an, which becomes central to the formulation of male guardianship (*qiwamah*). Once the verse is separated from its revelatory context and isolated as a self-contained principle, it is generalised into the pervasive criterion of marriage, and finally transformed into 'a cause for privilege, hierarchy and authority', rendering all men fundamentally in authority over all women.[6]

Other Muslim feminist readings have offered new possibilities for understanding gender in the Divine. YaSiin Rahmaan uses the gendered frames of Arabic grammar to reconceptualise the traditional grammar of divinity for gender non-conforming individuals. For Rahmaan, in language 'gender identity is a provisional linguistic assignment' and indicates fluidity rather than definitive gender assignment.[7] Where others have read Qur'anic Arabic references to the Divine and human subjects in terms that are either neutral, masculine or feminine, Rahmaan reads them as gender-fluid and argues that the linguistic fluidity of Arabic allows subjects of various gender identities to be simultaneously 'grammatically masculine or feminine when addressed' or referred to by others. This fluid grammatical assignment celebrates, reforms and destabilises gender. Pointing beyond gender binaries and heteronormative assumptions, Rahmaan finds possibilities here for 'radically gender equitable and queer readings of the Qur'an.'[8]

In contrast to God the Father, the possibilities for privileging the feminine in the Divine have also surfaced in Muslim feminist Sufi thought. Sa'diyya Shaikh's investigation of Ibn 'Arabī's gender cosmology brings this possibility to the fore in three aspects of gender subversion: in the possibilities for women to occupy the position of spiritual epitome, in recognition that femininity also functions as plenitude, and when the feminine is located in a narrative of activity and receptivity.[9] In parallels between women and God's essence as the 'source of all things', femininity offers 'a realm of being that is creative precisely because it encompasses both active and receptive qualities.'[10] The result is an 'ungendered human universality', a divine subjectivity that embraces 'both the male and the female in distinctive ways'.[11]

African, feminist and divine

In the academic study of religion, scholarship of and engagement with women's experiences in African religion remains limited. Oyeronke Olajubu's 2003 work, *Women in the Yoruba Religious Sphere*, characteristically marked by a study of female gods and women's ritual power, remains the most comprehensive reading of women in the context of an African traditional religion, its date pointing also to the slow uptake of gender-based readings of African religions.[12]

My assessment of this is not that women within these traditions have not already been questioning male normativity and gender inequality. Rather, African traditional religion generally has not received in-depth feminist academic study to the degree that, for example, African Christianity has, and the reasons for this are deeply embedded in the politics of coloniality and race. Many feminist approaches to African continental realities anticipate that African women eventually abandon African religion, as a sign of modernisation. Colonial approaches refused to consider African religious practices as religious or hoped that, however religious these practices may be, they would also soon be eradicated and replaced by Christian and Muslim religious practices. The women's march certainly replicated that dynamic, in the omission of African religion in the opening prayers.

A further reason for this limited engagement between feminism and religion is the rightful mistrust of feminist analysis that is brought uncritically into African religious contexts – namely, through Christian women's missions. Historical missionary practices of Northern women in the Global South have characteristically centred on white women's experiences, with the intention of extending them to African and other missionised women. Recent attempts such as Elizabeth Prevost's revisionist reading of the power dynamics of British women's missionary work to cast them instead as 'missionary feminists' do not successfully uncouple missionary women from the uneven power relations of mission work, however non-conforming some might have been in their own homes.[13] Rather they confirm that some of the early incarnations of the now banal triangle of white women saving black women from black men were actually in the context of white mission women saving African women from traditional African religious rituals and practices.

In recognising colonial histories of genocide, forced sterilisation of colonised women, and the discipline and control of mission schools as violent crimes against indigenous populations, however, post-colonial feminist readings of religion in the Global South have raised valuable critiques of the role of religion in sustaining colonial ideologies.[14] Focusing on the politics of the Bible as an imperialist text, post-colonial feminist Christian theology specifically interrogates the complicity of biblical scholarship in the colonial encounter.[15] It holds the texts to account at the intersection of three axes of power – gender, sexuality and religion – to take on what Kwok Pui Lan explains as the task of 'resignifying gender, requeering sexuality and redoing theology'.[16] In this way post-colonial feminist Christian theology pays attention to gendered symbolism in the scriptural texts, and to women in the 'contact zone', where the material reality of the colonial encounter is marked by conflict and inequality. It scrutinises interpretations that support the colonial agenda and responds with decolonial readings of sacred texts, paying attention to the 'politics and poetics' of location to gauge who speaks and who is constructed as the audience of the text.[17] African feminist post-colonial theologians such as Musa Dube have expanded the 'interpretive community' of the text to include 'the ordinary reader' – namely, women who do not engage the text as passive recipients of predetermined meanings.[18] These women use otherwise 'suppressed knowledges' to offer new interpretive strategies resisting colonial religious narratives of sexuality and difference.[19]

The Circle of Concerned African Women Theologians established in the 1990s by Mercy Oduyoye is not very well known outside of religious studies and theology scholars, but amidst the usual set of challenges attendant to feminist organising, it has produced various levels of feminist and womanist analysis of mostly Christian theology, including Oduyoye's *Introducing African Women's Theology*.[20] Also, starting in the '80s, feminist scholars of religion and theology offered rereadings and reimaginings, replacing traditional methods for reading texts with contextual readings, surfacing women's spiritual knowledge and experiences, questioning patriarchal church and ritual practices, and challenging the commitments of liberation theologies to gender equality. A rich genealogy of scholarship over four decades, through Bernadette Mosala, Denise Ackermann, Madipoane J. Masenya, Musimbi Kanyoro, Isabel Phiri, Susan Rakoczy, Sarojini Nadar and Nontando Hadebe, amongst others, demonstrates the growth and expansion of African feminist theological critique from the '80s into the present.

The work of Nokuzola Mndende remains central to the interrogation of the Christo-normative understandings of African traditional religions, tracing the challenges African religions faced moving 'from underground practice to recognised religion'.[21] Subsequent to Mndende, the rich articulations of African forms of feminism in recent years have opened up new readings for African religious practices that were once considered unintelligible to Abrahamic readings of gender and religion. Ideas of fluidity and the crossing of disciplinary boundaries have become significant in recent studies. There is a fluidity in the occupational practices of healers who go beyond the materiality of the body to also include spiritual healing. Similarly there is interest in the fluidity of health-seeking behaviours of people who consult both medical clinics and traditional healers or *izangoma*, as well as the convergence and tensions of Christian and traditional African religiosities.

Gender fluidity in the ritual practices of women as adherents and ritual leaders in African religion disrupts normative Abrahamic constructs of gender and religious authority. Women who embody religious authority as *izangoma* occupy a central space in the contemporary study of women in African religion. Significant studies on women in African traditional religion, such as Nkunzi Zandile Nkabinde's *Black Bull, Ancestors and Me: My Life as a Lesbian Sangoma* and her work with Ruth Morgan about ancestral wives, centre on the works and worlds of women *izangoma* or *izangoma* who are guided or called by women.[22] And perhaps that makes it even more concerning that there was no woman *sangoma* asked to open the formalities and to bring African women's ways of Being Divine into the march.

The women's march illustrated in sharp relief how, despite long-standing or emerging feminist readings of divinity in Islamic thought, Christian theology and African religion, feminist activist spaces either stumble carelessly when it comes to religious expression or remain oblivious to feminist readings of religion. The women who heckled the female pastor at the march could not identify with the divinity that had entered the march as a Father, yet it was incumbent on the organisers to enable this so that we marchers could find our location in a feminine Divine.

Divinity produced in a masculine imaginary delimits the divine possibilities available for women. Even when we are deliberate in creating male-free spaces, we are still challenged in creating male-God-free spaces. It is easy to ask men to stay away from spaces designed to empower women and gender non-conforming individuals, and we did. Shouldn't we also ask God to do the same, at least until we are able to find ourselves within our gods? Or until we're able to find feminist formulations for our divinities and envision our gods as non-conforming as we are?

CHAPTER 7

'Who Do You Think You Are to Speak to Me Like That?'

jackï job

Where I come from, expecting obvious answers is evidence of a complete lack of imagination. Indeed, questions are asked, either out loud in public spaces or silently through tears. One often asked out loud by my mother that rendered me to tears was, 'Who do you think you are to speak to me like that?' She asked this when she was angry, and she was angry often. Any attempts at answering her question were seen as disrespectful backchatting which exasperated her even more. 'What must people think? That's not how a lady behaves' would inevitably follow. Now, I realise that she possibly diverted her hurt and self-derision by placing the onus of her identity onto me. Then, providing a satisfying, compliant response felt crucial. In fact, I took her words literally and really began to think. Just who do I think I am? What do people actually think? And, how exactly does a lady behave?

Growing up, how and who I thought I should be were determined by two elements: family and religion. As the interrelationships in my family were framed by being Jehovah's Witness, my world view was ultimately defined by its tenets. Our religion signified the truth. In fact, Jehovah's Witnesses name it as such and, by design, this truth, as well as their insight of the scriptures, defines them as different and separate from everyone else. The truth, as purported by the religion, develops a particular self-imaginary, embodied in a mode of behaviour and enforceable public performance that ultimately shape a distinct understanding of oneself, others and the surrounding world. To support their assumed privilege as God's chosen people, Jehovah's Witnesses cultivate strategies of reasoning to turn others towards their perception of the world and purpose in life. For them, this is the way of the truth.

As an artist who has used and understood the body as a pivotal medium for creativity, I always wondered about the meaning of authenticity, particularly from unprescribed alternative perspectives of the human body. Thus, thinking about how to embody truth deeply impacted my life. Thinking, which I see as a process that shifts perceptions in between and across the body's sensibilities of sight, sound, smell, taste and touch, triggered unexpected notions and means of self-identification in my mind. Before long, my imagination moved beyond the frameworks of family, religion and its ecclesiastical tales. Much like the exercise of faith, my imagination rendered the invisible visible and expanded constructions and limitations of what I saw and how I saw it. I began to see how multiple variations of truths were played out, and indeed heightened, in the collective enactments of daily life in my community.

Insights into the everyday lives of the 53 homes comprising the 500-square-metre radius of my childhood neighbourhood exposed many meaningful truths. The kind of food eaten at supper time – tomato *bredie* (stew) with mutton, canned viennas and beans on white bread, or fried liver with mashed potato and braised onions – indicated not only the day of the week, but also the time of the month. Who kissed whom in cars parked outside the front gate after 10 pm was rudely revealed when Allison's name changed to Aisha, or Ronald became Riedwaan, much to his Christian family's chagrin, or Charmaine unexpectedly fell pregnant because she was 'naughty'. Grandeur by osmosis was seen when families spoke of their larney relatives who had emigrated to Australia, or grandchildren named after American soap-opera stars. There were also truths such as domestic violence, alcoholism and drug abuse. These details desired to be sealed tight but inevitably seeped through vinegary body odours or malnourished dry, scaly skin unsuccessfully hidden behind hand-flattened, slightly soiled outfits when the money ran out for electricity or a block of Sunlight soap. Living in Factreton, my imagination of myself and what it meant to be a lady was influenced by multiple versions of truth reflected in everyday lives in the community, as well as their collision against singular, insular narratives claimed through my family's faith.

Imagine, if you will, a debate between an elder of a Jehovah's Witness congregation and a community taxi guard, a *ghaatjie,* describing their perspectives of women, in particular a 'lady'. Both men navigate their lives with degrees of significance rendered by how their mothers, sisters, aunties and other women they may know inhabit and influence their worlds. A lady, however, is a particular kind of woman and, in working-class vernacular in Coloured[1] neighbourhoods, represents someone who is better than ordinary, exuding status and rank, like the British royalty as exemplified by Lady Di. A lady, therefore, garners and deserves attention. Could you just imagine how differently these polar ends of my world, an elder and a *ghaatjie*, would describe a lady?

Figure 7.1. *Of Dreams and Dragons,* 2017. Photograph by Cedric Leherle.

Scripting ladies

In my family's faith, the term 'elder' does not necessarily translate as 'an older person in church'. The term's reference to maturity is related to a man and his supposed superior knowledge and application of the scriptures. Therefore, a young man of 25 could be an elder and thus, at least in theory, assigned the role of guiding the congregation. Much like a shepherd, the elder is tasked with keeping the flock together. This flock includes women and men of all ages who subscribe to the idea that Jehovah God has assigned particular male elders as their leaders. With this hierarchical context and ultimate allegiance to God in mind, the elder supports everything he says by referring to 'the Word', the Bible. It is the book that claims to hold infinite knowledge spanning generations and worlds, and yet still remains applicable in contemporary times. The premise is that the Bible is a conduit, a capsule that holds one safe whilst being carried from one instruction to another. Reared in this environment, I readily picture an elder confidently referring to specific scriptures that describe a woman, or lady, as one who respects her husband, is passive and obedient to him, and even covers her head to indicate her submission to his authority.

To substantiate with physical evidence, he might refer to Lot's wife, who chose to disobey when they fled her burning city. She got distracted by her love of material possessions, looked back, and was punished by being turned into a pillar of salt. At this point, I wonder if she might have turned back because she remembered something, or someone. She might even have been called to the flames, like the phoenix, knowing that only fire could enable a rebirth by erasing her material self and a life that she may have been unhappy with. Perhaps she deeply sensed a profound truth related to her potential that involuntarily willed her body to turn away from obeying and following her husband. Of course, these reflections are merely of my imagination and not written in sacred text.

An elder would not see Lot's wife as a lady, especially against the figures of Hannah and Mary Magdalene, who behaved in ways that found favour with God. Hannah yearned to bear a son and, in her desperate plea for help, promised to offer him in service to God if he helped her conceive. Because of her sincerity and willingness to give God her greatest desire, he showed her mercy and she became pregnant. Mary Magdalene showed submissiveness by using her hair and expensive perfumed oil to wipe the feet of Jesus. The lesson, therefore, is that a lady is not selfish nor egotistical and always offers her best to God first, and not herself. These women pleased God and had their names recorded. They are remembered, whereas Lot's wife remains unnamed, recalled as a statue that serves as a deterrent for all who consider going against God's will, or the elder as head of the congregation and the man as head of the house. To listen and serve is what makes a lady admirable and good. Agreeable, like sheep, whom the Bible describes as being on the road to everlasting life, whereas stubborn and disagreeable goats are on their way to everlasting destruction.

Much like an elder, the *ghaatjie*, a young, scrawny, round-shouldered, gangster-type of man, also guides and guards an instrument that holds and carries people from one place to another. His job is to herd people into a minibus taxi, a controversial but necessary mode of transport for people living in breadline neighbourhoods. The *ghaatjie* watches over everyone and asserts his authority by determining who gets into his taxi and where they place themselves. He further displays his affiliation to different kinds of people by how he sees, names and describes them. The people he herds come from his community, a working-class Coloured suburb holding generations and worlds which play out in tales that stretch from the simple and mundane to the political and controversial, all of which animate the ride. These people and their stories ultimately frame his understanding of a lady.

For him, there are three clear distinctions. There is a girl, his *kin*,[i] the one that he knows *smaaks*[ii] him because she always accepts his

---

i   A cute girl that he likes in a physical, sexual way. [All translations in this chapter are from colloquial Afrikaans.]
ii To be sexually attracted to.

advances. When he whistles or licks his lips, she takes it as a compliment and shows off his admiration by sporting his love bite on her neck on Saturday mornings. She is almost like Mary Magdalene was with Jesus. She makes him feel 'all that', *kwaai*, important and in charge. She makes him feel like a man.

Then there is a mother, called Mummy or 'Mumz'. She is that aunty who, no matter what, will faithfully visit her son in Pollsmoor Prison, even if he raped and killed a girl, because he is her baby, and she knows that, deep down, he is good. She is forgiving. She quietly accepts, hugs herself by crossing over each side of her jersey, and carries on.

And then there is a lady. She is the one who arrives at the taxi rank and everyone knows *daai za lady* (that's a lady), and makes way for her to move unobstructed. She is wearing a blouse and perfume, has a clutch bag, and her clothing is out of this world. She seems untouchable and from another place. She might even be on her way to another place, but she gets into his taxi, and comes from his community. *Daai za lady*, and you have to give her space. In the *ghaatjie*'s account, the lady that gets the space is the one whose actions are not dictated by her son or boyfriend. However, I doubt whether her apparent difference can merely be limited to her nicely ironed and well-put-together fashion sense. Surely there are other women carrying clutch bags, wearing perfume, and on their way to places beyond the constructs of their community. Why does that lady, *daai lady*, not this one, *nie die nie*, but *daai lady* get acknowledged as a lady? This intrigues me.

When I look at the kinds of women I have been drawn to and for whom I have made space in my heart, or those who have planted irrevocable images in my mind, I notice one similar trait. They all have multiple secret scripts interwoven in their being. When I think about it earnestly, I can see how over time their way of being was a code that helped me unlock things complex and secret. They provide an answer to my mother's provocation of who do I think I am to speak like that, when I know people are watching and I have to be a lady. Gradually, I began to answer who I thought I was and deliberately, through the language of dance, designed my identity. I found a way to delve into and divulge secrets. My limbs spat it all out on the shiny, yellowwood floorboards of a dance studio in town. In the oh-how-I-do-believe-make-believe world of theatre, I was allowed to roam and dig into my stories. Like the Bible is for an elder, or the taxi for a *ghaatjie*, my body became the conduit to transport me from one set of circumstances to another and in singular moments inhabit multiple contexts and knowledges.

I make space for the lady who is not ashamed of her body. I see her pride in how she moisturises and makes her skin glisten with Dawn lotion. She is that aunty who can see more than the little in front of her and employs her imagination to turn bare basics into a feast. She dips six slices of bread into one well-beaten egg and, like Jesus, turns a little into a lot and feeds her family. I make space for that neighbour who wears Ackermans and feels glam. She calls it AC Kermans and laughs her head off. She is not defined by her body but defines it with her thinking and imagination.

She could be he, the *moffie*[iii] hairdresser down 7th Street, all camp with heightened femininity. Like my mother, that lady makes briyani and cooks all the ingredients separately. Some Pick n Pays might sell the ready-mix, but she knows that simplicity is laboured over time and layered with nuance. You feel love (a complex and ambiguous emotion with several manifestations in my community) distinctly in every mouthful of her briyani. *Daai lady* sees a relation in everyone. Her oddness is sexy and appealing. Her off-beat, off-centre nature attracts. When alone, she talks to herself, and in company, she is mostly quiet.

I make space for the girlfriend who sticks up two super-absorption tampons after having an abortion in the morning and still dances for paying customers and an undermining boss at night. She never begs, and when she does have to ask, resolutely feels no shame. Her circumstance does not define her; it merely inflects, colours and

---

iii A camp, effeminate man (often used derogatorily).

disturbs what remains too easily accepted. Want or gain is temporary. This too shall change is her mantra, especially when she is tired of being misunderstood by the stereotypical significations of her body in this place.

I make space for the *sturvy*[iv] aunty who rolls, sun-dries and swirls her hair, knowing that added flick and play with curls manipulates minds limited to first-degree logics and external appraisals of value. *Daai lady* does not ask if you know her name. She calls herself by name, and thus makes the space which she steps into. More than anything, that lady for whom I make space is the ultimate performer. She understands the value of an act, the doing of *something* and not everything, in order to achieve success on her terms. She knows how to keep a secret. In fact, her power is her subtext, and with that, she charges the atmosphere. She understands how performance packages intent. If she does not hold herself within those limitations, too much emotion, too much joy, anger and sadness, would gush out and sweep her across the floor. And when it does, she swims freestyle or backstroke.

Before becoming a young lady, when blood and discharge began to make regular appearances between my legs, I decided to keep it a secret and not tell my mother. The ambiguous term 'young lady' is used amongst aunties to describe a girl that has begun to menstruate and is at the cusp of embodying the expectations of being a real lady. 'Is she a young lady yet?' was an excitedly whispered refrain, and increasingly I felt the need to keep this apparently pivotal moment to myself. Fortunately, my body shape played along. My chest remained flat and my skin acne-free, thus giving no external evidence of abrupt transitions to ladyship. Thanks to Ms Fischer's sex counselling session at school, I knew that tampons would help preserve the secret. 'You can even swim with it and no one will know,' she said. However, irregular pocket money made it very difficult to procure those plugs, and therefore hiding inevitable panty stains required more cunning

iv   Someone that others perceive as wanting to be posh.

than my 11-year-old virtuousness could muster. It was just a matter of time before the termites ratted me out.

I imagine it started out all innocently, with one little foraging ant sniffing her way down the narrow cement path along my bedroom. Preoccupied with looking for food on the ground, she probably walked into the wall a few times, but motivated by the hunger in her belly, let alone the empty grumblings of a hundred thousand or so back at the nest, she was determined and decided to scale her way up to my window. Luckily, the timing of her landing on the pane and my stashing a soiled panty into a drawer was perfectly synchronised. The first whiff of my becoming-a-woman-ness must have been sweet, and I can just imagine how that ant glided down behind the curtain, fantasising on how ingesting this new blood could reverse her sterility. Overexcited, she tripped over her fifth leg, slid past the smell and landed on the carpet. After a brief pause for reorientation, she followed her nose up along the leg of my dresser to the secret smelly compartment, and 'Eureka!' After the first lick she was sure she had found the magic queen ant formula. Her working days were over. From now on she would be giving the orders. Oh, but the impact of this was way beyond her. Thousands of her infertile sisters would now have a future too. This ruby juicy find could change the status quo of her colony forever!

She took one large gulp and scurried back, following the route in reverse. She rolled and rappelled down the dresser's front leg, crawled across the carpet and scrambled under the fringes of my yellow curtain until she reached the bedroom wall. Despite the liquid load in her belly, she ascended the wall with ease. There was a slight downward draft that thankfully sped up her descent to the cement path which she had unrewardingly traipsed up and down for weeks. On arrival at the nest, she smugly regurgitated the ruby juice, patiently waited for a few sister termites to sip and, with newfound self-assurance, led the soon-to-be breeding mamas to the elixir.

Once word got out, the devotees were innumerable. Starting out from their nest in some crevice in the backyard garden wall, they incessantly and single-mindedly marched in a long-long line. They never faltered from the path laid down by their future queen. Backward and forward they came and went, each time swelling in ranks. And as great numbers tend to have a visibility flaw, it was not long before the queen of my nest, my mother, noticed the goings-on of something particularly odd. She followed the ants and, against her characteristic restraint, she opened one drawer. And yes, if this were the unrealistic Disney version, she would finally tell her friends that her youngest had indeed become a 'young lady'.

Rebellious women

In the Endemol Productions reality-TV Cape Flats version, my mother was convinced that I was hiding activities more shameful and carnal than my soiled underwear. In Disney stories, the fertile ant sits around plopping out eggs and giving orders, but with life being as it was in Factreton, my mother knew that once a woman's egg was fertilised, that was when the endless work began. She was frightened and lashed out because of the struggle she knew. Yes, in a Dr Phil-esque speech she might have been angry and felt betrayed as I unsuspectingly snatched her role as inaugurator of the first stage of becoming-a-woman from her. In everyday Diela-talk (my mother's shortened name), long cultivated righteous indignation erupted. She suspected me of not yet exactly doing – that was just a matter of time, of course – but already shamefully contemplating scandalous, salacious things so much more disgraceful in the ferment of pious religious observers.

My admission of occasionally having used those magic no-one-will-know tampons merely added fuel to her fire. My livid mother interpreted tampon insertion as preparatory measures for penis penetration and the smutty suggestions of that association frightened her. By comparison, if only penis insertion were as pain-free and functional, even when the secret is rudely discovered with messily

Figure 7.2. *Love Is . . .* , 2012. Photograph by Cedric Leherle.

stashed-away debris. Before the actual sticking in of my first tampon, I had memorised various positions that Ms Fischer promised would facilitate a smooth slip-in. 'See what works for you,' she said. 'Sit on the toilet, lie on the floor, place one foot on the mat and the other on the bath, basin or any other prop to create an upside-down "J" shape.' I did that, and in the end, the most natural position was similar to the quintessential pose of my primate ancestor – feet apart, knees slightly bent and buttocks pointed out.

Sex, on the other hand, came much-much later, but the first few times were no less creative. I often thought about doing it as a teenager but, as opposed to wondering about who with or how it would feel, I was obsessed with figuring out how one kept the choreography smooth and organic if shoes and clothes had to be removed and then one still had to climb into bed and get under the covers. Lying in wait between the sheets while he took his shower, like they did in the afternoon soapies, seemed too coy for my liking. And the contrast of ripping it all off just scared me, as I always suspected a savage was hiding in the lining of my hymen, just waiting to be agitated and torn apart. This detail, of course, I had to keep from my churchgoing family.

When the moment was upon my just-married, virginal, Mother Mary self, I was distracted by too many internalised misconceptions, fears and theocratic indoctrination. Peculiarly, I was not at all concerned about striking the correct position and was thus markedly surprised when after several attempts – in bed, harder floor surfaces and tabletops – it just would not go in. After several failed stick-it-in thrusts, we moved to more natural locales. When playing the birds and bees game, actually hearing them might be helpful, I thought. Still, I just could not relax enough to get it right. Then, I languidly soaked in a Radox bath and a light bulb exploded in my head. What was the epiphany? All is natural. Understanding three simple words changed my world. No matter the body pose or furniture surface, quiet acquiescence or barbarically out of control, there is no absolute, singular way.

I followed Ms Fischer's advice and found what worked for me, without the aid of a picture, pamphlet or, thankfully, theocratic advice. If the latter were the case, I might never have discovered how supremely satisfying an intimate tongue and all orifice relationship could be. Or, just how liberating enacting truths that lay deep in the imagination were. With dance as my language, I spoke those truths. With a head full of angry 'f-n-p'[v] expletives, cursing my body's shape, mourning my fatherless state and doubting my faith, I hopped and skipped about, splattering my guts everywhere, and then reimagined myself differently and put myself back together again.

Coloured, working-class, *kroes* (kinky and untamed) hair, English-speaking, good Christian girl were obvious descriptors circumscribed by the state, DNA and religion, but they did not speak of my wishes and desires, those secrets beyond the limitations of gaze which make me more than just this body. To answer who I thought I was to speak like that, when I knew people were watching and I had to be a lady, I burned the judges of good and evil and allowed nature to take its course. I stopped bewildering myself with certitudes of this means that and remembered how my very essence, my Liquorice Allsorts genetically mixed and messed-up history, refutes that conviction. I remembered that my inheritance is one where beiges and browns equal yellowpinkblue. Children born with halos and oral traditions are gospel. A bottle of *witblitz*,[vi] arthritis, *dik geroek*[vii] and teary eyes, normal. Sad secrets and *jou ma se*[viii] dirty jokes constitute life. Skin striped with blood and eating dirty, dry bread are things that never happened. These things have no hidden agendas. They are as they are because they have always been and everyone *mos* (actually) knows. These bizarre combinations tap

---

v   *Fok* (fuck) – *Naai* (fuck) – *Poes* (cunt).

vi   Potent home-made alcohol.

vii Being high on drugs.

viii A highly derogatory expression that references your mother's genitalia.

several variations of truths in my bones, and I could not stop myself from designing a few more. I rolled, jumped, kicked and turned on the shiny, yellowwood floorboards of the dance studio in town and sketches fuelled my imagination. Soon, I woke up not feeling pathological and good energy oozed from me without obstruction, as if I could give birth to five children at once. Life just wanted to gush from my guava, and before long I conjured an imaginary of self that insisted on my combination and formation of different sensations and everyday truths.

I am definitely more than just this body. Racialised, gendered impositions of any singular narrative on the construct of my being are inappropriate, unobservant and simply ignorant. My DNA is patterned with the meridians of latitude and longitude that have crossed and recrossed many times and many lives. As a consequence, the blood that flows between my legs contains fragments of multiple potentialities. Evolution *continua* . . .

Figure 7.3. *The Kiss*, 2004. Photograph by Cedric Leherle.

Daai za Lady

One Saturday afternoon I was walking home and suddenly felt depleted. At that moment a horse and cart hobbled by. The cart, relieved of its usual recyclable cables, paper and metal trash, bellowed my name. I jumped on and sat, like Laura Ingalls, the not-so-ladylike child in *Little House on the Prairie*, at the front, swaying in counter-rhythm to the horse's behind. As the horse gently plodded down Bunny Street, I found myself wondering how it would be if the reins were off her back, the bit removed from her mouth and the blinkers taken from her eyes. Can you just imagine how she would run? Whenever someone visualises a horse, words like power, grace and strength come to mind. That Saturday afternoon, however, the horse's head was hanging downward, because, I think, she knew who she was and what must people think of her when she most definitely was not behaving like the lady she knew herself to be. She probably felt 'in the eyes', a phrase that so pointedly places the subject as a recipient of negative judgement, and was possibly even grateful that the blinkers prevented her from seeing her adjudicators.

I also thought about how the sense we have of a horse seems so contrary to its physical shape. The head is long with tiny, pointy ears at the top and slides down to large, flaring nostrils and a wide, flappy, thick-lipped grin at the bottom. The eyes are relatively small and positioned at the sides of the head, just above seemingly oversized, muscular jowls. The neck and spine support a flat chest, a wide, round belly and proportionately skinny legs from which knobbly knees stick out, backwards. Furthermore, the impressive frame is carried by the tiniest feet. Despite this physiology, a horse is thought of as elegant and beautiful, with an intensity and sensitivity that is inviting, intoxicating even. If I were to describe a woman with the same features as a horse, would she be a lady? Could she appease my mother and behave right?

Would she be *daai lady*, the one for whom space is made? Or would she be of no consequence and derided for neither looking nor behaving appropriately?

That Saturday afternoon I decided to embody the spirit of a horse and exude grace, strength and power irrespective of my circumstance or shape. I wanted everyone and anyone to look into my eyes and see what their own eyes could not. No feeling 'in the eyes'. No pleasing their eyes by being a *lekker kin*,[ix] Hannah-Magdalene or nice 'Mumz', but intentionally living through my eyes, positioned all over my body. I conjured this alter ego and named myself Daai za Lady. I began to see beyond the obvious, *nie die nie,* but *daai,* that over there, broader than the nominal settings of prescriptive vision fields. Daai za Lady initially got into the taxi to travel to the studio in town, but soon I found myself performing hybrid tales everywhere. In travels to England, Germany, America, Singapore, Japan, I saw madams and masters, made friends, provoked fiends – and always, all of them were me.

I step onto the stage and survey the people and space with eyes at the top of my head, on my fingertips and under my feet. Immediately, I notice the overt boredom from someone expecting to be entertained in 'South African', feel the feigned enthusiasm from those needing to make the South African feel welcome, or hear the confusion from those claiming to know who and how I should be as a South African, and Coloured at that. I can taste all of these variations of truth and then, in dance, make the space and step into it, inserting myself and all the bodies I carry. I see these multiple versions of truth as a myriad of stories with lines criss-crossing my performance space. Only, these lines are elastic and give way with my touch. Daai za Lady is an attitude, an energy, that is honed and has grown on seeming dysfunction and contrariness. It comes from a place where nothing is

---

ix   A term used by men to describe a young woman in a sexually opportunistic fashion.

merely as it seems but contains a spectrum of nuance, ranging from what disturbs to that which emboldens and captivates.

Once as I was leaving the theatre after a performance, two people stopped me and said the most surprising and encouraging things. After performing an unconventional dance where I was focused on creating a sense of vulnerability and abstract lines with my movements, one woman was so happy that I could walk. Watching me on stage, she had believed I was disabled, an observation which hugely upset her partner, who saw me as a butterfly. That was when I realised that Daai za Lady freed me from remaining bound in one singular form. I could move beyond my skin and body, beyond *hotnot*,[x] gangster, wannabe, or the brutal mistake of some *baas*'s[xi] libidinous rights (essentially rape and pillage). I could be naked or wear flimsy clothes, not to provoke, but to feel the air move across and around my chest and thighs. Heavy and thick at one moment, and light wisps the next. Through Daai za Lady, portrayals of love could unfold, like *The Kiss*, set in 1852, telling the story of Johannes, an almost free slave, and Anna, the niece of a farmer, who fall in love. This story is narrated by Johannes for their child, Hope:

The night air had changed. There was a breeze. The air was light, filled with movement of the gentlest kind. Filled with promise.

'Imagine,' says Anna, 'imagine you can love and be loved.'

'Imagine you are,' I said. And together, gracefully, we float, glide, fly away.

Love, when alive, should be lived. Anna and I, we wanted to live, alive with our love. In Zandvlei, that would be crushed, downtrodden, killed by circumstance. And then there was you, Hope, to think of.

---

x   A derogatory term historically used to refer to Coloured people in South Africa.

xi   'Boss', specifically referring to a white man in a position of authority.

That's why we left. We made the trek to Wuppertal. On the back of a sympathetic horse, we slung our two blankets, bread and water. I felt as if we were leaving to be married. Our clothes were simple, but I believe they shouted of elegance. For ten days we journeyed. Zandvlei, now behind us. A new life, ahead.

From the first swelling we knew that you were a girl-child. You, Hope, you saved us. You joined us on the 1st day of October 1850 and greeted me with your shock of hair. Then you gulped the air and screamed a scream that filled your every cell with life. And after, you settled . . . mmm . . . and you smiled. I swear it. In the first hour of your first day in this life, you smiled. And inside the inside of the inside of me, I still see, feel, know your smile.

The horse that accompanied us to Wuppertal seemed to be aware of your preciousness. Daai za Lady was her name. She sensed your life in mama's belly. When mama mounted her back, she knelt, and arched to cradle her to rest. Her awareness carried over to you, Hope. I can see her eyes at the side of your head. I can see her limbs. They traverse across many miles. You, too, can live in extremes and play in the spaces in between. Your mind beckons challenge. Your heart is gentle, sensitive. Your soul, like the air, invisible, but always felt and absolutely necessary. It reveals the stories of much and will remind you when you need to recollect. Death, change, will always live inside of you and your life will flow with the energies of men, of women, of flowers, trees, birds and beasts. Take care.

My mother said that God is in the details, but details are not immediately evident. You have to look, carefully. And listen, like I learnt to do. Listen, especially to the silence.

Remember your namesake. You are Hope Daai za Lady Flowers.

Today is good, tomorrow will be better.[2]

Figure 7.4. *This Side Up*, 2003. Photograph by Cedric Leherle.

CHAPTER 8

Refining Islamic Feminisms: Gender, Subjectivity and the Divine Feminine

Sa'diyya Shaikh

As a South African born in the late 1960s, my experiences of religion and faith were complicated, contested and nuanced. I grew up nurtured by an enduring current of Islamic spirituality that was foundational to my sense of self. Among my cherished childhood memories are those of sitting on my father's lap, enthralled by stories about Abdul-Qadr Jilani, the eleventh-century Muslim saint active in Baghdad – he was a Sufi whose love and devotion to his spiritually accomplished mother was as celebrated as his transformative encounter in the desert with a group of marauding bandits. My young imagination was captured by this embodiment and model of human virtue whose gentleness, courage, spiritual discernment, devotion, integrity and equanimity inspired a radical internal shift of consciousness even in the most mercenary and violent of criminals.

In another vivid memory, I recall my excitement on the first night of Ramadan, draped in my favourite turquoise scarf, hurrying with my mother to our neighbour's home where a number of women from our neighbourhood gathered to perform *tarawih* (evening prayers) together, whilst the men went to the nearby mosque. My mum led the *salat* (prayers) for this women's congregation, and her melodious recitation instilled in me a love for the beauty of Qur'anic recitation and its aesthetic capacity to lift one out of the ordinary into the realms of celestial beauty. The sincerity and faith of this female community of prayer informed both my relationship to the Muslim ritual prayer and my experiences of being a woman. So did my early awareness that the 'official' public space of communal worship, the *musjid* (mosque), was a space owned quite exclusively by men.

Growing up in a South African Indian community in Durban, my encounter with religion became more complicated – sometimes sustaining and uplifting, and at other times confusing and frustrating. Despite moments of intense ambivalence, what endured was that Islam provided for me a way to grapple with questions of human nature and society, personal and public ethics, and the refinement of character and existential purpose. This feeling remained even in times when I was unsure of what constituted an Islamic position on a particular matter, or struggled with competing Muslim perspectives on the same issue.

As a young adult living in apartheid South Africa, my religious understandings of spirituality and the fundamental equality of human beings informed my commitment to the political movement against apartheid. In this period, my political engagement – as an intrinsic religious imperative – was influenced by ideas percolating in Muslim activist organisations such as the Muslim Youth Movement (MYM), the Call of Islam and Qiblah, which were all intensely engaged in the anti-apartheid movement.[1] Such Muslim perspectives also enabled my struggles, and the struggles of my religious cohort, against oppressive and unjust gender norms – often articulated in the name of Islam – within our communities.[2] I resisted sexist gendered norms within my community – and the strong, faithful women that I lived amongst were sources of inspiration even when they did not articulate resistance in the language of feminism that I was encountering in my studies.

As a Black South African women living in a context of political injustice and acute economic disparities, where human worth and possibilities were determined by a number of social hierarchies including race, class, sexuality and gender, the abiding existential questions became even more acute. What truly is human nature and what is our purpose? How do we foster morally ripe and sustaining forms of sociality? What are the underlying spiritual and ethical imperatives that demand our resistance to social injustice and oppressions in all their intersecting forms? I encountered questions of race and gender as intricately interwoven – participating in the anti-apartheid struggle enabled me (like many other women activists) to sharpen and hone justice-based concerns and apply these to issues of gender justice. All these questions continue to occupy me.

Islam provides me with an organic epistemology and ontology to grapple with existential and political questions of being human, it is the grounding for my aspirations for ever more inclusive visions of 'the good life', and it is core to my strivings towards justice and dignity in social terms. For a significant part of my generation of South Africans, the quest for racial, economic and gender justice was fundamentally a religious obligation. This was also certainly a strong imperative for Christian liberation theologians during the anti-apartheid struggle. Human rights discourses including feminism intersected and coincided with and enriched our understandings (albeit critically) of what it meant to be faithful Muslim women in our context.

Subsequently, in my study of various religious traditions during graduate school, I became increasingly aware of the insidious ways that patriarchy permeated so many religious traditions. I also learned how women of faith historically and contemporarily resisted patriarchy within their communities. Here I found solidarity, and indeed at times sisterhood, with women from diverse religions; women who powerfully claim voice and agency in each of their traditions; women who constructively, creatively live their faith distilling and foregrounding the spiritual imperatives of justice and collective human dignity.

One of my first teachers and mentors was Professor Denise Ackermann, a visiting professor in Christian feminist theology at the University of Cape Town in the early 1990s, who inspired me with her erudition and passion. I attended the meetings that she hosted of the local chapter of the Circle of Concerned African Women Theologians, a continental African interfaith group founded by the Ghanaian Methodist theologian Mercy Amba Oduyoye. In this space of sisterly solidarity, I learned about experience as constituting a feminist epistemological category, and how to centre women's religious experiences when engaging and developing a living, breathing theology. In my class seminars with Denise, she taught me to think of gender as an important category of analysis when engaging all parts of one's tradition. Hers was a pioneering South African Christian voice of 'radical critical fidelity' to her tradition.[3] Her critique of racism and sexism in the church was as strong as her voice of constructive feminist theology of love, inclusivity and justice.

Concurrently I was part of a reading group with local activist Muslims. We hungrily devoured the newly published, path-breaking gender-sensitive analysis of the Qur'an, entitled *Qur'an and Woman: Rereading the Sacred Text from a Woman's Perspective* by the African-American Muslim scholar Professor amina wadud.[4] To our delight, a year later, in 1994 – the year of South Africa's first democratic election – our mosque leadership invited Professor wadud to give the *khutbah*, the Friday sermon. This was a celebrated historic moment. It was the first time a woman assumed the role of preacher or *khatibah* in a regular established mosque in South Africa (and possibly the first in most parts of the contemporary world).[5]

Not only did the very act of a woman taking an authoritative position of religious leadership in a mosque signal a radical gender politics, the substantive content of her sermon was revolutionary. Prof. wadud depicted the deepest religious dimensions of Islam – the state of engaged surrender – through uniquely women's experiences of childbearing.[6] Her exquisite invocation of pregnancy, labour and childbirth as metaphors for engaged surrender resonated and echoed powerfully in my being as a young Muslim woman. This momentous historical event, and my subsequent relationship with the work and person of amina wadud, contributed meaningfully to my development as a Muslim feminist scholar and activist. In this journey I have been enriched by the works of a dynamic international group of scholars who have contributed to the emerging field of gender studies in Islam and debates on Islamic feminism.

amina wadud, a Muslim scholar, and Denise Ackermann, a Christian scholar, are two contemporary intellectual and spiritual pioneers who impacted and nourished not only me but a generation of feminists of faith. Their respective works are part of a valuable and growing global woman's theological archive. Within this feminist trove that traverses a number of faith traditions, one finds rich and robust broader feminist debates on the constructions of God, ultimate Truth, and issues of transcendence and embodiment.

Within the Abrahamic traditions in particular, it is clear that visions of God impact and influence how believers understand human beings – indeed, theology and religious anthropology are in fact intimate bedmates. Prof. wadud's evocative centring of women's experiences of childbearing when depicting the normative religious subject planted a resonant seed in my being to explore Muslim discourses on gender and the nature of God.

Historically, Muslim theology has been radically iconoclastic – God is not simply beyond gender but, for most Muslims, also beyond anthropocentric similitudes. The idea of God the father is simply not part of the dominant Muslim imaginary. Instead Muslim theology speaks of ungendered multitudinous divine attributes (or names) as a way for humanity to relate to the one all-encompassing God. The divine attributes are central in Muslim theology since humanity and all creation are ontologically lodged in and manifest varying combinations of divine attributes. So when engaging gender theologically, it becomes important to look at how the divine attributes are represented.

Also, despite a theological rejection of any form of gendered anthropomorphism, Arabic, the language of the Qur'an and earliest Muslim theology, is a deeply gendered language. Arabic nouns are generally either grammatically masculine or feminine, including inanimate objects, an animate being or an abstract concept, and thus in terms of pronouns one has to employ binary pronouns of either 'he' or 'she' since the gender neutral 'it' does not exist in Arabic. Allah, the Arabic name for God, is conventionally rendered into the masculine pronoun *Huwa* (He), which in Muslim theology is purportedly not to be conflated with any human attribution of masculinity. Through grappling with usage of a grammatically masculine Arabic pronoun for God as 'He' against the theological assertion that God is beyond gender, I decided some years ago to use both 'He' and 'She' in reference to God in my presentations – particularly as an attempt to refrain from promoting an underlying or unconscious valance of divine masculinity.

These gender-inclusive pronouns for Allah elicit mixed reactions amongst the varied Muslim audiences I have addressed. Some younger people find gender-inclusive pronouns for Allah compelling and exciting, whilst a number of older people have expressed deep discomfort with any feminine language associated with God. I have received diverse reactions when addressing congregants of the mosque that I belong to in Cape Town, the Claremont Main Road Mosque. To be fair, I did once have an older woman wink at me mischievously and encourage me to use the pronoun 'She' for Allah – she said she had not heard it previously but that she 'simply loved' it. We also agreed that we would have a three-way long cup of coffee with the Divine when we encountered Her, asking for some clarity and elucidation of Her plan, in light of the inordinate physical demands on women that range from menstrual pain and bleeding to pregnancy, childbirth and lactation. Then to top it all off – menopause . . . engaged surrender à la wadud aside!

In my view, the more general Muslim discomfort with using explicitly gender-inclusive pronouns for God might partly be explained by the fact that patriarchy within the Abrahamic tradition has rendered male imagery normative (even if only symbolically and linguistically). It has rendered feminine imagery for the divine as unthinkable or, at the minimum, dissonant. Muslims, like their Abrahamic siblings, have long histories of patriarchy – even though Muslims might not have images of God as father, there certainly is a long history of naturalised androcentrism, male authority, gendered hierarchies, and implicit masculine associations with the divine. These have had damaging implications for the full humanity of women and men. Ultimately, notions of the divine nature are intrinsically related to our notions of human nature and relationships.

Within a broad spectrum of Muslim scholarship historically, I have found refreshing resonance with the daring contributions of the thirteenth-century Muslim thinker Muhyi al-Din Ibn 'Arabī. In my feminist retrieval of his lucid egalitarian conceptions of gender, conceptions often unknown or marginalised in mainstream Muslim conversations, I am consciously reading against the grain. Significantly, this feminist retrieval not only illuminates the rich diversity of gendered ideas available in Muslim traditions, but also illustrates that gender egalitarianism is not simply the preserve of modern feminists. In reclaiming the gendered ideas of this luminous thinker, I find a distinctive and powerful poetics of creation, nurture, power and spirituality that weaves together the earth, maternity, femininity, women and the Divine Feminine. He states:

[The earth] gives all of the benefits from her essence [dhāt] and is the location [mahall] of all good. Thus she is the most powerful [a'azz] of the bodies . . . she is the patient [sabūr], the receptive one [qābila], the immutable one, the firm one . . . Whenever she moves from fearful awe of God, God secures her by means of (mountains as) anchors. So she becomes still with the tranquility of those of faithful certainty. From the earth, the people of faith learn their certainty. Therefore, it is the mother from whom we come and to whom we return. And from her we will come forth once again. To her we are submitted and entrusted. She is the most subtle of foundations [arkān] in meaning. She accepts density, darkness, and hardness only in order to conceal the treasures that God has entrusted to her.[7]

In this evocative set of images, Ibn 'Arabī presents the earth as a source of abundance and plenitude, one intimately linked with the divine. The earth epitomises the divine attributes of power, stability, strength, receptivity and subtlety – and constitutes an exemplary spiritual model for people seeking to foster their own faith, tranquility and certitude. Indeed, the earth mirrors an array of divine qualities that provide a form of instruction and teaching for the perceptive seeker to advance her/his own spiritual progress.

More especially, Ibn 'Arabī's depiction of the earth evokes an intricate spectrum of divine qualities that distinctly echo the Qur'anic descriptions of God. Calling the earth *al-Sabur*, the Patient One, a recurring name of God in the Qur'an, he creates for a Muslim audience an explicit resonance between the earth and God. Similarly, depicting the earth as 'concealing treasures' mirrors the well-known tradition (*hadith qudsi*) where God states, 'I was a hidden treasure and I loved to be known. Hence I created all things in order to be known.' Describing the earth as 'the mother from whom we come and to whom we return' is an unequivocal invocation of the popular Qur'anic verse (Q. 2:156) 'From Allah we come and to Allah we return'.[8]

In all of these descriptions, Ibn 'Arabī unambiguously and explicitly links the earth to the Divine, foregrounding the earth as the creative, benevolent, maternal source of the good. By reflecting on the human being's intimate spiritual and immanent physical relationship with the earth, he also brings into focus women's procreative capacities and the Divine Feminine. Moreover, by interweaving maternal, earthy and generative qualities with the majestic attributes of strength, power and immutability, Ibn 'Arabī urges his audience towards an integration and balance of what might be traditionally categorised as 'masculine' and 'feminine' attributes within the divine. A poetics where the earth reverberates divine presence, provides spiritual teaching, and is the locus of human origin and return, enables a re-evaluation of embodiment, materiality, mothers and spirituality.

For a feminist reader it is noteworthy that these images present a foundational integrity between the earthly and divine, and between embodiment and spirituality – elements that traditional patriarchies have often rent asunder through gendered hierarchies. Ibn ʿArabī's exalted portrayal of the earth – and its intimate neighbour the human body – presents an unequivocal rejection of traditional patriarchal binaries. Such dualistic binaries often devalue the earth as the realm of inferior lowly materiality and embodiment (often relegated to the feminine and women) – a necessary trap of human existence that one seeks to ultimately overcome. Instead, the body and the earth as maternal and generative realities are profoundly imbued with spiritual value, and reconfigure dominant gendered ideas.

Elsewhere, Ibn ʿArabī uses feminine metaphors of pregnancy, labour and childbirth to describe the origin of creation. In this cosmogenic myth, God is in a state of solitary Oneness before creation, when the yet non-existing entities within the One are heavy with potentiality and exert a metaphysical condition of pressure. Ibn ʿArabī describes this state of distress induced by the yet non-existing entities within the One with the term 'karb', signifying the process of labour during childbirth.[9] In response to this state of contraction, the divine creative force – described as the Breath of the Merciful (*Nafas al-Raḥmān*) – in an act of loving compassion, emancipates the non-existing entities into the sphere of existence. Like women who bear children, God births the cosmos and thereby reveals Her divine treasures.

Simultaneously, in his typically fluid use of gendered metaphors, Ibn ʿArabī also describes God as 'male', stating that all creation is ontologically 'female' in relation to God, who impregnates each being with existence. Boldly he states that, in fact, 'other than the Creator, there is not in this universe a male', and those who are generally referred to as males are all 'really female', receptive to the being of the divine creator.[10] Ibn ʿArabī's supple and relational use of maternal and paternal metaphors pushes his reader towards a more agile, fluid conception of gender as relating to divinity and humanity.

In Ibn 'Arabī's vibrant, corporeal metaphors, we encounter a God who desires and loves to be known, who experiences anguish without creation, and whose creative process is captured through images of pregnancy, labour and mothering. These metaphors invoke a vital aspect of deep connection, interiority, and nurture between God and humanity. Moreover, a God who *needs* humanity for the realisation, manifestation and fulfilment of divine possibilities subverts hierarchical patriarchal theologies that define God as primarily omnipotent, transcendent and independent of humanity. This is not simply an invincible God whose unadulterated power demands unconditional obedience, but rather a God whose love and yearning is the very impetus for creation. Confounding prevailing gendered hierarchies, Ibn 'Arabī instead presents a God–human relationship characterised by intimacy, closeness, love and mutuality, all of which contribute towards a nourishing theology, a theology which provides the ontological soil to cultivate a Muslim feminist ethics of relationality and radical interdependence.

Indeed, an ethic of relationality, interdependence and nurturing intimacy is one that is needed not only in South Africa but in the world at large in a time when toxic masculinities are running rogue. We are in dire need of generous intellectual and spiritual ancestors, creative interlocutors to sustain us in our battle against the tide of malevolent and rapacious male power wreaking political and social havoc. It is my view that underlying the widespread destructive forms of contemporary politics, fortified by hostile masculinist models of domination in a variety of contexts, is a spiritual malaise. It requires our careful attention, our concerted work of healing and expanding our spiritual repertoires, and of stretching the horizons of our imagination to integrate a theology, politics and ethics of justice and care.

I see my engagement with the work of a pre-modern Sufi luminary as a feminist friendship across time and space, what might be described in the Muslim tradition as an *Uwaysi* friendship with an innovative and daring Muslim thinker of the past.[11] In Ibn ʿArabī, we find a creativity and intellectual precociousness that speaks eloquently to the spiritual needs of twenty-first-century Muslim feminists. Within the heart of the Muslim tradition, this innovative thinker subverted and realigned the parameters of the dominant religious imagination. He offered generations of Muslims an intellectual legacy replete with vibrant 'conditions of possibility' to creatively address questions of gender, ontology and feminism.[12] For the ethical, religious and spiritual challenges of our time, we are in need of more sustaining gender-inclusive theological language that not only affirms women's subjectivities but also destabilises a masculinist symbolic economy.

My own constantly expanding visions of God and humanity, nurtured by engaging with Muslim tradition – its texts and spiritual lineages – as well as cherished relationships with and learning from contemporary feminist scholars and Sufis have tremendously enriched my life and being. Images of God as yearning, loving, just, righteous, generous and manifesting in all beings, as masculine, feminine and ultimately beyond any conceptions of gender or any constructions that I might fleetingly hold, demand a dynamic relational subjectivity. Within a Muslim feminist imaginary, in order to be continually transformed by the unceasing and ever-present Divine manifestations, we are each best served by consciously cultivating qualities of loving receptivity, humility and nurturing interdependence to guide our practice and our politics.

CHAPTER 9

Black Lesbian Feminist Thoughts of a Born Queer

Zethu Matebeni

It used to start with a whisper, two people mumbling a few words about what they think you are. Your closeness to another of the same sex was sufficient evidence to show them you are not like them. Then the whisper would grow louder; it would circulate among many until you look for proof of the word. Lesbian. They would tell you this is who you are. And you would believe them.

For days the dictionary would be your friend. It would reveal your existence, each letter spelling out your new name. Lesbian (noun). There you would see yourself, printed in black on white. A homosexual woman. A woman attracted to other women. 'This is me!' you would exclaim at the sight of yourself. The meeting would be an exhilarating encounter. Finally you have been reunited, with yourself.

Once you have accepted this name, things start to change. At first you ignore them – thinking it is just a passing phase. One day your best friend at school declares, 'I'm not sure I should play with you because I don't want to be a l e s b i a n.' She draws out each letter as if it leaves a bitter taste in her mouth. 'I'm not contagious,' you spit out as a response. She runs off without a goodbye. You do not chase after her but are unsure why. 'She will come back,' you console yourself. It is only a matter of time until she understands.

At home things are not easy. Your mother worries about you taking such a label. 'You are only 13,' she keeps reminding you. 'Maybe you will change your mind and you will be attracted to boys,' she says. It is too exhausting to argue with her. At her age, she knows best. But you know yourself too. In any case, there is no winner in this conversation, so it is better that you keep quiet. She believes she is right and you see through her fears. Your silence calms her. It makes her believe you are considering her wisdom.

Your father, who is always there, pretends to not know what is happening. Every day you look at each other deeply, in silence. He is your favourite guy, and although your sister would disagree, you are his favourite. Any conversation with him veers away from sexuality. When watching TV together, he stands up when he sees two women kissing, or sometimes an awkward giggle overpowers him. Each time you turn to him and say, 'Daddy, stop it.' He obeys and breathes out. In his own time, he will be fine.

Your mother is driving herself up the wall. Every day this word torments her. You want to tell her to drop the subject and get over it, but you can see she is not coping. She knows too much not to worry. But you do not know and she is not giving you time to find out. This is not her first time; she had years of training with her own sister, you think to yourself. Things are different, you want to tell her, but she is persistent. In her head, many things have already happened to you. She worries what people will do and what they will say. But you do not worry. You do not know and cannot live in her past.

The past, how strongly present it is. Everyone reminds you of how things used to be. Your focus is on how things are now: the sound of your new name, like an exotic fruit or a rare animal species, until your Gogo says it.

'*Heh mntanam*,[i] I hear you are a *lezibhiyen*'.

She makes you sound lazy.

'Lesbian, Gogo, lesbian,' you gently quickly correct her.

'Is it from school?' she asks.

Before you can tell her, she tells you of her friends in boarding school.

'Oh, *hayi nam wethu*[ii] I used to have *itshikin*[iii] when I was at school.' Your ears and eyes pop out.

'What is *itshikin*, Gogo?'

'A girl that I loved. She used to write me sweet letters and I would bring her gifts every time after holidays. Every now and then she would come and give me kisses. That was the best time for me, but we never saw each other after we left school.'

This is big news to you.

What else have you not been told? You wonder. What else can your Gogo tell you? You try to dig further, but she tells you it is in her past and you should focus on your present. She is more interested in knowing about your *lezibhiyen* things. You tell her you do not have a girlfriend, but you may want one in future. At the moment, you are just happy to know who you are. Gogo laughs. 'I named you Luyolo because you brought joy to our lives. You are a product of a proud and resilient people. We have always known who we are,' she says.

Perhaps you did, for a brief moment, forget who you have always been. The women in your family have always asserted their position. You learned this from your mother and aunt, who got it from your grandmother and her mother. There is nothing new in who you are, as Gogo reminds you.

Makazi is an interesting person. She is your mother's older sister and, like her great-aunt, has never had a husband or children. Although

---

i   Hey my child [Zulu].

ii Even I [Zulu].

iii A 'mummy–baby' relationship. Refers to romantic relationships between schoolgirls that happen at boarding school [Zulu].

she is very open, you have to know your story when you talk to her. She asks difficult questions. Like the day you were at her house and came out as a lesbian. She listened to your self-declaration and said, 'Cool, that's great, my baby, and so what does it mean for you?'

Now this question has no real answer. You tell her you will think about it and she agrees to give you time. She also gives you a list of books to go find in her library and read. It is an extensive library with many books on women, gender, lesbians and gays. This library is your favourite room in her house. It is after all where you find out about yourself.

You spend your school holiday reading these books. One in particular tells the story of the first lesbian in Mount Frere, near the village where Gogo lives. It is a sad story of a woman who, at almost your age, was given lashings publicly by a chief because everyone found out she proposed to another woman. You imagine the way she cried in pain, and suddenly understand your mother's worries. A bit of fear strikes you and you wonder if you really are a lesbian.

Another story tells of a lesbian gangster, a woman who was thought to be a man and sometimes dreamt of being a man. You're not sure of this. No. You know you're not a man; you make a note to yourself. Perhaps it may happen, but the way you feel about yourself and women now is not as a man.

It is the story of five women that draws you in. They all have different experiences as bisexual or even *isangoma*.[iv] There you read about an experience similar to Gogo's at boarding school. The writer shares her deep love of another woman at school and how normal loving another was. It is sweet and sad at the same time. In the same story she talks of rape, how gangs in her area would rape lesbians. Perhaps this is what your mother worries about. Why rape a person because she is a

---

iv   The term used to refer to traditional healers or a medicine men or women in South Africa [Zulu].

lesbian? For fun? To teach her a lesson? 'To change her,' they say. What is there to change? And for whom?

Makazi walks in as you contemplate these questions. She sees through your troubled heart. As she always does, she lights *imphepho*[v] for clarity and sits next to you on the couch. 'There are many ways to be lesbian, Makazi,' you finally declare as you draw your own meanings to this name. She agrees and holds you close to her. 'Yes, and you can be any. But always hold on to yourself,' Makazi says as she lulls you to sleep.

Time tells many stories.

It is your first year of university and you are away from home. Leaving was not easy. Your father found it the most challenging. He could not cope with not seeing you every day. Your mother, on the other hand, was happy to set you free. She wanted you to 'grow up and be independent', as she kept saying. Your sister could not believe you were leaving. She has always been by your side and could not imagine you alone. She kept asking you every day if you were sure you wanted to leave home.

Life at university is exciting. Living alone for the first time is exhilarating. Taking full responsibility for your time and life has its challenges. For the first few months you do everything by the book. You call home twice a week and never miss lectures, but the novelty soon wears off. You decide you want to excel, but your focus is also on enjoying your newfound freedoms.

In your gender studies course, you discover parts of yourself you did not know. You read from feminists of all kinds from many different parts of the world. You meet some of them on campus and in your lectures. It is an intriguing world. Makazi's name is on the reading list for one course. You feel completely at home in this environment. Feminism, like lesbian, has many meanings. The experience of being

---

v   *Helichrysum petiolare*, a variety of indigenous sage. The plant is dried and burned and used in rituals and sacred ceremonies [Zulu].

a woman, while diverse, demands an emancipatory politic. You settle on your meaning of lesbian as feminist. This decision feels powerful. It changes how you relate to others and your experiences. Your voice gets bolder, your opinions matter and you speak with confidence.

On campus there are different people from different places in the country, and you make new friends. One in particular is taking some lectures with you and often you spend time studying together. On this day he visits you in your room. It is a warm day and you are reading for your next lecture.

There's a knock and you slowly get out of bed, in your pyjamas, and open the door. It is your friend. He greets and comments that your roommate is not in. You notice a weird look in his eye and ask if he is fine. He does not respond. As you return to your bed he grabs hold of your arm. It is a tight grip and you try to loosen it.

In a split second he has pushed you onto the bed. You are on your back. The veins in his neck and arms are popping out. Your arms are above your head and you're not sure how they got there. Both his arms are pressing tight against yours. You lie still in your single bed. His legs are straddled around your body. You are not breathing. His bloodshot eyes are staring at you.

A soft and wet tongue pushes itself into your mouth. You almost choke. Breathe, a voice inside tells you. Your jaws lock as they bite hard into the slime occupying your mouth. The grip around your wrists tightens. One twist of your body shoots your right knee into his groin. You push him off onto the floor.

By the time you reach the ground floor of the university residence, you can hear your heart beating as fast as you ran down the seven flights of stairs. The warden's office is open and you rush straight to her phone and dial your mother. Her voice lets you cry out, 'Mama, he tried to rape me.' The rest of the conversation you do not remember.

Makazi arrives as you are curled up in the warden's chair. You have not said a word since hearing your mother's voice. Her arms envelop you in an embrace you call home. The cry you let out comes from your belly. She holds you tight while your weight is on her shoulders.

When you wake up Makazi is next to the bed. She has been watching over you. The smell of *imphepho* fills the room. You are awakening to your senses. No questions are asked and you know what you need to say. 'There's no need to go to the doctor. Please tell Mama not to worry.' These words slowly come out of your mouth. You both exhale as you decide not to open a case.

This day haunts you. At times you try to forget until weird reminders make your body shiver. You still see him on campus, at a distance and never in the same class. Friends tell you he no longer speaks. Friendships have become tricky. Casual hugs and hand-holding do not come so easily anymore. You walk about building a wall around yourself, but each day you try to break it down.

It is an endless struggle.

How do you hold on to yourself when you have been invaded? His presence in your body is like a disease. It refuses to make space for new lives. Sometimes you watch yourself brushing your teeth three times a day. It is a habit you've developed to rid remnants of him from your mouth.

Each day you yearn to come back to yourself. Yet fragments remain. Within the walls you build, you recollect yourself piece by piece. There is no completeness in ruins. He will not win, you tell yourself. You will own yourself.

Reclaiming yourself is a difficult task.

You did not lose yourself. Something was taken from you, a part of you. Even though the one who stole from you can never replace anything, the recognition of theft is an important starting point. How do you explain this theft, which is also an invasion and forceful inhabiting of another's body? Yes, he left parts of himself on you, and you refuse to carry them any longer. This is what you tell Gogo and Makazi when you meet at Gogo's homestead for the holidays.

When you are silent, your mother blames herself. This is not what she meant by independence. You have grown, yes, grown to appreciate her concerns and worries. Your father is angry because he does not know what to do. You decide to give him space.

Now you are finding your own way of dealing with things.

At your request, Gogo prepares *iyeza*.[vi] She tells you the ritual has to be done early in the morning, before first light. When you wake up, everything is ready. Makazi has started the recitations as *imphepho* burns. You hear some of the clan names she's calling for the first time. This is serious business, you gather. The smell of *imphepho* is stronger than usual and the smoke quickly fills the room.

You don't remember the taste of *iyeza*, but something happens inside your body after you drink from the jug. Your insides rumble and all you hear is the sound of Makazi's deep chanting voice. Perhaps you lose consciousness, you don't remember. But when your eyes open, a bucket in front of you is full of your stomach's contents. You are sweating.

Your sister lifts you from the floor and asks if you are ready. The two of you walk barefoot to the kraal. You can feel the wetness from the morning dew. The sun is not yet out. When she enters the kraal, she starts speaking. You are still dazed and not paying attention. She strips you naked and tells you to stand in the middle of the kraal. The cold air does not bother you.

With each scoop of *iyeza* flowing from your head as she pours, you start feeling light. Slowly, the weight is falling off your shoulders. The last scoop releases laughter inside you and you start dancing. Your sister starts her own praise singing while wrapping you in a blanket. She tells you not to wipe off *iyeza* as you walk back to the house.

As the first sun rays shine through, you feel whole again.

---

vi IsiXhosa term for traditional medicine, which is often a concoction of herbs and plants, used for their healing properties.

Conversations about Photography with Keorapetse Mosimane, Thania Petersen and Tshepiso Mazibuko

Ingrid Masondo

I am interested in how a series of photographs by different producers, with varied approaches that have no obvious thematic or aesthetic links with each other necessarily, can be grouped together in this essay form to suggest a coherence in theme and argument. I am also interested in how photographs with minimal narrative framing can constitute an 'essay' in which it is the reader or viewer who generates primary meaning. It is my belief that very often the conventional visual essay engages in interpretation that suppresses the profound and diverging meanings that can be generated by the reader.

This essay focuses on photographs as relational platforms. It asks of the reader to (re)consider what photography is. It also encourages active engagement from the reader in the relations and conditions related to the production, circulation and viewing of photographs. It is a provocation to the reader whose focus lies on reading the 'expert's' analysis as authoritative and definitive as though such an analysis lacked a subjective voice or agenda.

By drawing together the unrelated works of three photographers – Keorapetse Mosimane, Tshepiso Mazibuko and Thania Petersen – I urge the reader both to follow each photographer's vision and vantage point, as well as to consider elements that are beyond the surfaces of the photographs.

Figure 10.1. *Erasure 2*, 2017. Photograph by Thania Petersen.

Surfacing

The relationship between photography and the 'surface' has been a subject of concern, debate and experimentation since the invention of the medium. Some have focused on the camera's extraordinary ability to capture, expose and make visible the surface of things often invisible to the eye; and claims exist that photography has the ability to go beyond surfaces and capture essences and other existences. Others have focused on the material expression of the (printed) photograph, its sensitive and malleable surface. In this essay, I consider photographs that speak to some of these aspects.

Debates about surfaces in relation to photography have also found obvious resonance in questions about how ways of being, relating and narrating are shaped by racialised, gendered and classed lenses.

The histories of photography are deeply entangled with colonial and imperial projects and with bodily surfaces, especially the skin and hair. Deemed integral for racial classifications, photography was central in providing visual evidence (and fictions) about racialised difference and essence. I would argue that photography was instrumental in shaping ways of seeing and looking too. I do not engage with these histories (of colonialism and apartheid, or photography) in this essay. I am more interested in their implicit and explicit effects. How are we, the participants of this chapter, as well as the reader, shaped, enabled and limited by these classificatory categories and regimes? And how do our positionalities affect our vision and our relationship to photography?

In seeking notions and practices of photography that are not extractive, I have been inspired by several scholars, especially Ariella Azoulay. She critiques the fixation with the camera and the photograph (as an object and commodity, owned by a sole artist) in any discussion about photography, as well as the separation of the aesthetic and the political in art. She defines photography as a continuous event and

> a product resulting from the actions of many agents and that the photograph is only a sample of the relations between people or an effect of the space of relations between them. The existence of such relations cannot be reduced to the status of raw materials for, or mere objects of, the artistic image . . .[1]

Below, the three photographers and I attempt to mark some of the relations and economies that are implicated in this conceptualisation of photography, which include networks of participants and institutions, technologies, contexts and discourses. The reader is part of this network, is not solely a spectator or consumer, and is thus urged to be conscious of the political act of looking and the potentialities therein for action. What actions are possible from our individual and collective reflections on the above, and from our interrogations of our relationship to photography?

Figure 10.2. *Androgenia – a beautiful boy*, 2004. Photograph by Keorapetse Mosimane.

The call to rethink our notions and engagements with photography is especially critical at this historical moment. Advances in digital technologies have expanded access to the tools of photography and the capacity to produce, process and circulate photographs in unimaginable ways. This presents opportunities and challenges in the fields of communication, media and the visual (especially with regards to surveillance and control). These issues, however, are complex and not the focus of this essay. The consideration here is about particular tools, cameras in this case, having certain effects. The aim is not to centre the camera or establish hierarchies between the different types of tools and photographies that exist, but to acknowledge and grapple with the different kinds of labours involved in producing photographs in particular ways, contexts and times. These reflections also help me to consider the possibility of a different set of expectations made on certain photographies with regards to the relational fields, the outcomes, authorship and ownership, and so much more.

The three photographers featured offer some reflections on their artistic journeys and aspirations. Will these journeys be perceived differently if I reveal that all three photographers do not identify as feminist? Alternatively, what does framing them or the photographs in a volume about being black and feminist do? This essay does not hold the answers to these complex and often paradoxical and contradictory sets of issues. I ask these questions as an ongoing exploration about the possibilities of a humane photography.

Modes of working and seeing

In separate discussions with the photographers about their creative processes, our conversations drift between intention and style, to the politics and ethics of the representational, to the place of the artist and the visual in their lives. In one of the conversations with Mosimane, she tells me that she locates her practice within street photography, in a particular context and time. I am surprised by this because in the two confrontational images included here, it is clear that this is not a photographer snapping away at a distance, perhaps even invisible to those being photographed. There has been some discussion and thought about producing these photographs. Before she even confirms it, I had assumed that the photographer and those photographed are known to each other. At the time of production, one lives on the same street as her, and two are her friends. Perhaps it is the recognition of shared enquiries into and the refusal of fixed gendered identifications and performances that brings their worlds together in the first place: to see each other, to talk, to even agree to make these photographs together.

Once a photograph is made and has been seen by many, is it possible for the participants to speak of their original intentions and desires unaffected by the outcome, the photograph that they have made and have now seen? For Mosimane, the moments of clarity, of happiness and satisfaction, were in the moments of creating the photographs. With *Androgenia – a beautiful boy*, she recalls how she knew when she 'got the shot' after pressing the shutter. Later, when she saw these photographs, after they had been processed and printed and were about to be exhibited publicly, these moments were less clear and raised a lot of questions.

Speaking about *Androgenia*, Mosimane remembers her shy young self, being called a tomboy for not acting in ways that are prescribed and expected of those identified as girls. She shares that Sakhile, in *Androgenia*, styled himself for their photo shoot and was certain about how he wanted to be photographed. This is clear to me looking at his portrait: a dare-invitation to be seen, to participate in the celebration and memorialisation of a way of being in the world, of innocence, of beauty. There is also something else in Sakhile's eyes that I cannot read.

With *B(e)aring our Load*, an exploration about 'how far lovers will go at pleasing each other and making each other comfortable', Mosimane has to sit back and let her friends decide what to reveal.

Perhaps they too don't know how far they will go, and how much the photograph will reveal beyond their intentions. One thing is agreed upon at the beginning of this photo shoot – that her friends' faces will not be revealed in the photographs. During the negotiation and making of both *Androgenia* and *B(e)aring our Load*, no one – including the photographer – knows what the final photographs will look like, where and how they will be circulated, and who will see them. Is it because of the warmth and intimacy in these relationships that these concerns are not part of the creation of these photographs?

Listening to Mosimane recount the making of these photographs, the focus, the energy, the expectations . . . I begin to get a glimpse of the kind of street photographer that she sees herself as. She would be casually walking down her street, shyly, camera invisible in her backpack, and a resident would randomly appear and declare, *'Awung' shuthe lapho'.*

Mosimane's reflections remind me of some of the photography practices and relations I witnessed growing up as a child in Soweto where those photographed and their photograph were not removed from each other. In most cases, the photograph was their possession. They had the right to use or destroy it, choose who saw it and determine the conditions of the viewing. Her work also reminds me of townships as complex spaces that have embraced expression and difference.

Mazibuko's photography training and mode started off in the documentary tradition. It was after someone who was looking at her work observed that she mainly photographed men that she genuinely considered the dynamics of representing others. She says, 'I started thinking about how I impose myself in other people's spaces, impose my politics on them, maybe as a metaphor to speak about myself . . . When I looked at my images after that, I realised that I had so much anger about the current situation in the townships and how some people have to live.'

Figure 10.3.
*Mazibuko family,
Thokoza*, 2016,
from the series
Gone and There.
Photograph
by Tshepiso
Mazibuko.

These reflections prompted her to experiment and explore a new visual language. For some time, she turned her gaze on her family history and where she is from: Thokoza, east of Johannesburg, which in the late 1980s and early 1990s was plagued by political factionalism and violence. Many in her community, including some of her family members, disappeared as a result of this violence. She claims that even if she did not witness this period, there are traces of the turbulence and devastation in the space to this day.

With the series *Gone and There,* her journey of self-reflection, Mazibuko plays with some photographic processes. She recreates old family portraits with available family members in the same locations, with similar clothes and gestures. She messes with her negatives (which are meant to be precious) deliberately. She superimposes her new family portraits with the old ones (by unknown photographers, usually) to create multi-layered photographs that speak to the 'presence of unspoken tensions, with the past and present spilling into each other . . . displaying something that is there but not there'. What started as a tribute to her grandmother who had passed on has resulted in a commemorative gesture for other family members who are not there. The layering and defamiliarisation in *Gone and There* is critical to disrupting views of photography as a mainly realist mode, and of photographs as mainly evidence and testimony.

Petersen's practice has been focused on creating vivid, colourful, site-specific self-portraits, still and moving, that challenge the idea that what we look like (our bodily surface) is related to place, to a specific space where we belong. The way in which she creates photo studios, assembles the sets and costumes – as well as her own presence in the photographs – has been crucial to her enquiries about identification and her family histories, particularly in relation to how dominant historical narratives have constructed these. In speaking of her practice, she constantly refers to 'we' (not 'I'). When questioned about this, she clarifies that 'my family and community are my biggest influence. My aunties, the way they arrange their homes, their flowers, their drapes . . . the way my other auntie ties her *medora*[i] . . . the way my grandmother dresses and applies her make-up and does her hair . . . this is in all of my work.' Having immersed herself in this mode for several years, grappling with her relationship to her body and image (and place), she notes that she eventually felt ready 'to take back my image and move away from representing it in particular ways'. She adds, 'I think the point of art is to liberate ourselves. It is a therapy . . . when you claim back your image, make whatever work you want, that is freedom.'

Figure 10.4. *Erasure 1*, 2017. Photograph by Thania Petersen.

It was through the series *Erasure* that she could test this freedom and redirect the gaze from herself to the site of enquiry: Elmina Castle in Ghana, one of the key sites in the Atlantic slave trade. Although she had done extensive research and preparation for her presence there and the photo shoot – including dressing in black to symbolise mourning – she was still struck by how the space, which she considers

---

i In the artist's experience, this is a ceremonial headdress that is worn in some Muslim communities in the Cape during naming rituals: of babies, and of women at marriage, and after pilgrimage. The scarf is sometimes passed down from generation to generation. She also notes that in her research, the scarf and tradition is said to have its origins in Borneo in Southeast Asia.

a graveyard, affected her movements and performances, and the creation of the work. While there, she was also struck and saddened by the tradition of turning such sacred spaces into tourist attractions. 'We are complicit in our own erasure, the erasure of our experiences and existences . . . I think this reflects on our relationship with our ancestors, our lands, and our histories,' she says.

The effects of Elmina Castle extended to how Petersen looked at and experienced the photographs she made there. In post-production, she converted them into black and white and adds that 'other forms started to emerge as I erased all the colour, got rid of all the trimmings and left the bare minimum. I have never experienced that before – I always add more, not subtract, in my work. With the kinds of feelings I experienced there, I just could not think in colour.'

The lives of photographs

I asked each photographer to reflect on how surfacing spoke to their work and/or practice. In response to the title, not her work, Mosimane shared that the concept evokes 'a picture of someone in water, submerged and nearly drowning, held down by chains and stones. Then, as if something is suddenly released, little bits of the body start to appear slowly: the nose, the feet . . . ' This image remained with me for weeks after speaking to her and made me reconsider surfacing as related to survival. Who or what is meant to survive?

Reflecting on this, I engaged the three photographers about image circuits, networks and structures of support. They all shared experiences and concerns about art markets and other image industries, especially with regards to the promotion of photographs as mere commodities or isolated sources of knowledge. Unlike with Petersen, whose practice is focused on self-portraiture, for Mosimane and Mazibuko, this is seemingly more challenging when photographing others, and especially in one's community. In photography, why are those who are photographed rarely considered in negotiations about the different currencies that are generated from a photograph such as knowledge, profit and other value? As curators, scholars, publishers, editors – and more – how have we been complicit in contexts where artists are invited to offer their labour or artworks without compensation, in exchange for exposure? And how can we contribute to photographers fostering habits and relations that are not exploitative?

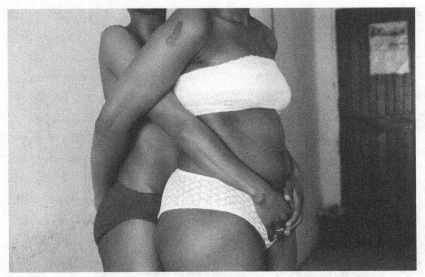

Figure 10.5. *B(e)aring our Load*, 2004. Photograph by Keorapetse Mosimane.

Contemplating the lives of those she has collaborated with in creating photographs, Mosimane laments how the 'township condemns us to particular lives' and how we (photographers) often leave behind those we photograph. 'We hardly return to even communicate about the lives of their images,' she adds. In another instance, she recalls her dismay at a collector who wanted to buy one of her photographs. This was at a time that she was still studying photography, in 2004, and was also the first time that *Androgenia* and *B(e)aring our Load* were exhibited and seen publicly.[2] She also recalls stumbling upon one of her photographs online some years back, inscribed on the surface of a ceramic pot, without permission, credit or compensation.

These complex experiences and relations are not unique to Mosimane and highlight how the lives of a photograph can differ vastly from the lives of those who created it. Mosimane has not considered herself a photographer or produced photographs in a long time – not the laborious, analogue kind – and she has not kept and maintained an archive of that creative journey. I wonder if she had had all that she needed, if she would have pursued photography further, and if so, in which ways would she have done so? Beyond the basic needs, there are many other resources and levels of support that one needs to be a photographer that include grappling with ethical dilemmas around participation, ownership and compensation. In response to all of this, Mosimane wonders about the photographs she would create and the issues that would consume her in the present.

In her engagements with art markets as an independent artist, Mazibuko clarifies that her participation in some exhibition and artistic residency programmes, especially in far-off places, has felt like she was living some sort of double life: 'one returns to the same context, to the township, still with no money . . . and you are expected to live on a per

Figure 10.6. *Neo le Katleho*, 2016, from the series *Gone and There*. Photograph by Tshepiso Mazibuko.

diem'. She adds that because some of the photographs are visible and circulating in the public domain (as in this essay) and because of her opportunities for travel (albeit limited), there is an expectation in one's community that one is doing well financially. She also points to how artistic practice and approaches can be influenced by market forces. She refers to a contemporary aesthetic where clean, slick, refined and processed photographs are more valued. As a result, the market would typically dismiss the photographs from *Gone and There* as illegible and imperfect.

Pointing to the ageism that exists in the industry, amongst many other challenges, Mazibuko declares that 'as an emerging photographer, it feels like the industry has a tradition where you can only sit at the big table and be heard and paid well when you are older. Many important people don't take you too seriously but you have to engage them and be nice. It can be tiring.'

One would assume that Petersen does not share these challenges of invisibility, survival and ethics. But she speaks about the pressures of international visibility and claims that it is much better for her not knowing if and where the work will go than knowing. She also confesses that when she made her first extensive body of self-portraits as an independent artist and did not consider where and how her photographs would be seen, except by her children, she was freer. 'With gallery representation, there is pressure to create continuously and for the work to sell, which can impact the creative process,' she adds.

Both Mosimane and Mazibuko do not speak in detail about the labours and resources involved in the creation, preparation, transmission, care and storage of photographs. This I found interesting, especially with the added demands of having to maintain and care for both analogue and digital archives. For Mosimane, the inclusion of the two works in an archive and museum's permanent collections facilitated easy access.[3] Mazibuko did not dwell on her challenges in submitting images for this essay. What was apparent were issues of access to other resources: time, transport to and from affordable and stable internet connectivity. Petersen is the only artist who spoke directly about the labour and the technical and financial resources required to create just one artwork – both before and after the photograph exists in various formats and scales, and different platforms. She clarifies that 'selling work is one of the avenues for recovering costs and for enabling more work to be created'. Petersen says:

> I really don't think that art should be sold and I believe artists should get a social grant to create and live . . . I have learnt that there is no science to what sells and that I cannot seek validation in sales only.

She adds that 'sometimes, you find an artwork that did not sell on the market having more lives and impact . . . it can travel and get seen and experienced by people who could never afford to buy it. Just to witness people engaging with your work in public and being moved can be more rewarding.' Unsurprisingly, her earlier bodies of work have been exhibited and collected extensively.[4] However, the series *Erasure* has enjoyed minimal exposure. 'Many curators and collectors have found the work too haunting,' she says. The photographs included here were accessed with ease from her gallery, whatiftheworld.

All three photographers spoke of kin, of communities that have inspired and supported them, enabling their creative expressions and survival outside of the markets. Mazibuko and Petersen share the sentiment that royalties and appearance fees should be a norm so that photographers do not have to rely largely on sales. The need for care, support and survival extends to those who are photographed too. Sadly, many who are involved in photography are invested in the fiction of the individual author and owner, including photographers themselves. Who and what is erased in the creation of 'self-portraits' that are so dominant in particular photographies (beyond the mobile phone selfie)?

Figure 10.7. *Erasure 3*, 2017. Photograph by Thania Petersen.

The ways in which photographers talk about their work made me reflect on how they make sense of the conditions (and inequities) under which they labour to make photographs.

These conversations have made me consider my choices about who and what I have brought to the surface in this essay: which participants have surfaced (the photographers, those photographed, and others present during the creations); what information is shared and withheld; and which photographs are exhibited and how. What informed my decisions? What privileges and power dynamics were at play?

Conclusion

The work of black photographers, especially black women photographers, is seldom seen as separate from their personal histories. Is it even possible to experience their work differently? If we were to consider Azoulay's conception of photography as not simply being about the photograph but a broader space of politics, how might our expectations that photographers operate in a more humane way extend not to just black women photographers but to *all* of us implicated in the (re)production, care, circulation, presentation and interpretation of photographs? If we changed our methods of working in this way, then surely this would disrupt the exploitative relations, contexts and structures that have become so normalised in photography, in art sectors and in our society generally.

About the artists

Tshepiso Mazibuko (b. 1995, Thokoza) studied at the Market Photo Workshop in Johannesburg and continues to work independently on personal projects.

Keorapetse Mosimane (b. 1973, Soweto) studied at the Market Photo Workshop in Johannesburg and currently works as a provincial civil servant.

Thania Petersen (b. 1980, Cape Town) studied at Central Saint Martin's College of Art in London and is represented by whatiftheworld gallery (Cape Town).

2.
Positioning

CHAPTER 11

What We Make to Unmake: The Imagination in Feminist Struggles

Yewande Omotoso

In *Outlaw Culture*, bell hooks writes that the function of art is to imagine what is possible. I once used her thoughts on creativity and the imagination as my defence on a panel I participated in alongside two African-American men in March 2018. The panel was in Durban at a literary festival called Time of the Writer. One of the men, Salim, was facilitating a conversation between myself and another writer. In fact, it was not, in the end, a conversation. Instead, Salim conducted two parallel conversations. I've facilitated panels before and I know what it's like when the facilitator decides, 'I won't try to have one conversation, I'll just speak a bit to this one and then speak a little to the other and then change and then change' and so on. That was the kind of panel I was a part of. At one moment, Salim turned to me to challenge me on the relationship in my novel *The Woman Next Door* between Hortensia, a Bajan woman, and Marion, a second-generation South African woman. Hortensia has retired to Cape Town; Marion's parents, Jewish, fled Europe from the terrors of Nazi Germany and settled in South Africa. The novel, I like to say, is about the 'hateship' between these two octogenarians. It is also an experiment. Salim challenged me on the nature of the relationship, as he struggled with the fact that Marion, a racist woman, remains 'unsympathetic' throughout the story. 'At no point,' he said, 'did I manage to relate to her.' He also struggled with a particular scene in the novel when, unable to comb her head of short tight curls, Hortensia allows Marion – for a few seconds – to run a comb through her hair. 'A black woman would never let a white woman touch her hair,' declared Salim. I was surprised that Salim felt comfortable to speak *for* what black women would and would not do with their hair, an authority I, a black woman, would never even give myself. He seemed to carry the assumption that there is one Black Woman Hair Guidebook and all black women have signed up to it.

In addition, I was saddened. Saddened by two possibilities: 1) that Salim's imagination had so failed him or 2) that I had failed to write a work that could ignite his imagination. And perhaps the truth is a combination of the two. But let's say, for this argument, that I had done my job and yet somehow he, as a reader, failed to allow for what I believe is the work of fiction. In a blog post titled 'No Love in the Wild', bell hooks says that movies do not just mirror the culture of any given time; they also create it. The same can be said, I believe, of novels. Even if the scene I rendered was so unimaginable, then, I would argue, is it not my job, perhaps, to create just that? To create a culture in which two old women can tend to one another, where even amidst prejudice and pain, tenderness can prevail? Are we not, these days, so desperately in need of such?

Along with the complexity of the struggles we face, these days call for unmaking, and I find nothing more well equipped for unmaking than the creative endeavour itself. The employment of imagination, using the act of making to unmake the ways of sensing and thinking that are often at the root of so much of what doesn't work in our lives and societies. I want to talk about my own methods of unmaking, however humble, and my obsession with both unlikeliness (unbeknownst to Salim, I was deeply complimented by his perplexity) and unlikeability.

I want to preface what I am saying and what I am about to say by quoting Ama Ata Aidoo, one of my favourite authors. I once attended a workshop where she was present. The event was held in Accra, Ghana, in March 2014. At the gathering Aidoo recalled an anecdote relating to her novel *Changes*. She mentioned that after the book was published, her friend read it and said, 'You're telling our stories.' Aidoo spoke about how this notion (of telling our stories) was not, in fact, front and centre of her mind when she was writing the novel. Similarly with regards to the feminist politics evident in all her work, she doesn't write thinking, 'I'm a Feminist, I'm a Feminist', because in her estimation to do so would result in not a novel, a piece of literature, but rather a tract or political pamphlet. Instead, Aidoo speaks about what she calls a 'politicised imagination', and this is certainly what I aspire to. It is not that my mission is to write out my feminisms in my novels; it is rather that I believe and tend towards a politicised imagination. My hope, then, is that the work that erupts from such an imagination is not a tract but rather a story imbued with the nuance of storytelling and also propelled by a mission; a delicate one that contains doubts (I believe in the aesthetics of doubt) and spaces and gaps which allow for ignorance and new information. I interpret Aidoo as putting her politics through the thresher of imagination so that something pure is retained and it is powerful without being overtly didactic. I believe stories, when done well, contain an endless source of instruction. You don't have to wield a heavy stick to achieve that; you simply have to abide by the lore of story.

A hateship between two octogenarians

I won't pretend that much of what instigates my stories is premeditated. Mostly, rather than having the capacity to prescribe to myself what to write, I find suddenly (on waking up one day or on walking along a certain crowded path) that a story is in my head, requesting attention and tending to. That said, I know that I do have certain interests and these are often not disconnected from the kinds of stories I end up telling. For instance, I seem to be particularly interested in women over 50. In the case of *The Woman Next Door*, as already mentioned, Hortensia and Marion are in their 80s. I'm often asked to explain this, which is perhaps a well-meant question that unintentionally (or intentionally, who knows?) affirms a world where such a focus is strange and different. I want for a time when it's not a spectacle to have 80-something-year-old women as the focus of our narratives. When asked the question, I often stumble, the way one might when providing what had previously seemed to be obvious information, unpractised in explaining what had never felt in need of explanation. In answering, I might mention my own grandmother, whose voice certainly echoes through some of the dialogue in the novel. In truth, though, even without the inspiration of my grandmother, I am infinitely intrigued by the lives of such women. Women who have survived adolescence, who've pushed through the objectification of their 20s. They've either had children or not had children and endured all that *that* means, they may have tempered their ambitions or, depending on era and culture, pushed back against notions of what they can and cannot aspire to. I'm interested in their fatigue, their disappointments and bitterness; I'm interested in what mistakes they've made, especially the seemingly irrevocable ones. Of course, a story about older men could be just as intriguing, except, knowing what we know about what it means to be a woman in this world, I believe the story of old women carries something distinct, a distinct set of scars.

In March 2017 at the Virginia Festival of the Book in Charlottesville, at the end of a presentation of *The Woman Next Door*, a writer came up to me. Why, she wanted to know, would I write about women fighting? She hadn't read the book, but her impression from my presentation was that I was somehow creating a spectacle for people to gorge on; she made my novel sound like the literary equivalent of a bitch fight. Of course, that this is, according to her, even something to be avoided is arguable. Men fight all the time on paper, screen and real life. Their fights are not to be hidden or deemed shameful. When they fight, it's called a brawl or, at the most insane of levels – war. To write a novel about two women fighting seemed a betrayal of sorts. This is not the first time a person would appeal to me for what I think of as a 'decent depiction', but I will come back to this later.

A lost boy and the love of his father

In my first novel, *Bom Boy*, I wrote about Leke, a baby of mixed heritage whose mother, a poor white South African woman, is unable to care for him, both financially and emotionally. She leaves him in the unsuspecting hands of an older, much wealthier white woman who goes on, along with her academic husband, to raise Leke as her own. Leke's biological father, Oscar, a Nigerian man, is in jail in South Africa at the time of this exchange. At the centre of the story, now with Leke as a young man, is a series of letters Oscar writes to his son, expressing a deep love that Leke would only ever experience second-hand, almost 20 years after the letters were written. The question I am often asked about this story is: isn't it odd to be writing about a young boy coming of age, being a woman myself? It seems the birthplace of these kinds of questions (the one about writing about 80-something-year-olds and this one) is a place that says you ought to write to type, write according to what you are. As awful as that directive sounds, surely it must be the expectation of this that makes any departure from it deserving of such enthused interrogation. What does it say about us that we think it necessary to remark? Have we somehow misunderstood, as, I would argue, had Salim, what it really means to imagine, what the real work of the imagination can be? While I will always have sympathy for such a line of engagement, I do think its recurrence underlines something troublesome about how we live and think.

I recall a funny story. *Bom Boy* was my master's thesis, which I undertook at the University of Cape Town between the years 2008 and 2010. While I was completing my studies, a visiting lecturer came through. We were asked to schedule one-on-one sessions with him, which I did. When I met up with him, after he'd read a few pages of my manuscript, the first thing he said to me was that I need not worry about getting the voice of the boy correct; that I had done so convincingly. And it was so interesting to me because up until he mentioned it, I didn't know that was something I ought to have been worried about.

It had not been premeditated: I had not thought it through first and then decided to write about a young boy. Instead, the story had descended upon me and I was left to grapple with it. Having written the novel, I kicked myself – surely as a feminist I should have written about a young girl! Of course, we know it's not as simple as that. In fact, feminist struggle is as much for the boy child as it is for the girl, the gender non-conforming, the anyone. At the festival I mentioned earlier – Time of the Writer – I spoke at a workshop at the Tongaat Central Library. Children from a local primary school attended. When we engaged and invited participation, young girl after young girl shot her hand up. The boys all sat in the back, serious-faced and stoic; it almost seemed as if creativity was something they were now suspicious of or, even worse, deemed unworthy of their concentration, their gender. There was one young boy who sat amongst the girls in the front row, soft-faced and gentle. When we commented on the absence of participation from boys, he tentatively put his hand up and read what he'd been writing during the workshop. I felt tender towards him then. In observing his utter gentleness and observing the slightly older, more reserved and hardened (scared?) boys, I felt I could see the fate of this young man. Short of a miracle, society would see to it that he 'manned up' and subscribed to the one dimension of what that has come to mean. In many ways, *Bom Boy* and the story of Leke is an attempt to take a lost boy and see whether he might find himself. Find himself not emotionally shut down or closed off, but find his centre, find his heart and learn to love, to imagine.

Class, race, gender, ability, sexuality

During a panel at the same Time of the Writer book festival, this time at the Elizabeth Sneddon Theatre, a person challenged me on the representation of a blind woman in *The Woman Next Door*. In the novel, a key aspect of the story is that Hortensia's husband is unfaithful, and that in fact there is a child he's had with his lover. A child whom Hortensia, on her husband's death, is called to contact. Eventually the child – now all grown up – does arrive and she is blind. My challenger felt that I was using a blind woman, using disability, as a prop in the story. She cites the 'sweetness' of the character, her guide dog that she travels with, the fact of her very few lines (she arrives and leaves within a few pages) as problematic. I really listened to this critique and took it on, acknowledging her, accepting guilt and suggesting that there is an ongoing process of attempting *not* to make work that flattens humanity versus expanding it. As she asked her question, new images came up in my mind, the possibility that the blind daughter was addicted to porn or cigarettes or slowly trying to drink less alcohol each day and struggling. Perhaps she was bitter instead of sweet and forgiving. Of course, none of the details of how I envisage the character had to change, just a handling of character that would arrest the sense reached by this one reader (and perhaps others who just haven't said) that the portrayal was one-dimensional when more dimensions were not only called for but imperative to push back against stereotypes. It was interesting to me that in a book where I work to portray the sexual lives of 80-something-year-old women, where I make them complex and whole and care not for whether the reader ends up *liking* them or not (I can think of nothing more asinine than this ambition), in this endeavour I also fail to portray a blind woman as a whole somebody versus a useful moment. In fact, a small defence, I was not trying to do what bell hooks describes as 'commodify Otherness'.[1] A key theme of the novel is judgement versus redemption, and in many ways this child's entry into the story marks a moment of Hortensia's judgement/redemption. 'Justice is blind' was what I was going for. Hortensia dreads meeting this woman, whose existence is the seat of her torment, proof of her husband's infidelity. But upon meeting, in contrast to Hortensia's meanness and her expectation that that is what the world will serve her, the child is kind and open, she withholds judgement. I understand, however, the critique that this all seems too easy and convenient; having been corrected, I understand the error in my design.

In *The Woman Next Door*, I explore what it means that my two main characters are working women, women who pursued careers in the '60s and '70s. Marion is an architect and Hortensia is a textile designer. I explore their domestic spaces and how they grapple with those. The fact that both women are successful and extremely wealthy – from their own achievements as well as the success of their now dead husbands – allows me to explore issues of class. Marion hires a woman – Agnes – to keep her home. This is a not unfamiliar relationship that has been explored (and sometimes idealised) in films like *Driving Miss Daisy* or books like *The Madams*, *Remains of the Day* or the rather problematic *The Help*. Perhaps in the same way I was taken to task about the portrayal of a woman who is blind in my novel, this portrayal, by me, a middle-class person, of a working-class woman might be fraught with error. I was pleased, however, when a woman I respect commented on a certain section of the novel. She said that in only a few words (excerpted below) I managed to sum up the interstices between race, gender and class:

Marion fought with herself, in her head. The reason she hadn't wanted Agnes to bring her child to work was because the child would be a distraction – that was the reason. And the reason she suggested Agnes not wash her clothes in with the family's load was because this seemed sensible, to keep things separate. *Why complicate the washing?*[2]

A mother who is not a mother

In my forthcoming novel *An Unusual Grief,* I explore the life of a mother as she mourns the death of her estranged adult daughter, Yinka. The woman, Mojisola, is approaching 60. On the news of Yinka's death, she is deeply and permanently bereft. With no knowledge of how to grieve, she leaves her cheating husband in Cape Town and aways to her daughter's apartment in Johannesburg, where she occupies Yinka's life, goes on her blind dates, takes care of her cat, and so on. I really wanted to write about a woman who struggled with motherhood and who blames her estrangement from her daughter – and her daughter's eventual death – on that struggle. Now in grieving, the mother who wasn't a mother must come to terms with herself, her past, the silent judgement of society and the unique relationship she had with her daughter; she must make peace with motherhood through grief. Mojisola must forgive herself, forgive her daughter and forgive a world that provides only a box so big for mothers to fit into, and if you don't fit, then you (and not the box) is seen as wanting.

In keeping with every novel I've written thus far, when I read a short piece of the manuscript (still a work in progress at the time) in August 2016 at the Writivism Festival in Uganda, a man asked, 'Are you a mother?' I said no and he seemed to be satisfied with my answer; he asked me no further questions. Of course, I wondered whether he thought the fact that I wasn't a mother disqualified me from writing about them. This would be absurd. I wondered whether he objected to my insistence on writing about a woman who did not feel motherly, whose existence opposed this notion of the natural motherness of women. Perhaps I have to finally conclude that this question which stalks me, sometimes mildly hostile, sometimes admiring, of writing beyond my own immediate experience must be at the heart of what my work is. And yet it is also what we have come to call cultural appropriation. I am in full agreement with bell hooks when she says:

> Acts of appropriation are part of the process by which we make ourselves. Appropriating – taking something for one's own use – need not be synonymous with exploitation. This is especially true of cultural appropriation. The 'use' one makes of what is appropriated is the crucial factor.[3]

In the end, my acts of appropriation will either be to good use or, as my challenger found with regards to my cursory portrayal of a blind woman, to bad.

Say nice things about us

While I was in Durban in 2017, I visited another community library, this time in Austerville, and spoke about *The Woman Next Door*. I read a few pages from the book. At the end of the presentation, a woman came up to me. We spoke and she shared with me about her challenge, having lost her daughter about a year before. She was clearly in pain and I was deeply moved by what she said and the emotion she conveyed. Towards the end of our conversation, she told me her age. She was about to turn 80. She told me that she was happy to hear I was writing about older women and she beseeched me to 'please say nice things about us'. I found this so interesting and it reminded me of the story I told above, of the middle-aged American writer coming to chastise me for allowing women to fight on the pages of my novel. Both incidents in turn reminded me of the African-American comedian Wanda Sykes, who does a skit in which she talks about being young and her mother taking her and her siblings out, and they would inevitably start to misbehave and the mother would pull her children close and scold them by saying: 'White people are looking at you!'[4] This recurring appeal – spoken and silent – for decent depiction or representation. Don't make me look bad. Don't make *us* look bad. Don't make *us* look bad in front of *them.* I hear this appeal and I have compassion for it, I even identify, recognise myself in it. However, it is not my job, and to fall prey to that as a writer is to fall prey to the tract writing Ama Ata Aidoo guards against. But is this at odds with what bell hooks says, the duty to depict us not only as we are but as we can be? Don't make us look bad, make us look better, show us what's possible. Maybe these two tenets are at odds, which presents a golden dilemma that could preoccupy me for a lifetime. But let's say, for a moment, that they are not. Let's say, rather, that these two notions are in a kind of twirl on the dance floor of the Imagination. The one tempers the other and vice versa. Images matter. That's why the strong appeal for a good one. Except, I believe if I am *really* doing my job, commodification of Otherness is absent, and what we are and what we can be is fully present. I'm pushing back against the tyranny of singularity, and we look bad and good and bad and good and bad and, ultimately, we look ourselves purely and truly with all our longings and fragility and wonder. I think this dynamic carries its own integrity and is all I can or should hope for.

CHAPTER 12

Breathing Under Water

Danai S. Mupotsa

There has been important work on Black South African women's poetry and the ways that experience, the body and memory are central to its formal, political and ethical commitments. This essay is laced with these traces; they reflect my location as a non-citizen South African Black woman, teacher, writer and poet. But this essay is also much more.

The dreamland

My daughter sits like my great-grandmother Esther.

She does it like she knew her and like she breathes her spirit back to life each time she folds one leg over the other, ending up with them flat on the ground in a way that seems impossible. But if you are a child descendant of Esther, you know how. This is how my daughter sits.

My great-grandmother breathes warm air against my ear, says nothing. I know that she is deeply grateful that I bring a daughter who sits in a way so close to her deepest expression.

She breathes deeply in gratitude for the angel-light born to us. My grandfather, her son Edgar, laughs. His father, Isaac, says nothing. Always. Heartbroken perhaps?

Or perhaps it is always and only my wish for the dead, who left scraps of kin strewn across territories, leaving us only the explanation of national borders to gather our sense of being. Perhaps they left nothing because they had no other option. Any other explanation feels too cruel.

In *Conscripts of Modernity*, David Scott talks about the feeling that I describe as cruel, as a problem of narrative. For Scott, anti-colonial movements rely on the narrative of overcoming colonialism in articulating demands for a better future, and that when this future of freedom arrives, it can only be understood as an overcoming. These stories of overcoming make the history of the nation, and its time of independence the only story that we know. And it seems that all we then have is a repetition of the same narrative of overcoming.

Panashe Chigumadzi begins *These Bones Will Rise Again* with a reflection on the coup-not-coup that saw President Robert Mugabe finally deposed after 30 years in as president. She reads this moment as a 'Fourth Chimurenga'. Not even a year after, people in Zimbabwe took to the streets against the new government. Those who spoke out were beaten in their homes, in public; thugs visited the ones who were not yet dead in the hospitals. Those who worked in the hospitals dare not speak.

Everyone lives in repetition of the same.
And yet, long live the hope for the nation.

M. Jacqui Alexander poignantly writes: 'Breathing grief for a lifetime can be toxic. Breathing only grief simply kills.'[1] The grief of hope is what I feel, is that which is cruel. But it is also the nation and its time that feels the same. But it becomes our only language. How else to speak of the dispossession of land, of value, of kinship, of language, of self?

My father, Isaac, wishes he could reach me across the bridge of stubbornness wedged between us. His mother, Hilda, rests her spirit body against the pillow next to my face, begs me to see her and to be kinder to her son. But gently, Hilda mostly wishes that her children could learn the language we speak between those living and those dead. Hilda died in 1976 alone. I never met her, but I have known her my whole life as the woman who burns fire in my stomach.

I first met Hilda as the feeling of a wind:

The girl runs slightly away from the other children and lands upon a curved piece of rock that has broken its way between the earth and the water. She tries to sit down, but the stream of water to her left begs her to stand tall and reach her eyes upwards towards the sky. She looks up, then behind her, then back at the surface of this rock that breaks earth and water and seems to also climb right up into the sky. The wind comes to join her, rushing wildly in circles. The girl is only six-years-old, but a deeper knowledge rests inside her. This voice tells her she has landed on a njuzu's rock and begs her to greet her kin. She glances at the water while the wind still draws her up, up and up. She thanks the njuzu for this reception. This memory will rest inside the girl's stomach for the rest of this lifetime, it is the first time she meets a place that gathers her like she is home.

Never knowing about Hilda in my stomach, my father always feared that my stubbornness was the fullest expression of the connection between me and Edgar. It is possibly quite true.

The phone call arrived at night. The girl was playing with her sisters when she suddenly felt the world turn over her head. She picked up the phone, even while her mother yelled for her to let an adult answer. On the other end, she heard her father weeping.
There was a deep despairing spoken between them.
Grandfather had died.
The girl wept for her father,
this kind boy

the world always sweeping his childhood
from under him.

That night, when the girl finally stopped weeping and fell into the
dreamland, grandfather arrived by her bedside. He sat with her and
told her stories about his journey. From then on, the girl would always
mourn for him for her father, whose heart seemed from this point to
be too broken. Her grandfather climbed into her stomach where he
mourns for his kindest son.

> utata waits for me inside a drum
> i cannot reach him   until i peel him off the tractor blades
> piece him together   scattered on a maize field
> carry him home in a wreath and broken string of white beads

> umakhulu warned him   against spilling calamine
> playing too close to the river
> she hid a drum   inside a kist   in the shed
> to protect him
> I cannot reach it without red and white beads.[2]

Questions of power

Not everyone can afford to breathe for a living.[3]

I was 19 years old the first time I read Bessie Head's *A Question of Power*.
This was for an undergraduate course, and I was expected to write an
essay about the connections between Head's biography and the context
of her writing. It was Head's novel that made the men who then decided
whose work was worthy open up a space for other African women's
writing to be included in the canon, as I was told in this class. These same
men found the work of women writing before her lacking in complexity.

It was not Head's 'complexity' that drew my attention. It was not
an agreement with the misogynistic and racist assumptions of what

qualified as 'the novel in African literature' that drew my attention. *A Question of Power* struck my senses in a way that I had no language for. Reading this novel felt like a possession. Much like Elizabeth, Head's protagonist, who falls into what my professor told me was a mental breakdown, failing to distinguish between day time and night time, or wake time and dream time – I felt myself fall into the very same state. As I read along with Bessie/Elizabeth I felt the same awakening.

Awakening, in the ways that Christina Sharpe introduces the idea of 'the wake' as a problem for thought.[4] For Sharpe, to be in the wake is to be in a state of consciousness. Bessie/Elizabeth's consciousness awakens them to their own biography, their respective out-of-placeness within the confines of national time, but also awakens them to a consciousness of the dreamland. An awakening out of 'national/historical/linear' time and an awakening into the consciousness of the dreamland.

One of the most enduring ideas of modernity, or what Lisa Lowe calls 'liberal modernism',[5] along with the narrowing down of notions of political freedom to the question of the nation state, is what Lowe describes as 'colonial division of intimacy, which charts the historically differentiated access to the domains of liberal personhood, from interiority and individual will, to the possession of property and domesticity'.[6] While autobiography, like the novel, becomes one of liberalism's genres par excellence and the technique used to articulate the temporality and masculinity of the nation, Head is among a range of women whose writing takes up this form, and diffracts the individual subject borne out of such a division of intimacy.

In her biography of Head, Gillian Stead Eilersen draws connections between the time of the publication of *A Question of Power* and the states of consciousness Head was experiencing at the time. Vangile Gantsho's poem 'schizophrenia' offers three useful definitions to rest beside this understanding of Head's various states of being awake:

> a serious mental illness in which a woman forces her ten year old daughter to wash in a river during winter for buying sweets with her two cents change.

a psychotic disorder characterized by a fifteen year old girl trying to calm her mother from attacking a baby she believes is the devil on a bus. also known as *inherited paranoia*.

the co-existence of opposing voices. example, *she may cook and sew curtains as service, but may not serve as a leader because she is divorced – Assemblies of God.*[7]

Eilersen describes Head's writing at this time as preoccupied with spiritual phenomena and mental confusion. She reads this as Head resisting logical sequence. Logical sequence, when and where it does appear in parts of *A Question of Power*, comes to be the language Eilersen reads as Head's attempts to make her experiences legible; however, these experiences of wakefulness intensify, and lead to an 'undoing'.[8]

The personality of Head's protagonist, Elizabeth, disintegrates, and Eilersen argues that 'Bessie uses the device of externalising, even dramatising her psychological scars and suppressed fears and aspirations in a series of dream visions'.[9] Elizabeth crosses over to the dreamland, where this disintegration in one view could be read as a dissociative condition, where her psyche splits into various characters and 'there is a fragmentation of the "characters" in Elizabeth's inner universe, which increases the pressure on her mind'.[10]

This splitting apart, a diffracting of the subject Bessie/Elizabeth, betrays a colonial division of intimacy and the optimism of national time. This betrayal, then, is a different kind of opening, one similar to what Trinh T. Minh-ha calls 'how to write an ending',[11] where she invites us to write the wounds of our time, or what she calls 'the work of *resonance*' – 'the way different events, both natural and man-made, vibrate across times and places, tune into one another, and deeply affect life processes'.[12] The work of resonance, she continues, is when 'language meets its edge, [its] pain and at its worst, even especially when it can't be silenced, is first and foremost a word'.[13]

You remember it because it's a wound.
A cut, twenty cuts, the name
for the canings on the palm,
on the knuckles, on the buttocks,
a finely graded order of pain
that we who should not exist
were assigned for our failures.[14]

. . . it seems there is only a climbing blackness that wraps itself around my
corners to break each scene between its fingers . . .[15]

when the sun sets

blow the whistle

and signal for help[16]

Girling

I'm standing in the middle of the road trying to drown out my mother's
voice. She tells me I'll go to hell for the men who come in and out of my
bed. She doesn't know about the women. I wonder if there is a worse kind
of hell for people like me.[17]

The first time I felt I might be a feminist was during a telephone call
with a friend in high school. I struggled to find my place during that
time, despite finding my way into various groups of friends. On the
first day of school in Form 1, I sat in the seat I had been assigned to and
watched the other girls arriving, quietly. I was shy and awkward. And
if I am totally honest, even though I think I am the funniest person I
know, it's probably just my dad and sister Mudiwa who know how to
laugh properly when I tell stories. So I was not always sure that I could
rely on my sense of humour to make friends.

But friends came.

At first it was all of the most awkward girls and there was something intensely familiar and at the same time there was a not-enoughness about those friendships. The social scientist in me now can better describe this feeling as an affective structure of female friendship. This is a cruel affective structure, as I remember it, where friendship is informed by awkward forms of recognition where 'this recognition precisely brings the comfort or pleasure of recognition itself, but that this cannot be confused, say, with being known, or with happiness'.[18]

For those of us who attended girls-only schools, we know the range of intense friendship and feelings established over the years. I sometimes mention examples of this to my students when I am introducing the concepts of sex/gender. I try to help them recognise that the ways that we are sexed and gendered is a relation to expected time, events and markers of progress that lead up to the promise or expectation of heterosexual couplehood, and social and biological reproduction.

I often also talk about the letters we wrote each other in school. You would be sitting only a few desks away, but four or five letters could be exchanged in a single day. These same intense friendships were also rivalries, because the general expectation was that friendship was the foundation from which we would mature into women and support or betray each other in establishing proper relationships. We would keep each other's secrets for protection and for what was also proper. We would betray each other's secrets. We would covet each other's lovers. We would fail to name the moments, feelings or touches that broke the many rules spoken/unspoken.

The women I grew out of
Laugh to feel they are still here,
They open their mouths
tell their stories
and vomit tales they were forced to believe.[19]

In her essay 'In Sisterhood and Solidarity', Awino Okech traces how female friendship and intimacy have been useful political locations for the awakening of feminist consciousness and the work of solidarity. Okech also cautions us that within these solidarities an enduring compulsory heterosexuality structures the expectations of friendship and intimacy, with no place to articulate desire. I did not have Okech's clarity as a teenage girl, but I learned to be a girl and to do what was proper against the will that burned inside me, feeling like an ongoing intentional arbitrary dispossessing violence.

You call them your friends.

In the opening passages of her book *Willful Subjects*, Sarah Ahmed presents 'The Willful Child' by the Brothers Grimm:

> What a story. The willful child: she has a story to tell. In this Grimm story, which is certainly a grim story, the willful child is the one who is disobedient, who will not do as her mother wishes. If authority assumes the right to turn a wish into a command, then willfulness is a diagnosis of the failure to comply with those whose authority is given . . . Willfulness is thus compromising; it compromises the capacity of a subject to survive, let alone flourish. The punishment for willfulness is a passive willing of death, an allowing of death.[20]

Ahmed's figure of the willful child rises again in her book *Living a Feminist Life*, where she describes girling: 'becoming a girl . . . is about how you experience your body in relation to space. Gendering operates in how bodies take up space.'[21] Girling, she continues, 'is enacted not only through being explicitly addressed as a girl, but in the style or mode of address: because you are a girl, we can do this to you. Violence is the mode of address.'[22]

Like Head, who re/forms the *Bildungsroman*, Chinelo Okparanta's more recent novel *Under the Udala Trees* uses this form through the story of a girl, Ijeoma. Ijeoma's meets her first love, Amina, when she first moves to Nnewi, and then they meet again at boarding school. The frame for a lesbian love story makes one of those enduring stories told and untold about female friendship/intimacy and the range of institutions where we become girls.

The novel has received important praise, as part of a swelling of queer African literature, but more explicitly because Okparanta uses the form of the novel and not the short story, which has formally preoccupied a lot of queer African writing. Set against the backdrop of the Nigerian-Biafran War, Okparanta locates Ijeoma's 'coming out' within Nigeria's national time and as central to the emergence and ongoingness of that violence. When Ijeoma's intimate friendship with Amina is discovered by a schoolteacher, Ijeoma is sent back to Ojoto, where her mother takes to teaching her the Bible as punishment for her actions. During the months when Ijeoma receives these lessons, her wilfulness continues to grow.

Ijeoma's mother, Adaora, anticipates that her biblical lessons will 'correct' her, but instead it is in enduring her punishment that Ijeoma becomes more aware of reading as an act of critical consciousness. Ijeoma's smartness (to smart as also to hurt, to hurt in relation to history) is also my deep burden.

smallgirl with hands of spades
smallgirl dreams too much. hopes too much
wants to plant and grow
smallgirl thinks she is the ocean
smallgirl is a stream

smallgirl will break her heart with all this want
smallgirl is not even the wind[23]

Later in her life, Ijeoma has a new lover, Ndidi, a teacher she visits at her home at night. During her visits, she spends many hours reading novels. The critical awareness she has about novels and their forms again, like her reading of biblical texts, becomes the language of her awakening. In this way, whereas Bessie/Elizabeth diffracts the novel, Ijeoma's tactics splinters the form and occupies the gaps.

a pink cotton invitation under the table
the ill-timed blood on a lover's fingers

the smell of impepho in the middle of the night[24]

I do not find tragedy romantic at all.
I do not think playing dead is empowering.
Or good for my ego even.
I love you.
But
I'd rather be alive.[25]

Like Ijeoma, for me, without knowing its name, it was through learning how to read/write/breathe against the grain that I first learned ways to language the burning in my stomach. This finding a name, or a form of articulation for the burn in the stomach, is located in the ways Desiree Lewis thinks about the work of the radical imagination. That is, that a name, or what formally will be called identity politics, carries potentiality in the moments of its wake. This wakefulness risks being occupied by the very structures of power from which one wakes.

Edgar, his mother Esther and the woman he wed when she bore my father, Hilda: her voice rests whispering in my ear, on the surface of my skin, in the bottom of my stomach she is reaching for herself across all of my mess and dense. She probably finds me basic. She left her husband, but also her children. She died alone. Her grave a pile a sand eroded over time until she haunted my dreams for so long, we were forced to remember her.

Today there is no black. No dark. No light.
Today there are only blues and blood. Hope and heart.
    a half-done face in a coffin.
a brewing storm of smallgirls coming[26]

Breathing under water

I'm told my lungs are made of water
That a snake coils around my spine
and I carry hives of bees inside my breasts[27]

little girl runs through the crowd dances
like her feet are pulled to the sky laughs gently
little girl plays with her friends dips feet in the water
claps her hands with another asks her questions
little girl catches the eye opens her mouth even wider stares close to
the ground
little girl whispers[28]

In the final days of Audre Lorde's life, her work was preoccupied with what it means to be alive, animated in *The Cancer Journals* and *A Burst of Light*. While she continued to work through many of the stomach-burning questions that had animated her writing and political life prior to her diagnosis, the question of life, or liveness, is more concretely torn open in the work that comes towards the end. This final collection includes poems written between 1987 and her passing in 1992.

Your hunger for rectitude
blossoms into rage
the hot tears of mourning
never shed for you before
your twisted measurements

the agony of denial
the power of unshared secrets.[29]

Until one day I began to write
and I wrote until I could not forget
myself anymore
On the page appeared
each breath and gesture, each posture
of the body I had torn away
On the page appeared the years
and the words I could not speak
On the page appeared the pages
and the emptiness I had erased
On the page appeared my bones
and my memories
and at last I stepped again into my body.[30]

One of the little girls that I first read, and thought myself through, was the young Audre, then Audrey, in the opening chapters of her biomythography, *Zami: A New Spelling of My Name.* Like Head's *A Question of Power*, this was not an easy book to read and I was completely overwhelmed by it. I was overwhelmed in the way that poetry has always been overwhelming until it takes me like a possession.

One day I sat with a large sheet of paper and tried to map the journeys Lorde made, and how they brought her closer and yet further from a sense of home. I thought about Afrekete, the figure of the trickster that 'smarts' like Ijeoma and connects Audre/Zami to a dense lineage of Black women. Then I tried to trace my own journey. Writing/living and teaching as a 'feminist scholar' is one trace of this journey.

The blind little girl in the opening pages of *Zami* feels quite alone and quite misunderstood. She seems overly aware of girling, and because of this, she is overly aware of when she is punished for it. She also can't seem to take control of her body, her period leaking through her clothes, making the sorts of mistakes that I still make. It feels too easy to simply name her a killjoy and let that be the resting point for my sense of affiliation with her.

> This is what might have been lost   this is how my bones seize up
> This is my only way to you[31]

As the story in *Zami* develops, the erotic/sacred language intensifies but it also becomes more and more complex. This complexity intensifies the connection with the personal and political and the personal as spiritual.

Just before her passing, Lorde discovered that she had twin half-sisters in Grenada, where her parents lived before they moved to the United States. The girls were born the same year that Lorde's parents were married. In Grenada, their existence as Byron Lorde's children was an open secret, but Lorde and her sisters, Phyllis and Helen, were only told about them in 1991, once their parents were both dead.

> This is me being carried   a woman being carried out to sea
>
> See how the sun fills my eyes
> See how I hang here[32]

M. Jacqui Alexander offers that 'the purpose of the body is to act not simply . . . as an enactment of the Soul, but also as a medium of spirit, the repository of a consciousness that derives from a source residing elsewhere, another ceremonial ritual marking'.[33] This marking is etched across Lorde's work, but also in me in the ways I have felt her and Head and every woman whose words I place here; these are my hauntings. Like Ijeoma, who animates the smart in me, that seeks sequence within the splintered gaps of how we come to knowledge.

I have titled this essay after Gantsho's poem 'breathing under water' because it gathers the intuition I have about decades of feeling as though I am in the wake. Gantsho is a poet, publisher and healer. She was also the woman who edited my collection of poems, *feeling and ugly*. It came to me, out of me, from the form of experience in the way that Alexander offers in her account of the body, where the 'Sacred becomes a way of embodying the remembering of self, if you will, a self that is neither habitually individualized nor unwittingly secularized'.[34]

Gantsho's collection *red cotton* is formally written as a novella, but different forms and parts stand alone, just as specific figures like the smallgirl run across the narrative. The collection was first drafted while she completed her MFA at the university currently known as Rhodes, and I remember sitting with her at a bar, at a moment when she was stuck in eRhini. The Eastern Cape is a place that haunts my own family's history, albeit unspoken. It was my first time there and I felt spiritually too open. The wine opened us further.

During our talk, I told her of a dream I had had. I was by a rock and a pool appeared. The faces of two njuzu sat before me, and below a huge crocodile looked up at me in anticipation. For a long time I had been asking about what it means to be 'under water', which for Gantsho has been her journey to becoming igqirha. In that moment in the dreamworld, I recognised the crocodile as my kin and allowed myself to be swallowed into the water. Finding my poet voice was this accident that happened in my dreams, came against my will, and is both diffracted and splintered by the voices of my kin, living and dead. Yet in my dreams it is the resting rocks where the most recent of my ancestors lie, where I am called to find the resonant language of a feminist consciousness and the work of the Sacred.

Gantsho's stuckness came to an end when she allowed herself to be swallowed by the dreamworld.

Audrey/Audre's early life is a running away from her kin.

This is the same as mine.

My kinship with Gantsho was intentional in the way that she edited the collection, and our books were launched together. But this kinship is also again, against my will, etched onto my body and mirrored in our stories and our dream visions.

Her in her prayers
Me in the water[35]

CHAPTER 13

'Do I Make You Uncomfortable?' Writing, Editing and Publishing Black in a White Industry

Zukiswa Wanner

The journey to my first novel, *The Madams*, is a story I have repeated often in interviews, charmed as it seemed to be. In 2004, a year after returning to South Africa from Hawai'i where I had been studying, via the United Kingdom, unable to find a job in the field of journalism which I loved, I started working at the Alf Kumalo Museum in Soweto. It was here that I met the late writer and essayist Lewis Nkosi during a small staff braai Alf hosted. Lewis emailed a 'returned safely, 'twas nice to meet' note on his return home to Switzerland, and a literary friendship was born. Every time something on the South African political scene riled me, I would write the sort of outraged, if dark-humoured, pieces that I wished I could have written for South African newspapers, if any of them had responded in the affirmative (or at all) to just one of my application letters. Instead, I would send my opinions off to Lewis.

Reminiscent of my old faculty editor and journalism professor at university, one Larry Le Doux, Lewis would take time to engage, then fill the pieces with notes on what had failed to work, and what points should be teased out further. Although the pieces had lots of editorial notes, he would also be complimentary of what worked. In that way, he never shattered my confidence, and I learned to take the criticism in my stride. Invariably he would end each of these emails with, 'You should seriously consider writing fiction.' And I would retort, 'I am too much of a realist to write fiction.' And he would return, 'That is the greatest bullshit you've ever written and the best fiction you use to keep trying to convince yourself.' In February 2005, Lewis was yet again in Johannesburg. I was unaware, and bumped into him at a Dumile Feni exhibition at the Johannesburg Art Gallery. He was chatting to some relative of the then president.

'Have you met Zukiswa Wanner?' Lewis asked the man he was in conversation with.

'No, I can't say I have.'

'She is one of the best young writers we have in this country today,' Lewis responded, hyperbolically.

I don't think Moeletsi Mbeki recalls this meeting, and although I have repeated this story often in interviews, this is the first time I am naming him. So Moeletsi gave me his card and said, 'Please email me. I would love to read what you have written.' I made sure I did not lose that card, and the very next day, a Friday, I selected what I thought were my three best pieces of writing and emailed them to him. Five days later, I received an email from Moeletsi. It was a generous email, but I can't recall everything he said in it, except the phrase 'you should consider writing fiction'.

I often joke that both men, both essayists (Lewis was a novelist too, but it's his essays that have always spoken more to me), decided to shove me off to another form of writing because I wasn't impressive enough as an essayist. And yet, on a serious note, I am grateful to both of them.

That Wednesday 9 February 2005, with little to do in the office, I started writing the very first draft of *The Madams*. It was, interestingly, inspired by the controversial old 'Take Another Look at Mzansi' SABC 1 advert, where the white folk were in the townships and the black people were in the suburbs. One of the sequences has a white maid chasing after her charges, black suburban children, and I decided I wanted to write her story. Except I wanted her to be younger and to have the sort of agency that I would want anyone to have, whatever their job. I completed this first draft of what I wasn't naming a novel just yet, within a two- to three-week space. Sadly, despite the amazing works it had, there really were not many people coming to Alf's museum unless they came with him, so I had plenty of time to work on the manuscript. When I was done, I sent it off to retired *Drum* veteran Doc Bikitsha. Within three days, he called me with some advice: it was the best stuff he had read in a while in South African fiction (he obviously wasn't reading much). He sent his driver back with some notes on what I should improve, and a list of five publishers to send the manuscript to. Of the five, as I repeat often, three accepted the reworked manuscript, and one was enthusiastic enough to fly up from Cape Town for a lunch meeting with a contract and some more notes.

I don't remember whether I signed the contract there and then, or if I pretended I wanted to look at it and would email it back. What I do remember is that I was so excited about the contract that when I finally signed it, I agreed to everything. Ten percent royalty fee. World rights. Translation rights. Filming rights. I was getting published, that's what mattered.

Sigh.

If I had known then what I know now, I would have been slower to sign. I would have consulted Kagiso Lesego Molope or Sindiwe Magona or Fred Khumalo or Niq Mhlongo or Mandla Langa or Zakes Mda or or or . . .

I did not. And yet despite that, it was a beautiful journey.

It would be over a year of working and reworking *The Madams* to make it the product that people bought in shops across South Africa from November 2006. First came the publishing director's notes. Later, considering the commissioning editor's input. Finally, three drafts with the editor assigned to me, one Jacqui L'Ange. Fourteen years later, I still refuse to publish a book before it has gone through five drafts, and it's due to my experience with this team of women who took on my first manuscript and loved it as I did. Throughout the process, I interacted with not a single black woman. But what's interesting is that I did not find it odd at all. Such is the way the South African publishing industry normalises the abnormal. At last I met a black woman on the team: Samu Mavimbela, my publicist in Johannesburg.

It went like this.

Samu came to deliver my author's copies to me. Yay.

I asked her when we would have the launch.

She said she would check back with the publisher.

Then she got back to me with the bad news.

There was no budget for my launch. Nay.

So I walked to my then home, Xarra Books in Newtown, and asked, 'Would you do a launch for me?' The co-owner, June Josephs, asked for a blurb and a copy of the book, and then informed me that everything was in place. The launch would happen. They had my discussant, the snacks and the wine. On the second Thursday of November, *The Madams* was launched.

I was now a writer.

I decided to do what many writers are warned against. I quit my day job so that I could pursue this writing thing full-time. I needed to treat it like the profession it was supposed to be. At that time, as a single mother with a one-year-old child, it was perhaps not the wisest idea, and yet I felt I owed it to myself and to this writing that I loved to try it full-time.

Writing

The reviews were generous. The love was there. But I was touted as 'the first black chick lit writer', and the term riled. When a contemporary white writer who had used that very term to review me in the *Sunday*

Times was surprised at my annoyance, I couldn't help but break it down to her at a literary festival. She was ghettoising me, I said. I am black. And I am a woman. But I want to be a good writer primarily. Did my work stand up on the global stage or not? Or was it good enough for black women only? And if black women are the majority in South Africa and I am therefore the standard, shouldn't it just be called a good book? And I was chick lit versus what? Could she point out to me the male authors in South Africa whose books she'd referred to as 'cock lit'? Take Coetzee, with his women characters who aren't well rounded and don't seem to have any agency; was he cock lit?

'Oh gosh, Zooks, I'm so sorry. I didn't realise that it was that serious.'

I looked at her and smiled, 'No, of course not. It's not that serious.'

Of course it was that serious. But 'we wear the mask that grins and lies', as Paul Laurence Dunbar wrote those many years ago. After all, it would not do to offend.

By this time my second book, *Behind Every Successful Man*, was out with another publisher; my first publisher had closed shop less than two years after the release of *The Madams*. Miraculously, I had got the rights back. Although my new publisher had some black writers on their books – Niq Mhlongo, Maxine Case, Kgebetli Moele – just like my former publisher, those in charge were white.

A reader's report praised the manuscript. They had shared it with one of their black staff members, a young woman who was a big Zukiswa Wanner fan, and they had enjoyed it. The reader had enjoyed it immensely too. 'Zukiswa Wanner is truly the Dorothy Parker of Soweto,' madam wrote. Because, of course, Zukiswa Wanner is incapable of being the Zukiswa Wanner of wherever she stays, and every black woman in Johannesburg must be from Soweto.

The white male editor I was assigned had some questions. Somewhere early in the script, the male protagonist, Andile, is remembering his late friend while sitting in his study, and he pours cognac on the Persian rug. Did I not mean to say he 'accidentally spilt the cognac'? Nee, baas. I did not. My editor was younger than I. Surely, he knew black people the world over poured out liquor in memory of the deceased? If he chose to be deaf and blind to black South Africans, surely he had listened to Tupac?

Evidently not.

The publishers were not messing with the label. To them, I was chick lit and chick lit I should stay. So I got the pink cover, despite my experimentation with voice, and narrating the story from the perspective of both the male and female protagonists. I admit, though, that my feminist bias deliberately made Andile come out hotep-y, but then he did mirror quite a few men in our society.

The sales for these first two titles were not great. Everyone in my grandmother's street in Orlando West Extension read *The Madams*. They all read the copy I had given my cousin Nomonde. It was not ideal, and I could not keep asking my mother for some money to help with the bills. She was running out of patience. 'We all learnt to write in first grade, Zukiswa mwanangu,' she once said to me. 'Aspire to something better. Get a real job.'

So I took on a job at the National Electronic Media Institute of South Africa teaching writing. My relationship with them lasted a term. I refused to improve the grades of students to whom I had given a syllabus and my marking rubric at the beginning of the term, but who failed to adhere to it. People who did not turn in assignments and presentations did not deserve a pass mark. It was a sad insight into South African mediocrity. They did not call me back for the next term.

I was back to being a full-time writer. And as had become clear, I had to work smart. Full-time writing meant deciding what writing jobs to take on and what to charge. I was on the writing team for SAfm's first radio soapie in English, *Radio Vuka*. Because we admire everything that's from abroad, it was dubbed as the South African version of the BBC's *The Archers*. The work I had to do was not nearly in sync with what I was getting paid, so I excused myself after six months. Then I started writing a column for a magazine, but the monthly take-home was not ideal, and that was when they remembered to pay me on time. But still I wrote. When a new editor came to the magazine, I decided the chance had come to try to get paid a bit more. I had first-hand knowledge of what a friend who was also writing for the same magazine was getting paid. I gave a figure similar to his, but was informed that there was no budget. I was worth nothing if I was writing, and still had to worry about submitting work consistently that would not pay a single bill in totality. So I stopped writing for the magazine just as my third novel, *Men of the South*, came out.

With three male protagonists, the blurb still centred around the one woman they were all connected with, but at least I had graduated as a writer. A white male literary academic then at Stellenbosch University, while moderating a panel at a literary festival, referred to the books of Thando Mgqolozana and myself as 'great books for black teenagers'. I generally dislike classifying books, but if I had to classify my work, and Mgqolozana's up to that point, I would be hard-pressed to refer to it as Young Adult. But yay, perhaps I should have been glad that he didn't refer to me as a writer of 'great books for black teenage girls'. I don't put much stock in literary prizes, but I felt as though *Men of the South* gave a middle finger to this academic when it was shortlisted for the Commonwealth Writers' Prize: Best Book for the Africa region. Right up there with writers that I suspect this same academic would have shown respect to – like Aminatta Forna and Helon Habila – because they are not black South Africans.

Years later, I would recount this incident on Facebook. His then wife, also a literary academic, who had not been present at the panel, took umbrage, and decided to take Panado for his headache. Years later, after they got divorced, she would send me a message apologising for her defence of him. Then, on New Year's Day 2019, I got a message of apology from the academic. I am still, as the young'uns would say, *shooketh*.

I was lucky that I had a group of writer friends who helped me (and still do) ensure that I get the best possible financial deals despite some of the disrespect outlined above. Someone once referred to these friends of mine and me as the Brat Pack of South African Literature. Every time I was offered a job and I quoted an amount, I would blind-copy Angela Makholwa, Sihle Khumalo, Ndumiso Ngcobo, Thando Mgqolozana and Siphiwo Mahala. We had all had our debut books come out within the same two-year period, so are contemporaries in that way. When the person making the request stated that my figure was too high, I would respond, 'I'm sorry but that's what I charge. I am happy to give you names of my contemporaries so you can see whether they may charge less.' Invariably, when offered the gig, they would go higher to ensure I got the tender. I would do the same for them, and in this way, we learned that the strongest pillars of support for writers are other writers.

These solid writer friends notwithstanding, I am aware that there is a hierarchy in both publishing and freelance writing in South Africa.

White Man.

White Woman.

Black Man.

Black Woman.

I, as a black woman, am at the bottom of the totem pole of the industry in both journalism and publishing. Black brothers who have not written nearly as much as I have will get paid more than I do. I am no longer surprised when I chat with white women and white men, and I hear how much they are getting in advances versus their black and white counterparts, even when our book sales are more or less on par. And this totem pole is not unique to South Africa.

Even the rest of the continent has, until recently, believed this, perhaps in the same way as the world seems to believe white Americans are superior to their black counterparts. After *Men of the South* came out, I applied for a literary workshop in one of the other countries on our continent, less to get writing tips and more to form a network to better market my work beyond South African borders. I did not even get a reply, but noted that white South African writers were consistently invited to be part of this workshop, whether as facilitators or as experts-in-residence.

A year after I moved to Nairobi, Kenya, the same residency emailed me. They wanted me to facilitate a workshop. I am unsure whether my leaving South Africa suddenly made me more acceptable to my non-South African siblings. Did I perhaps no longer fit the stereotype of the angry, Afrophobic black South African with a superiority complex towards other Africans?

And yet I am delighted to report that, thanks to social media, there has been greater engagement between black South African writers and the rest of the continent. Indeed, one of English-speaking Africa's premier festivals, Aké Arts and Book Festival in Nigeria, has consistently had black South African writers in the last six of its seven years in existence. It has also been gratifying for me to get some editing jobs from the rest of the continent. Although I am primarily a writer, I enjoy editing immensely.

Editing

The love for editing was born while I was in university under the aforementioned Larry, who taught me to look keenly at the work submitted when I was a sectional editor for our college newspaper. It is this same sort of eye that I bring to manuscripts. And yet, despite that, only one mainstream South African publisher has ever trusted me with their manuscripts, and then only for reader's reports. I choose not to do them anymore.

They didn't pay enough for the work that I put into them. What they pay is not enough to warrant anyone taking the time to do them, unless it's purely for the bragging rights of having read something by some writer first. So here is how it was with me. Whenever I got a request to do a reader's report, I worked on both content and structural edits, hoping that the effort I had shown would stand me in good stead and move me up the ladder so I could get some editing gigs. Unfortunately, this is not a job that is easily entrusted to black women in particular and black people in general in South Africa's mainstream publishing industry.

A few years ago, I got wind that a younger writer whose manuscript I had read was about to get published. I immediately got in touch with her. 'I really liked your manuscript but saw some oversights and problems in it, did you get my notes from the publisher?' I enquired. She had not. And so she gave me her email address. Luckily, I still had the notes on my computer, although it was a good year later, and I sent them to her. She called me after she had gone through my feedback. She wondered whether I would be open to being her editor, as she was now writing the final draft of the manuscript. As a matter of fact, I would be very open, I said. This was a manuscript that I saw potential in when I first read it.

When she asked the publisher, the answer was negative. They already had an editor assigned to her. A white man. I wasn't surprised. I had worked with this publisher before. When I had asked for a particular black editor to work with me, the publisher had initially refused. They said they had a white woman editor who had worked with me previously and was standing in the wings to work with me again.

'Is it Jacqui L'Ange?' I asked.

'No, it isn't,' publisher replied.

She was the only white woman I had worked with.

'Please ask them what manuscript they worked with me on,' I wanted to know.

I never got a response. I couldn't help but be amused at the chutzpah of this woman who claimed to have worked with me, and who, when asked for more detail, suddenly went mum. To be white in South Africa is to be believed until proven otherwise, and even then, given the benefit of the doubt. Despite this, it still took my threat to withdraw my manuscript before the publisher permitted me to work with the black woman editor I knew would understand the context of my work. This publisher, like many in South Africa, seemed to work on the editing principle of black is bad, white is good.

I dare anyone to enquire and report back on whether there have even been ten black editors in major South African publishing houses since 1994; and how many of those were brought on board at a black writer's insistence, and how many through the independent initiative of the publishing house itself.

So back to my story with my young sis.

'No problem,' I told her. 'However, send me the manuscript when he's done so we can get certain aspects of black lives in context that I think he may overlook.'

She agreed. Unfortunately, it was over a weekend that was particularly hectic for me, and she had been given less than 72 hours to return the manuscript for typesetting. So I did what I could. The printed copy still had some problems. I would later see the publisher. There was no thank you, no acknowledgement of any pointers given to their younger writer. Fortunately for me, I was already in a political space where, if white folk dig and respond to something I say, cool. But my focus is primarily on engaging with black folk. It is from this perspective that I published my last book and got into publishing.

Publishing

Before I finished writing *Hardly Working* in 2017, I had chatted with Duduzile Mabaso of the indie publishing house Black Letter Media. 'Would you be interested in publishing me?' I asked her. She said she needed to read the manuscript first, and if she felt it worked for her list, she would be happy to do so. I respected this and sent her the manuscript. Respected it because, given my longevity in the literary industry, there are those who will publish me even if I were to write rubbish just so that they can claim to have published me. After reading, she said she was keen on publishing it, and would send some editorial comments. There was just one problem, so I told her to hold back until I had sorted it out.

Kwela, with whom I had been in a relationship since 2007, had right of first refusal on my manuscripts. They had already received the manuscript and were keen to publish it. How to get out of it? Aware of what some of the paler and maler authors were getting as advances, I asked for the same. They agreed to what I asked for . . . for two manuscripts. We reached an impasse and amicably parted (sounds like a Hollywood marriage, doesn't it?). I was now free to enjoin myself to Black Letter Media. My sixth adult book was due to be published by a black woman publisher a few months before I turned 42. Her company could not afford to give me an advance like the company I had just left, but I knew we would make a good team. I was keen to prove that leaving a white publisher was not a mistake.

She was keen to prove that, in light of the Bonang controversy of the year before involving a black woman publisher, another black woman publisher could turn the narrative around and publish a good book. The Bonang controversy revolved around a memoir of South African radio and television persona Bonang Matheba, which was released to much fanfare but had to be pulled from the shelves of bookstores because it had too many typos and editorial errors. And therein lies the problem with the publishing industry and South Africa. Despite black women comprising the majority of the population, any mistake from any one of us represents the race and not the individual.

I had just taken back all the rights of all my novels, and was reissuing them under my own publishing house. I had no money in my account to justify having been a full-time writer for 12 years. All I had was my name, my work, my networks. Fortunately for me, I have never been scared of being poor. As I recount in *Hardly Working*, I had my fair share of waking up early in the morning with my cousins in Zimbabwe to stand in the queue for relief parcels during a drought. It can be painful to fail and start again, but I have never feared doing so. And so for the first time, my politics and my professional life were in alignment.

My publisher and I decided to put in 101 per cent effort to publicise *Hardly Working* and sell it. And South Africa was generous. In less than four months, we were on our second print run. But the market had also changed since *The Madams* was published in 2006. Back then, the target market was middle-class white women. Now the biggest reading and book-buying demographic was sisters who looked like us. It is a marvellous transformation to see, and a beautiful time to be alive and writing. While these sisters are sympathetic when we are not perfect, Duduzile and I also felt because they were us, we owed it to ourselves and to them to give them the very best.

As a publisher, I live at a time when the continent is speaking amongst itself, and with networks in a few of the English-speaking countries on the continent, I am equally elated. Late last year, I published my first new (rather than reissued) book, *Story Story Story, Come*, a children's anthology with 12 stories from 12 writers from eight African countries. I have the East and Southern African rights, and my friend, sister, Aké Festival Director, Ouida Books publisher and brilliant author, Lola Shoneyin, has the West African rights.

Where I have rights, I have chosen to try to get as many translations as possible done so that we don't run the risk of having only English-speaking children able to enjoy the stories. It's early days yet but thus far, *Story Story Story, Come* has been translated into isiXhosa, Shona, Tshivenda and kiSwahili. If I can add three more languages in the next two years, I'll be a happy publisher. I have also published my first adult novel, a reissue of Mukoma wa Ngugi's *Mrs Shaw*, which we retitled *We, the Scarred*.

As a black woman from a country where the publishing industry is white, I don't know where the publishing road will lead me, and

I do not want to fail. But if that happens, I will do so knowing that I tried, and I can still hold my head up high. As a publisher, I would like to continue publishing until I take my last breath. As an editor, I shall continue nurturing young writers, and as a writer, I won't stop writing either.

In ending, then, I paraphrase our late sister Maya Angelou:

Do I make you uncomfortable?
Does my ambition upset you?
Still, *I write*.

CHAPTER 14

Echoes of Miriam Tlali

Barbara Boswell

Encountering a womxn who dared to dream

My entry into Johannesburg on a frigid day in July 2006 is not
set in the mould of the triumphal, Jim(or Jane?)-comes-to-Joburg
narrative. As I find myself waiting in the forecourt of a petrol
station in Newtown, with an insufficient coat offering little protection
against the Highveld winter, I am overcome with dread: the fear
of being alone in an unknown city; the anxiety of knowing I
have an important and what will turn out to be a life-changing
appointment, without knowing how to get to the place of this fateful
meeting. I am in the discomfiting position of being a stranger in my
own country, having spent the preceding four years in Maryland
in the USA, where I completed a doctorate in women's and gender
studies. Now I am returning briefly to an unfamiliar city, at once
an insider and an outsider, to do a series of interviews with Black
womxn writers, the topic of my dissertation.

My appointment is with Miriam Tlali, the first Black South
African womxn writer to publish a book-length work of fiction in
South Africa. During my doctoral work and before, as an MPhil
student at the University of the Western Cape, Tlali had occupied
a large part of my imagination, and became for me an icon. I was

almost 30 when I first read *Muriel at Metropolitan* (1975), the debut novel that would secure her place in history and in my heart, and it forever changed the way I thought and still think about literature, its political and cultural value, and its beauty. The novel produced for me an epistemic break – leading me to consider, for the first time, questions about the value of certain voices, the circuits of publication and dissemination of Black womxn's literary writing, and the sheer courage it took for a Black womxn to articulate a creative work against the backdrop of one of the most repressive political systems of the twentieth century, bent on destroying Black womxn and Black families.

How can I fully begin to tell the story of what Miriam Tlali has meant to me? It is a story I will grapple with for the rest of my life, as her multiple meanings and significations in my personal, political and professional life continue to unfold. She was a pioneer, a trailblazer – a Black womxn who carved a path for that little girl – me – who decided at six that she wanted to be a storyteller and writer; who let go of the dream as she grew older and examined the world and saw no one who looked like her, writing. A girl whose world was turned upside down by the discovery of Miriam Tlali and the worlds she created in her fiction. I was the girl who became a scholar of Black womxn's literature; able, much later, to carve out a professional path in an unforgiving system, due partly to Tlali's life and work. And I was the scholar who, later in life, dared to dream into being my own fiction, inspired by Tlali's courage and light.

But all of this was still to come. I quivered with cold and anticipation as my Johannesburg friend arrived and escorted me, an hour later than agreed, to the home of Mam' Tlali in Rockville, Soweto. Tlali welcomed me into a modest but pristine home. She lived alone in a small house framed by a neatly clipped lawn, and filled with comfortable, homely furniture. It was in this house that she started writing and completed *Muriel at Metropolitan*, as well as most of her other written work. Her living space centred around an old coal stove, which radiated warmth throughout the small house on a blisteringly cold day. She was friendly, yet reserved; and her eyes seemed, at first glance, filled with sadness. It soon became apparent why: Tlali had lost both her husband and son within the short space of two years and was clearly grieving. She explained how the loss had compounded her poor health, and often mentioned that she felt unwell.

The most poignant moment of our time together came when she showed me what looked like a brand-new study annex built in her backyard. Her life as a wife and mother, a caretaker of children, a husband and ailing in-laws, had allowed very little time and space to write. As she painfully expressed in an interview with Pamela Ryan, when asked about the dearth of Black womxn novelists during apartheid, Black womxn did not have time to dream:

> For a black woman, I don't think it is very easy unless you have complete peace inside, which is something I strive very much to get. You have to analyse situations, and all that needs peace of mind and time. It needs a long time and you have to think about it. And you have to dream about it and black women do not have time to dream.[1]

Her study at the back of her house represented a space-making practice that would allow her time to dream – to sit and write in peace now that apartheid was finally over and her children had grown. She recalled:

> I didn't have a study, I would always sit and write on my lap and my husband was quite happy with that. And then when I asked him, you know what it is like, you know the political system[i] . . . I could not very well say to him, I want to build something . . . But it became

---

i In those days (and until 2006), Black womxn who married according to customary rites were legal minors under the control of their husbands.

inconvenient for me and when I asked him to build a little study he wouldn't, he refused. So after '94 I could now take a plan, building plan to the office and tell them I want this and so on.

Tragically, her husband and son died upon completion of the project, leaving her alone in her home and rendering the study space obsolete. It was in a wistful voice that she recalled her dream of a balanced home and work life, one that would finally bring a talent restrained by apartheid and patriarchy to full fruition.

Tlali's work: From womanism to radical feminism

Miriam Tlali's oeuvre reveals a womxn deeply committed to using her art in the service of fighting structural oppression, be it racism, economic oppression or gender oppression. Her death on 24 February 2017 warrants a critical reappraisal of her contributions to both literature and Black feminisms in South Africa. Though she would claim feminism and name herself a feminist quite early in her career as a writer – a career that thrust her into prominence internationally after she became the first Black womxn to publish a novel in English within the borders of apartheid South Africa – Tlali was careful to temper this identity. She stated that she was a feminist, '. . . but not in the narrow, Western way of speaking about feminism . . . Our liberation [as Black womxn] is bound absolutely, with the liberation of the whole nation, so I'll always combine the two.'[2]

Tlali's works collectively give us an insight into a developing Black South African feminist consciousness that found expression in her fiction, essays and journalism, and document the formation of her critical theory, in the form of fiction, around race and gender which deconstructed and challenged both white feminism[3] and Black patriarchy at key political moments in South Africa's history. Her feminist writing portends the development of a radical Black feminism, articulated especially by young Black feminists in student movements such as #RhodesMustFall and #FeesMustFall, where Black feminisms have been invigorated by the fight for decolonial and free tertiary education in South Africa. Exploring her feminist consciousness and her theorising-through-fiction by analysing selected works, I trace the evolution of her feminism from what can be described as a womanist articulation at the beginning of her career, to a radical Black feminist position by the time she penned her last published work.

As Black womxn generally were excluded from formal knowledge production spheres, I consider her work a site of theory-making in which she refused easy dichotomies and binaries. Tlali's feminist praxis is a significant precursor to contemporary articulations of radical Black feminism in South Africa. In this chapter I further trace some points of intersection between Tlali's radical feminism and iterations of Black radical feminisms in the 2015–2018 student movements in South Africa.

Muriel at Metropolitan

Muriel at Metropolitan was the first novel to be published by a Black womxn within the borders of South Africa. Based on Tlali's own experience working in a furniture store in downtown Johannesburg, the novel was rejected by several publishers, and lay 'at the back of the dressing table, gathering dust'[4] for years before Ravan Press published it in 1975, though only after excising five chapters, causing Tlali considerable distress. The novel was banned upon publication, beginning a period in Tlali's life where she was routinely harassed by the apartheid regime's Special Branch police, to the extent that she took to burying her manuscripts in her backyard to avoid them being confiscated and destroyed.

Muriel at Metropolitan is aimed largely at showing a global audience the inhumanity of apartheid and the exploitive labour conditions experienced by Black South Africans and African womxn specifically.

The novel is set within the extreme confines of Metropolitan Radio, an electronics store in downtown Johannesburg where the title character, Muriel, works.

The reader encounters and negotiates the space of the store through the movements and confinement of Muriel, the only Black womxn staff member. Because she is not allowed to sit in the same space as the white womxn who work as clerks, Muriel is initially given a workspace, which she shares with men, in the attic above the shop floor, giving her a vantage point that she enjoys. Muriel's movements between the attic and the store eventually become too time-consuming, forcing her boss to bring her downstairs to sit with the white womxn clerks. This inaugurates a series of increasingly vicious arguments with the white womxn, who patronise and humiliate her daily – pointing to the impossibility of a nascent feminist solidarity between them because of the white womxn's racism. One such encounter occurs early in the novel, when the white womxn send a Black man, Johannes, to the shops to do their shopping. Before he leaves the furniture store, Johannes asks Muriel whether she too requires anything from this errand, to which she responds with a no. She ruminates later that 'I was reluctant to send him. How could I? He was a man and I was a woman. According to our custom, a woman does not send a man. We reserve a place, an elevated place, for our men.'[5]

In Muriel's action and theorising, Tlali demonstrates an unwillingness to side with white womxn in order to degrade Black men by sending them on frivolous errands. Muriel, instead, displays race solidarity with Black men, as both Black men and womxn were likely to be on the receiving end of racist provocation and humiliation both in the shop and outside of it. Tlali here articulates a womanist standpoint within her fiction – a standpoint offered by Chikwenye Okonjo Ogunyemi as an analytical lens for reading African womxn's fiction. Ogunyemi defines womanism in the writing of African womxn as explicitly contrasted with white, Western feminist articulation:

> ... while the white woman writer protests against sexism, the Black woman writer must deal with it as one among many evils; she battles also with the dehumanisation resulting from racism and poverty ... The politics of the womanist is unique ... for it addresses more directly the ultimate question relating to power: how do we share more equitably the world's wealth and concomitant power among the races and between the sexes?[6]

Even though Tlali describes, to a limited extent, abusive and violent behaviours by Black men in *Muriel at Metropolitan*, she is primarily concerned in the novel with exposing the inhumanity of apartheid. Muriel thus demonstrates an ethic of solidarity with Black men who are her co-workers, rejecting any incipient sense of belonging to the category of womanhood articulated by the white womxn at the shop. The novel can thus be classified as womanist, rather than feminist, in its approach to gender relations and its analysis of the impossibility of womxn's solidarity across racial difference.

Amandla

In *Amandla* (1980), Tlali's second novel, she takes a different approach to Black masculinity. A finely textured, polyvocal account of the 1976 Soweto uprising from the perspective of a number of young revolutionaries of the time, *Amandla* offers a critique, albeit a gentle one, of the Black Consciousness Movement (BCM) articulation of masculinity which establishes itself at the expense of Black womxnhood. The novel depicts the 1976 Soweto uprising and its aftermath, delivering commentary on gender dynamics between men and womxn caught up in the wake of the initial protests. Both Pravin Ram (1992) and Asha Moodley (1993) show in their scholarship how womxn who were part of the BCM resisted and strategised against sexist treatment by men, leading to their formation of the Black

Women's Federation (BWF) in December 1975, a Black womxn's organisation that united womxn classified as Indian, Coloured and African, while remaining affiliated with the BCM.[7,8] Fatima Meer founded the BWF's precursor, the Natal Federation of Black Women, in 1973, and the organisation expanded nationally after a delegation of womxn travelled from Natal to Soweto to meet with womxn activists there. Thus, a national body, the Black Women's Federation, came into being as a 'response to the urgently expressed need for women to form a united front'.[9]

Given the prominence of two Soweto residents – Sally Motlana and Ellen Kuzwayo – in founding the BWF nationally, it can reasonably be assumed the BWF's concerns about operating autonomously from both Black men in the BCM and white feminist organisations may have percolated through activist communities in Soweto in the period leading up to June 1976. The circulation of such a Black womxn's viewpoint may provide insight into why Soweto resident Tlali's early output, including *Amandla*, is so firmly rooted within the Black Consciousness tradition, while also demonstrating ways of integrating Black womxn's experiences, oppression and interests within Black Consciousness politics. *Amandla* thus theorises, through the central male character, Pholoso, a model for a politically engaged Black masculinity that refuses gender dominance and patriarchy. Pholoso, for example, urges his fellow male comrades to encourage womxn to read and partake in debate, and holds them accountable for womxn not attending political meetings because of the prevalence of sexual harassment on the streets of Soweto. In asserting this vision of Black manhood, the novel offers a model of masculinity that accommodates and encourages Black womxn's autonomy, equality and leadership in political structures, while disavowing violent masculinity. The work also engages the fraught issue of domestic violence, demonstrating a communal response to violent masculinity that does not fracture Black unity at a time when it is sorely needed.

'Fudua-a-a!'

Tlali's next book-length publication was *Footprints in the Quag* (1989), also known as *Soweto Stories*. I focus on one story – 'Fudua-a-a!'. *Fudua* is a chant, meaning 'stir the pot', sung by distressed commuters on packed trains moving out of Johannesburg, as they wriggle their bodies to try to create space within the grossly overcrowded trains. This short story traces the dialogue of three Soweto-bound womxn – Ntombi, Nkele and Mashidi – as they wait for the crowded train at Johannesburg's Park Station on a Friday evening. They reflect on how, as African womxn, they are treated worse than dogs by their white employers during the day at work. But on their journey home by train, they face an additional danger: sexual assault on the overcrowded trains by Black men.

Tlali situates the three womxn as 'looking on and reflecting, anxiously waiting their turn to be caught up in what was virtually the "front line" of a black woman's battle for mere existence in the bustling city of gold'.[10]

Black womxn here are positioned at the coalface of oppression, having to negotiate both whites who treat their dogs better than Black womxn, and Black men who sexually harass and abuse them. As they are waiting for the train, Nkele remembers and relates to the two other womxn the first time she was sexually assaulted on a train. She describes commuters singing hymns and clapping along to the rhythm, which produced a deafening noise that masked the abuse taking place:

> I wanted the music to stop because . . . the very noise was being used as a shield. I was trying to scream that someone was busy massaging my thighs and backside, trying to probe into my private parts and nobody was paying attention. It was embarrassing and awful! . . . you see, with so much congestion it was impossible to see who the culprits were. We suffocated and suffered in that terrible torture of it all, and there was nothing we could do. By the time the train got to Park

Station, we were too hurt, too shamefully abused to speak. Who could we speak to? Who could we accuse? Who would listen to us even if we tried to complain?[11]

The story ends with the three womxn's train to Naledi arriving as the story is concluded. The womxn alight from the train, but this time, having spoken the shame that should remain unspoken, they know how to protect themselves and each other:

> The three women had succeeded somehow in battling their way in. They had at last found space to stand next to each other. It was an achievement and a victory which deserved to be celebrated. Alert and as watchful as ever, they stood smiling into each other's faces . . . They had 'won'.[12]

Zoë Wicomb (1996) reads the short story as a kind of compromise, letting men off the hook, so to speak, for the sexual abuse. She sees the mode of narration, and the unnamed perpetrators, as a 'female reluctance to name black men'.

> the ambiguous 'they' can refer both to men who control female discourse and to the authorities who create conditions in which abuse becomes possible – that is, 'they' may create extenuating circumstances for men. Concealment, then, becomes a trope for the woman writer who has to negotiate the conflicting loyalties of race and gender.[13]

My own reading of this short story differs. Far from concealment, Tlali holds Black men as a group responsible for the sexual abuse on trains. The 'they' Wicomb focuses on is, indeed, an ambiguous focus on the simultaneous oppression of Black womxn by whites and Black men. It is white capitalism that enables the overcrowded, dehumanising conditions which allow Black men to abuse womxn without being held accountable for their crimes.

An encounter with dreams deferred

In 2010, I completed my dissertation, 'Black South African Women Writers: Narrating the Self, Narrating the Nation', and, as promised, sent a copy to the womxn whom I had interviewed for the study. I did not hear back from any of them immediately, but in March 2011 received two letters from Miriam Tlali in response to my work. In the first letter, she praised my work, stating 'of all the material I have read so far, your presentation, approach and analysis of our Black womxn's writings in South Africa is unique and far reaching'.[14] She gave me her blessing to publish the work, and invited me to present it at the Miriam Tlali Reading and Book Club, which had been started in her honour.

A second, much more personal letter followed. In it, Tlali documented her failing health – a compressed nerve running the length of her spine had left her in great pain and unable to walk – lamenting that, with her condition, 'I cannot continue to do my writing. Without writing I can't even recognise myself anymore. The pains even disturb my passion and pleasure of reading! I feel totally cut out of my inner self – my writing – and out of the outer world, reading and reflecting on what is happening around me and the broader world.'[15]

Tlali wrote to me about two incomplete projects she wished to bring to fruition: a complete manuscript for a work of fiction, *Bleeding Shoulders*, which was to be '[her] fourth major work'. She noted: 'From the moment it became known that I was about to complete it in the late 1990s, it was hunted down . . . Let it suffice for me to say that ultimately I was forced to momentarily set its publication aside as I had discovered that a manuscript of the book was in the hands of an academic individual abroad . . . Without my permission, "someone" was already in possession of the manuscript without me having been informed.'[16] She felt profoundly betrayed by the prospective publisher, as well as the academic who had taken the manuscript without her permission. She also shared details of an autobiography in-progress,

Mamello (Patience), named after a house her mother built 'in her old age'[17] in Lesotho, 'the culmination of a long-struggle story'.[18] She reflected on the state of the nation too, and expressed the need to enter public political discourse, especially through engaging younger womxn:

> Is it the South Africa we fought and endured harassment from [an] oppressive system for? This is the discourse I want to continue to be active in. I so desperately want to pass on the baton to the younger upcoming writers, especially young women, that in my state I feel really frustrated. This society needs creative writers with a critical eye, lest we forget what we fought for.[19]

Bringing Tlali into the room

I see myself now as one of the young womxn to whom Tlali passed the baton she mentions in her 2011 letter to me. I did not think of myself in that way when first reading her words, but I claim that position as one of the handful of Black feminists in this country trying to assert the vital importance of her work.

I felt her influence particularly in April 2015, when, as a contract lecturer at UCT, I was asked by the students of the #RhodesMustFall movement to facilitate a session around feminism, womanism and their meanings by students occupying Azania House. Kopano Ratele (a feminist scholar of masculinities) and I were asked to conduct a dialogue around feminism and masculinities, a conversation necessary for a number of reasons: one of the womxn occupying Azania House was assaulted by a man in that space, and when she asked him to leave, she discovered other men coming to his defence and protecting him. A queer Black womxn was also threatened with rape. This kind of sexism and gender-based violence is not new in liberation struggles, but to see it play out in the space of Azania House – to hear the excuses that men use to disregard patriarchy or claim it doesn't exist, and to assert entitlements over womxn's bodies, sometimes violently – was a shattering experience.

Kopano and I decided the best course of action would be to separate the students by gender, conducting two separate workshops with them, and then bringing both groups together to start a dialogue about the gender relations in the room. I started my session by discussing feminism and womanism and their various articulations in African contexts in particular, along with providing a definition of intersectionality, as well as a short exercise on mapping intersectional identities and oppressions. In my group of womxn, there was very little consensus on the need for feminism or the harms of patriarchy, but after two hours there was strong agreement on the need for womxn to feel safe. After heartfelt discussion, the group agreed on the following principles for engaging in dialogue with the men who formed part of the group: 1) they were speaking out of a place of love for Black men; 2) they wanted a Gender Desk that could monitor and enforce some sort of code of conduct around gender relations; 3) they needed to have continued conversations about what their freedom entailed, and how to imagine freedom for all in the movement; 4) that an intersectionality auditing subcommittee would be started; and 5) that ongoing educational spaces be created to explore how colonisation impacted ideas around Black femininities and masculinities. When the men re-entered the room, Kopano and I facilitated a protracted discussion around patriarchy, violence, masculinities and femininities.

I brought my feminist teaching praxis into the space of Tlali's gender theorising because she is part of a tradition of Black feminism on which I drew in conceptualising and facilitating this discussion. As I often do when I teach, I invoke and summon the spirits of Black womxn, alive or departed, who have shaped my feminist politics, silently entreating them to guide my thoughts, words and actions for the ultimate end of gender, race and economic injustice. Walking into that room, I brought with me the spirits and influence of key feminists whose words and actions have impacted my life, including Lynn Bolles, Elsa Barkley Brown, Amina Mama, Pumla Dineo Gqola, Elaine Salo and

Miriam Tlali. I summon them as feminist and literary ancestors whose collective works in my life constitute a form of knowledge not always recognised in the academy, but a way of weaving unacknowledged epistemes into the fabric of often violent knowledge-making spaces. It is here that I was guided by the consciousness of Tlali, as expressed in her writing, to attempt to make visible ways of thinking through and theorising Black feminisms at a particular location in post-apartheid South Africa. Within my mind and body, my readings of her (and other feminists') work had found a place, a space of sedimentation and maturation, until they could then be passed on to other womxn who might be seeking new ways of seeing and languaging the world. I wonder if this could have been what Tlali envisioned when she wrote of passing on the baton to younger womxn, as part of her dreaming?

Contemporary radical Black feminism: Echoes of Tlali's radical feminism

Returning to the question with which I started this essay, I propose that Tlali's feminism is a radical Black feminism, which started as womanist ideological articulation, as seen in *Muriel at Metropolitan*, but became more radical in its critique of Black men and racism as her body of work develops. When referring to radical feminism, feminists generally mean a strand of second-wave separatist, lesbian North American feminism. Radical feminism has also come to stand, in the North American context, as trans-exclusionary and transphobic. Yet the term as articulated by African feminists has come to signify in completely different ways, including trans, non-binary and queer identities within the category womxn. Simidele Dosekun (2007), for example, defines radical African feminism as an ideology and movement that

> pursues substantive equality between men and women in Africa where gender inequality persistently reigns . . . [T]his feminism is not just for women. Its purpose is not to replace men with women, nor

even to include more women in men's worlds. Its purpose, rather, is to transform the very structures of our societies which produce and perpetuate gender inequalities in the first place.[20]

Articulations of radical feminism generated from within the South African student movements foreground race, naming itself Black radical feminism. Black radical feminism stems directly from the South African #RhodesMustFall and #FeesMustFall movements. Wanelisa Xaba traces the movements' ideological influences as 'Pan-Africanism, Black Consciousness, Black radical feminisms, queer theories, and decolonisation',[21] while Mbali Matandela, one of the leaders of the student movement at the University of Cape Town, articulates Black radical feminism as forged in the crucible of student politics against racial, financial and political exclusion:

> After the movement's first meeting, myself and a small group of *black radical feminists* [author's emphasis] decided that we needed to stake our claim in talks about the university and its institutional racism. We began speaking up at meetings about what it means to be a black woman or LGBTIQA people in an institution that still celebrates misogyny and white supremacy symbolically with the statue of Cecil John Rhodes. We knew how easily patriarchy can dominate any context, even protests about equal rights, and we were not going to let the RMF movement become one of them. We were not going to let only men lead the movement.[22]

Looking at this formulation, men are not excluded as in separatist feminism, but are seen as part of mobilisation towards racial justice. However, men should not be the only ones to lead – leadership roles need to be shared equitably between genders. Rather than separating completely from men, here Black men are held accountable for their political leadership and organisational practices. In this conceptualisation, there is again a willingness on the part of Black womxn to come together strategically, using their intellects and bodies, to stake a claim, much in the way Tlali's three womxn create a space for themselves in the congested train. Though this type of feminism declares itself radical, it is still willing to work with men, in the way in which the womxn of Tlali's *Amandla* work with men in the BCM while still highlighting sexual abuse and harassment. In a similar way, womanism has space for men within its articulation.

Matandela furthermore links Black radical feminism to the emergence of an 'emancipatory discourse linking the past to the present, and imagining a future that is beyond a political climate that has not adequately addressed the substantive representation, leadership, safety and dignity of Black womxn and queer bodies in the process of democratisation'.[23]

When looking at Tlali's fiction along a continuum, it is possible to trace the development of a feminist consciousness that is, at first, concerned with solidarity with Black men against the exploitation of apartheid. By the time she writes *Soweto Stories*, it has morphed into a much more nuanced analysis of Black womxn's oppression under apartheid. At the beginning of her career in the 1970s, she focuses on the conditions under which Black womxn labour in *Muriel at Metropolitan*, which is a womanist concern preoccupied with the overwhelming and dehumanising racism Muriel experiences. With *Amandla*, the womanist consciousness is even more pronounced, with Tlali centring Pholoso and using him as simultaneously a Black Consciousness and feminist consciousness raiser.

Yet by the time Tlali writes *Soweto Stories*, a marked ideological shift has occurred in her thinking about gender. She has embraced both womanism and a kind of radical Black feminism that calls men to account for their deviant and violent behaviour. Unlike in the case of Pholoso, where men address men and try to conscientise them, the three womxn on the train in 'Fudua-a-a!' see the value of addressing themselves to 'call out' Black men's sexual harassment and assault, speaking the unspeakable act of sexual violence, an act that locates the shame of sexual violence with the perpetrator, not the victim. Here, instead of concealing Black men's culpability, Tlali points to the way it reinforces white supremacy. Her analysis of the womxn's plight on the train is thoroughly intersectional, gesturing to the ways in which white supremacist capitalism intersects with Black sexual discrimination to produce the conditions under which Black womxn's bodies suffer. The story ends on a victorious note – 'they had won'.[24] It may seem a scant victory, but in highlighting it, Tlali points to the numerous daily acts of resistance and creativity that Black womxn deploy to protect themselves and each other. In a social order filled with hatred towards them, protecting each other with the very bodies which are objectified, abused and vilified, the victory of travelling home unscathed is an enormous one for the three womxn in 'Fudua-a-a!'. This speaking out is used to strategise towards their own safety on the train. It is an act that makes the front line of battle for the Black womxn making her way in Johannesburg a bit more liveable, through sisterhood and camaraderie.

Ten years after that first meeting, I would visit Miriam Tlali again in a frail-care unit in Parktown, Johannesburg, where it was evident that she was dying. Her autobiography and fourth novel remained unpublished; her existing fiction was out of print. Though we had kept up a correspondence, she did not recognise me or Pumla Dineo Gqola, with whom I was visiting. She begged us to take her away from this place, and back to her beloved home in Soweto, a homecoming that was not to be. A few months later, Miriam Masoli Tlali would cast off her earthly body, preceded in death by her husband and both her children. Her spirit, I believe, remains in what it teaches us about our own capacity to dream, despite oppression and constraints. This, and the rich legacy of her words, remain.

CHAPTER 15

My Two Husbands

Grace A. Musila

I used to tick the 'single' box on forms interested in my marital status. This was the truth. It was also true that I had two husbands. I acquired both of them at birth, though I met one of them posthumously. I loved and continue to love different things about my two husbands. I loved my living husband's particular brand of craziness. His chronic political incorrectness is in a class of its own, even by the standards of older Black people, who often dispense with common politeness as they age, and say and do as they please. In his 90s, my husband's offside thoughts and utterances were second only to his belief in hard work as a moral principle. Yet that sharp tongue, caustic wit and immodest swearing is a deceptive shell of toughness, beneath which lies the gentlest, most generous old man who has ever loved me.

But if my cantankerous husband taught me to look forward to that age when I could flout all social expectations of politeness, my posthumous husband taught me something even more precious: he showed me a different face of death. Before meeting him, death meant a confusing mix of grief, adults' tears and their insistence that good children went to heaven and enjoyed all those impossibly fresh fruits – some of whose names I didn't know – and played with cute lion cubs and lambs on green gardens beside fresh blue streams, as

The Watchtower magazines promised. True, I longed for those perfect fruits. Somehow, the juicy passion fruits and creamy avocados from our garden looked apologetic beside these Jehovah's Witness fruit baskets. And yes, I wanted nothing more than to play with those lion cubs as I dipped my feet into those infinitely blue streams. Still, I remained unswayed by this version of the hereafter. Even at that tender age, I had soaked up the spiritual arrogance that marked the Catholic children of my parish. We knew we were the chosen ones. And instinctively, we considered these *Watchtower* heavens a little too syrupy.

But my late husband introduced me to a different face of death. He had been laid to rest under a smooth gravestone, right in front of his house, that bore his name and date of death. With that gravestone, he taught me a lot about death. With him, death meant literally resting at your doorstep, and therefore remaining a part of everyday life. It meant hearing children's laughter as they played on your smooth resting stone, and daily eavesdropping on your daughters-in-law's gossip as they sipped their four o'clock tea on the stoep and prepared vegetables for supper. Death was a lovely smooth cement gravestone which generously lent itself to all manner of important needs a child has. Like a nice smooth surface on which to practise basic mathematics with colourful pieces of chalk liberated from the classroom floor; and cousins showing off their cleverness to each other by writing out 'Little Miss Muffet, sat on a tuffet, eating her curds and whey', in questionable spelling, in between arguments about what whey must taste like. Death involved a nice cool gravestone on which to lie down on your back – when the adults were not around – and count the mangoes in the old tree that protected my husband from harsh sunlight, and dulled the chilly pelt of hailstones. In my considered opinion, therefore, death was pretty decent; interesting even, as you got to be part of everything that went on in the homestead, without having to lift a finger.

As a child playing on my husband's beautiful gravestone under the ancient mango tree at my grandparents' doorstep, I often wondered what kind of man my dead husband was. Did he like mangoes? How did his voice sound? What was the texture of his hair? Did it go grey with age? Or did it, like my father's, one day simply decide to stop growing and, for good measure, never go grey, so that my father's hair throughout my childhood was the exact same length, never once needing to be shaved? My father never needed to trim his beard either. It also just stopped growing, and never considered going grey either. Between them – my father, his hair and his beard – they seemed to have reached an understanding of sorts: no growing, no greying, no cutting. They met each other halfway on the combing though: only his head got combed daily. His beard enjoyed its sovereignty, curling and uncurling as it pleased.

So, in between counting the young mangoes in the tree above and feeling sad that, yet again, by the time they were ripe, school holidays would be over and my parents would have whisked us back home a long trip away, I often wondered whether my dead husband's hair grew grey. I wondered too, whether he would have liked me if he had met me in person. And would he like me better than my other co-wives and namesakes – some older, others younger, than me? Of course I knew I was the nicest, kindest, best behaved, of the young co-wives named after my grandma. And I had my Catholic confirmation card to prove this.

But my namesake – my grandma – didn't get this memo. Sure, she liked me enough to make my favourite meals whenever we visited. And she allowed us way more playtime than our parents would permit back at home. But she seemed fonder of my brother than me. She called him her little husband and spoilt him rotten. I resented this. I was her namesake; I was a girl. I was the one who helped her out with chores when we visited, while her young husband disappeared with his newly acquired band of best friends and cousins, all day long, often returning in the evening, with half the buttons missing from muddy shirts.

In hindsight, I know she loved us all equally. I suppose this was a case of couple jealousy. I mean, my brother's wife – our grandma – could speak aloud to him, while I had to content myself with listening very carefully to what my husband had to say as I placed my cheek on his smooth gravestone. My brother could see my grandma's tall, thin, slightly stooped body; feel the texture of her soft, sparse, grey hair; and smell her perfectly rolled tobacco, while I had to speculate about my husband's hair. Still, I remained secretly proud of the fact that it was my namesake, and not my brother's namesake, who knew how to roll her own tobacco, despite having lost her eyesight to age. My namesake was a clever old lady. Even more delightfully, she only smoked her cigarette with the fire on the inside of her mouth. I was incredibly proud of her. She was clearly cleverer than the 'bad women' back in town, who smoked shop-bought cigarettes and couldn't put the burning side into their mouths. She was my heroine. And since she was my namesake, it surely meant I was just as clever, regardless of what my school reports claimed. So, with this secret insight in mind, I allowed my small brother to bask in my namesake's doting, knowing that he would never be able to roll his own cigarette when he grew so old, his eyes opted out of seeing. And I knew he would always smoke his cigarette with the fire on the outside, while I would naturally inherit this special skill. After all, I was my grandma's namesake and co-wife.

Turns out neither of us would grow up to be smokers. I still wonder about my late husband's hair though.

●

My second husband – my maternal grandfather, my *kuka* – has always been a big supporter of my education. Alert to the perils of teenage pregnancy at a time when the imaginative powers of the education system could not stretch far enough to conceive of young mothers resuming schooling after the birth of their surprise babies, he worried about my successful completion of my education. We all knew his *msomos* (lectures), as they tended to be repetitive and chronicled the transgressions of various family members which his mind refused to forget; but he also refused to remember that he had told us these exact same complaints the last time we visited, and the time before that. Behind his back, we dramatised these *msomos* with each other and had an entire shorthand of disses and phrases everyone in the family knew. But his lectures were also customised to each person's life trajectory at any given time. Mine was customised around education. So, from the time I got admission to my high school – whose name he had never heard before, but someone helpfully explained that it was as good as a famous boys' school known to him; and so, he simply hyphenated the boys' school's name and added my school's name – he took a serious interest in my education. As I left for boarding school at this newly hyphenated school, he told me that my books should be my husband. I understood him. He meant I should focus on my education and not be distracted by boys. At 13, and a late bloomer in matters of the heart, I found this advice redundant, but I listened and nodded like the good wife I was. Since then, at every opportunity – I visited him at least thrice a year, during the school holidays – he issued the customised lecture, ending with the reminder about books being my husband.

The *msomos* continued when I went to university. By now, I could tell when he had added a word or rephrased another one. I was intimately familiar with my customised lecture down to the pauses. And then I completed my undergraduate studies, with honours, and immediately applied for a master's. To be honest, the master's was not a thought-through decision of someone with clear life plans to join academia. It was what was available to manage empty time, especially since there were no jobs, not even volunteerships. I had been repeatedly rejected as a volunteer at schools and orphanages because I was overqualified, so the master's came in as a welcome next step. When I visited *kuka* to tell him about my plans; I expected my usual *msomo* about education being my husband. I thought he would be immensely pleased with me. Instead, he told me he had a question for me: but who will marry you? I was astounded at this question, whose meaning I would only grasp years later. What astounded me at the time was my *kuka*'s change of tune. Here was a man who had invested serious amounts of thought and money in my education, with greater conviction than I myself had about its value. Here was my one-man cheerleader, who believed I had a great future ahead of me, who had, for years, insisted that I marry my books, now making a sudden change of tune.

Although he asked it as a rhetorical and part-humorous question, my *kuka*'s question would only sink in for me much later. I have since had occasion to understand what he meant. It took me a while in part because I had never given marriage serious thought. While by then I was a serious connoisseur of Mills & Boon and Harlequin romance novels and, like every self-respecting young woman, fixated on Ridge Forester and the goings-on in *The Bold and the Beautiful*, I had never given marriage much thought. I would discover later from a good friend that apparently most girls had a vision of their fantasy wedding dresses and wedding rings from the time they are little girls. I had no such vision. Belatedly, I tried to remedy this lapse of conjugal fantasy on my part, by taking an active interest in wedding dresses and wedding magazines and wedding shows and the entire industry. But I couldn't fully integrate into the fantasy. It turns out you cannot fake aspiration to bridal bliss. I liked the dresses, I loved the beautiful cakes, the flowers, the music, the joy, the romance of it all, but try as I might, I have been unable to see myself in a wedding dress or a wedding ring. I had the good sense to quit trying to force it, and simply continue enjoying the aesthetics of these experiences without the pressure of arrested fantasy. But with this mental wiring about marriage, I can see why I didn't hear my *kuka*'s rhetorical question in its deeper sense.

Thanks to a lifetime of thinking, reading and observation, I have now come to understand my *kuka*'s question. He was telling me about men's fragility. He was telling me about men's difficulties with women's success. He was telling me I was narrowing my dating pool of men. He was telling me that while my education could husband me – in the traditional sense of husbands' labour of provision and security – it would soon become a liability. He had a point.

Thinking about my *kuka*'s question, I am reminded of two things. Firstly, I recall the young Jamaican musician Omi's track 'Cheerleader', which was a hit song in 2017 and remains a popular dance track in clubs across Africa. In the song, Omi declares that his girlfriend is his cheerleader and motivator who grants his every wish, like a genie in a bottle. Long before Omi declared his precious find, my *kuka* was telling me that men need cheerleaders who can channel their life energies towards making them feel good about themselves, motivating them and being loyal and granting all their wishes. In his reckoning, my master's would complicate my cheerleading capacity.

I am also reminded of the *mikayi* (first wife) phenomenon from back in undergraduate days. This was an ironic name for student relationships in university where the female student performed what were considered wifely duties for their boyfriends, in the belief and hope that these relationships would consolidate into marriages after university. The women students, who often shared classes with their boyfriends, regularly left class early at lunchtime to go and prepare midday meals for their boyfriends so they would find lunch ready when they left class. They also did the men's laundry and were sexually available to these men. In most cases though, after university, these male students found a girl from their home regions to marry immediately after leaving campus, conveniently ending relations with the *mikayi* just before graduation. University women could not be trusted to make good wives; they 'knew too much' and were simply too much for men. They were not 'decent' 'marriageable' women, never mind that they had lost their supposed decency and marriageability to these same men, and never mind that the real issue was that they were unlikely to brook control by men once married.

These men were hardly setting a new precedent in Kenyan public discourse. Thinking back, I see them as descendants of Wangari Maathai's husband, Stephen Mwangi Mathai, who officially divorced his wife ostensibly for unfaithfulness, but as far as Kenyan media and public perception was concerned, it was really because the outspoken first PhD holder in East and Central Africa, with a fine academic career ahead of her, was 'too educated, too strong, too successful, too stubborn and too hard to control'.[1] While he may not have made these specific utterances, Maathai nonetheless believed these views resonated with her husband's perceptions: despite being an educated, seemingly exposed man, her husband's thinking was still shaped by the wider patriarchal Kenyan discourse which deemed highly educated women a problem for male control. This is what my *kuka* was referencing: educated women are a problem for male control. Even when they self-consciously teach themselves to be cheerleaders to their men, as Maathai did, in support of her husband, the embedded sense of threat in men's psyches proves difficult to dislodge.

The discourse of respectability and supposed decency is central to these logics of Black women's relationalities to Black men. Few novels capture this as fluently as Toni Morrison does in *The Bluest Eye*, in her description of particular kinds of girls. She describes them as brown girls who move through the streets without a stir, who observe strict hygiene with their skin and their hair. These girls do not drink, smoke or swear; both their formal and cultural education are aligned with the cultivation of high morals and good manners – 'in short, how to get rid of the funkiness'.[2] Men keep an eye on these women, knowing that if they marry them,

> they will sleep on sheets boiled white . . . there will be pretty paper flowers decorating the picture of his mother . . . they feel secure.

They know their work clothes will be mended, washed and ironed on Monday, that their Sunday shirts will billow on hangers from the door jamb, stiffly starched and white. They look at her hands and know what she will do with biscuit dough . . . What they do not know is that she will give him her body sparingly and partially. He must enter her surreptitiously, lifting the hem of her gown only to her navel. He must rest his weight on his elbows when they make love, ostensibly to avoid hurting her breasts but actually to keep her from having to touch or feel too much of him.[3]

In African-American feminist history, the tensions between the respectable women's movement and the blues women captured these gendered logics remarkably, as Angela Davis described in her *Blues Legacies and Black Feminism*.

Who will marry you? I would remember my *kuka*'s question in subsequent years in the dating scene on campus. In one instance, having worsened my matter by registering for a PhD after the master's was completed, I noticed how the man I was dating at the time kept evoking my PhD whenever we had a difference of opinion: 'Is it because you are doing a PhD and I am only doing my master's, that you think your ideas are correct?' I found this comment baffling because I had consciously chosen to downplay my PhD studies. In the end, we would part ways, as it was an unsustainable situationship.

Years later, I would realise that one of the strategies of survival organically inherited by women across generations – especially Black women – is strategic navigation of Black men's fragility and narcissism. Just as historically, Black survival has depended upon Black observation of white people's lives, worlds and thinking in close detail, as bell hooks has noted; Black women's survival too has relied on similar powers of observation and careful manoeuvring around Black men's fragility and their readiness to displace their rage and humiliation onto Black women's bodies. As Toni Morrison notes in *The Bluest Eye*, Black women bore the brunt of abuse from both the white families they worked for and their Black men who both resented them for witnessing their humiliation and counted on them to absorb and nurture their wounds and restore their dignity. Black women's bodies and hearts have historically sponged up Black men's shame and humiliation. Because of this history, Black men – even more so middle-class men – often expect women to minimise themselves. Part of my feminist journey has been learning to minimise myself and my achievements, then eventually recognising the pointlessness of it all. Between a Catholic upbringing and the patriarchal scripts that informed my cultural upbringing, I had absorbed the potentially co-opting wisdom that humility is next to godliness. But looking back at the women who surrounded me in my growing years, I now realise that they performed this script without necessarily believing it. They minimised themselves in the eyes of men, not because they believed in their inferiority, but because they recognised their inner toughness, which could easily crush their men's fragility. They knew their men were a whole lot weaker than they projected themselves to be; so they played along with the script of inferiority, all the while navigating their own pockets of freedom and making choices and exercising power in surreptitious ways that escaped the men. Here, I am reminded of the saying often attributed to the Nobel laureate Margaret Atwood: 'Men are afraid women will laugh at them. Women are afraid men will kill them.'[4]

Part of these logics of relationality are embedded in what Elizabeth Freeman terms chrononormativity, which frames gendered bodies' relationship to time.[5] Within heteronormative frames, women's respectability is gained or lost in relation to the disciplining of their bodies to obey societal temporal contours that prescribe distinct transitions from one stage to another. My *kuka* had never heard of Elizabeth Freeman or the word chrononormativity, but he subscribed to its logics. His anxieties about my marriageability were as much about my capacity to be a cheerleader as they were about a strong investment in my respectability. It was all well and good that I had not fallen pregnant as a teenager out of wedlock before completing my education, but there nonetheless remained a danger of transgressing the temporal scripts that contour a woman's life and dictate that she be 'spoken for' by a certain age. While these scripts also apply to men, who are considered to have remained boys if they don't settle down and start families by a certain age, there is relative flexibility in men's temporal contours, in part because men's power increases with age and wealth and there are limited concerns about reproductivity, while women's viability within these logics is closely aligned with their most reproductive ages, which also overlap with their optimum desirability to men.

My *kuka* was concerned that I would lose respectability if I was 'unspoken for' for too long. He needed me to secure my third husband.

CHAPTER 16

Hearing the Silence

Panashe Chigumadzi

'Mbuya?'*

'Woye?' My maternal grandmother's soft reedy voice reassures me about the tentative start I am making.

'Mbuya, there are things I would like to ask you about your life tomorrow evening. Please be prepared.'

'About my life?'

'Ehe.'

'What exactly do you want to know?'

'Things like where you came from, where you were born, what was your mother's name. Things like that.'

'What are you going to do with it? Are you writing a book?'

It is late on Christmas Eve. I'm lying in my maternal grandmother's bed. It takes time to convince Mbuya Chiganze. I explain that I had done something similar that very morning before we had left kwaMurehwa. My father's youngest sister, Tete Evie, my grandfather's three surviving sisters, Tetes Ena, Evert and Venencia, and I sat together to draw a family tree five generations back to Tateguru Chigumadzi, the first of our family to come to what would become Murehwa communal lands.

---

* A version of this essay was delivered as part of Chigumadzi's 2019 TEDxEuston talk, also entitled 'Hearing the Silence'.

Driving from Murehwa to Gandiya village, around 85 kilometres west of Mutare, my family and I had already gotten the sense that this Christmas, the first 'post-Mugabe' after the coup named 'Operation Restore Legacy [of the liberation war]', felt a little different. The roads were full of motorists cutting corners and overtaking on blind curves, impatient to spend Christmas kumusha.[i] We were delayed by the seemingly kilometres-long queues at the Rusape toll gate. These delays meant that, despite our mid-morning departure from Murehwa, we failed, as usual, to arrive in Gandiya village before nightfall, much to Mbuya Chiganze's dismay.

As soon as the familiar sign in front of Mbuya Chiganze's gate, 'NDAPOTA VHARAI GHEDI!' (Please, close the gate!), appeared, I had already begun trying to persuade myself to ask her about her personal history. The tall matriarch stood waiting to welcome us with my mother's only sister, Mainini Foro. I continued to bargain with myself until we retired for bed.

Although there are several spare bedrooms, with long stretches between visits, I prefer the intimacy of sleeping with Mbuya and Mainini. Mbuya refuses, as usual, to sleep on her bed. She lays out her mattress, while Mainini and I take the bed. This evening there is much activity on the dust road. Kombis going up and down with relatives coming from town. Lying in the dark, we listen out for the sound of my uncle, Sekuru Timothy, the oldest of this house, arriving from Harare. Mainini and Mbuya agree that this is one of the busiest Christmases in a while. The 'new dispensation' seems to have given a new confidence and hope. People seem to be spending money and making the journey home to celebrate and enact the hope of good times ahead.

As we listen to the night's activities I'm still bargaining with myself. Eventually, the sting of my regret over not having spoken to Mbuya Chiganze finally pushes me to make a tentative start. Suspicious

---

i At our ancestral home, usually in the villages located in what settler colonial land policies demarcated as the 'Tribal Trustal Lands' or the 'Native Reserves'.

though she is, Mbuya Chiganze eventually agrees. Sometimes we stumble over language. Mainini is a bridge between Mbuya's deep Manyika and my Manyika-Zezuru hodgepodge. Mbuya repeats the phrase 'Bhabha wedhu wekudhenga' (our Father in heaven), imitating the anglicised Shona of the white Anglican priests. She says this is what I sometimes sound like. Sometimes she gets frustrated with my line of questioning. 'Zvimwe hazvibvunzwe'. Some things are just not asked. 'How could I have asked my own mother such a thing?' Sometimes I am not sure how to continue asking as she relays difficult experiences.

It feels cruel, voyeuristic, to ask her to tell me more about what it was like for her and her family to be put into the lorries that carried them from their original musha to a place they did not know during the forced removals of her girlhood. Or to ask her to describe how she felt when she saw the school trunk returning home on top of the bus without its owner, her third-born son, just 14 years old, confirming that he had not started his second year at St. Faith's as they had expected, hitchhiking instead to Mozambique with friends to join the Chimurenga.

'To cry? You could not. You just had to keep it to yourself. This was war.'

•

Often, because I am a Black woman writer interested in work that centres Black women's narratives, I am asked to talk about voice. I am often asked about the importance of African women, Black women, telling their own stories. On one occasion, the one that triggered these reflections, I was asked to explore why African women need to write their own stories for themselves and as a gift to future generations.

It is a question that belies the ways in which the dominant culture values speech over silence, presence over absence. The trouble with this bias for speech over silence became apparent to me in the process of writing my second book, *These Bones Will Rise Again,* which in part entails an attempt to reconstruct the early life of my late paternal grandmother as part of my search for both a personal and national account of Zimbabwe's liberation history in the wake of Mugabe's fall. As part of this, I had to speak with and interview women of various generations.

One of them was my maternal grandmother. In the weeks that followed my conversation with Mbuya Chiganze, I spoke to various women related and unrelated to me. Some women were unsure of their authority to speak and referred me instead to others. Other women were militant in their refusal to speak because I'd failed to follow the right protocol. Some did speak to me, but there were certain things they were unwilling to talk about.

Very often I had to fill in the gaps by parsing together facts learned by speaking to other people or through history books because these women were unwilling to talk about certain things I asked about. Through these many conversations Mbuya Chiganze's words continued to reverberate: Zvimwe hazvibvunzwe. Some things are just not asked. While the queer feminist poet Audre Lorde rightly taught us that our silences will not protect us, these women's refusal to speak, even when asked, reminded me that silence often remains a state into which the world forces us.

At a time when younger women of my generation have greater access to platforms for telling our stories, it's often tempting for us to declare: 'We did not inherit our mother's silences.' But how true is this? For one, this ignores the fact that long before us, there were generations of women who did refuse silence and spoke out. More than this, it ignores the many silences that today's generations carry.

•

A little while before I was to have the conversation with my grandmother, there was something else that had gotten me to start thinking seriously about paying attention to the silence. It was the decisions made by Black women to remain silent in light of the cultural reckoning brought on by the #MeToo movement founded by Tarana Burke in 2006, which developed into a broader movement, following the 2017 use of #MeToo in the wake of the Harvey Weinstein sexual abuse scandal.

In October 2017, it had been a little more than two weeks since a pair of investigative reporters, from the *New York Times* and the *New Yorker*, exposed decades of sexual harassment and assault claims against Hollywood mogul Harvey Weinstein, when A-list actress Lupita Nyong'o came forward with her own ordeal with Weinstein. Nyong'o explained her motivation for sharing her story, saying, 'I felt uncomfortable in my silence, and I wanted to liberate myself from it and contribute to the discussion.'[1]

Before Nyong'o's story, something that had struck my friend and me was that no Black women had come forward with their own accounts of abuse by Weinstein or any other famous men in Hollywood since the allegations first came out. We were struck by this silence. What did it mean? That no Black women had been abused? We knew that couldn't be it. We just knew that the answer was something different. We knew from our own experiences – his as a Black queer man, mine as a heterosexual Black woman – that the silence could not be an indication that nothing was happening.

With the help of the vast amount of knowledge created by Black women activists and scholars globally, we were able to make sense of Black women's apparent silence in that #MeToo moment. Books like Pumla Dineo Gqola's groundbreaking *Rape: A South African Nightmare* outline how historical ideas of who 'can rape' and who 'can be raped' are shaped by aspects such as one's race, class, gender, sexual orientation, ability, age and profession. Historically, there have been certain bodies that were deemed 'rape-able' – white women, because they were held as pure and sexually chaste. There were certain bodies that were deemed 'unrape-able' – Black women, because they were held as dirty and sexually deviant.

Then and today, the logic of who 'can rape' and who 'can be raped' is further complicated by aspects such as age, class, ability, sexual ability and profession. For example, a sex worker cannot be raped, whilst a baby or an elderly woman is the undisputed victim of rape. Historically, this has meant that the execution of Roman-Dutch law during South Africa's slavery and colonial years ensured that neither a white nor Black man was ever tried for raping a Black woman.[2] The continuities of this are best seen in former president Jacob Zuma's high-profile rape trial in 2005. Standing as an 'unrapeable Black woman' who dared to accuse one of South Africa's most powerful men, the late Khwezi, or Fezeka Khuzwayo, was subjected to scrutiny that undermined any sense of her trustworthiness, sexuality and, most of all, her humanity.

It's no surprise then that even as the #MeToo movement implored the world to *believe women*, women marginalised because we're not white, rich, heterosexual, able-bodied or of the 'right profession' understood that we were less likely to be *believed. We were weighing up the consequences for speaking out differently.* Our instinct about differing consequences for speaking out was validated when, after dozens of women accused him, Weinstein directly issued a statement denying Nyong'o's claims. A few weeks later, he would do the same with Mexican-American actress Salma Hayek's account. Hayek later stated that she believes the difference in response to herself and Nyong'o is because they're not white.[3]

More than a year later, a clip from African-American journalist dream hampton's *Surviving R. Kelly* documentary went viral. In it, Chance the Rapper rationalised working with Kelly, saying, 'Maybe I didn't care because I didn't value the accusers' stories because they were Black women.'[4]

Later that year, the BBC's *Sex for Grades* documentary, led by Nigerian journalist Kiki Mordi, placed the global spotlight on the decades-long battle against sexual harassment at West African universities. The intense debate that followed exposed one of the familiar silencing tools used against women speaking out against abuse from within historically oppressed societies. Detractors made the familiar charge: 'You are being used by our oppressors to bring down our community.' This kind of claim echoes the backlash Anita Hill received from the Black community for speaking out against Clarence Thomas in 1991. In the case of *Sex for Grades*, the victims were supposedly tarnishing the image of their countries by speaking to the BBC, the broadcasting network of their former colonisers.[5]

While neo-colonialism certainly does exist, Mordi's documentary highlights just how important it is to have our *own* empowered local media spaces that can override the pressure to remain silent even in the face of overwhelming evidence. Importantly, her documentary forces us to ask: *who else* has been silenced? What *other* abuses have our leaders helped bury by limiting local press freedoms and infrastructure?

•

I want to invite us to think about hearing the silences. To understand that what *is not* said is just as important as what *is* said.

I want to invite us to interrogate how we *hear* silences that echo in the aftermath of traumatic pasts and presents.

Silences have frequencies.

I want us to ask, 'How can we learn to hear silences that echo *loudly, softly, or in code?*'

•

To begin with, we need to pay attention to the ways in which our silences are shaped by race, class, gender, sexuality, ability, religion and nationality. It is important to pay attention to the power dynamics that play out between different bodies across history.

We need to be attentive to the many forms that silence can take. At the end of 2017, Dr Sindi van Zyl, a renowned Black woman medical doctor, who has made her mark by sharing HIV-related knowledge and other health information with the public on social media and other platforms, shared an anecdote on Twitter about why she mostly refers Black patients to Black doctors. One of the most important reasons she gave was communication. Through her post, she relayed a conversation she had with a 65-year-old Black woman patient, from whom she needed to draw out a sexual history. To do this, Dr Van Zyl understood that she needed tact. The conversation, shared on Twitter, went like this:

> [Dr Van Zyl]: Mama are you in a relationship?
> Mama: No. My husband died 15 years ago
> [Dr Van Zyl]: Do you have a 'friend'?
> Mama: Yes I do have a friend
> [Dr Van Zyl]: How often do you 'visit' your 'friend'?
> Mama: Mostly month end
> [Dr Van Zyl]: Do you use condoms? Yes? No? Sometimes
> Mama: Sometimes.[6]

Dr Van Zyl understood: some things are just not asked. Without crudely asking, 'Mama, are you sexually active?' she got the crucial information she needed. Another doctor without her cultural awareness and knowledge of Zulu would have missed Mama's indirect way of speaking and simply moved on to the next question. Dr Van Zyl appreciated that AboMama don't have boyfriends or sides. They have 'abangani' – 'friends'.

What Dr Van Zyl highlights here is the importance of paying attention to the silences that are created by language and cultural differences. This is particularly true for our post-colonial situation where those who hold power are often unable to speak or even *hear* any of South Africa's indigenous languages. Many will go to great lengths to learn French or even Mandarin before ever being able to go beyond sanibonani (hello), celi'amanzi[ii] or, if we are particularly unfortunate, nkalakatha.[iii] Beyond transmitting functional information, our languages carry our experiences, our values, our world views. *If you cannot understand our languages, you cannot hear us.*

Importantly, these coded silences exist not just between isiZulu and English, Setswana and Afrikaans; they are also embedded in the modes of speech and languages that marginalised people use as a means of survival. This can take the form of languages queer people may use to communicate with and identify each other in places where there are threats such as social exclusion, prosecution and even death. Often I, as a heterosexual woman, miss many cues when I'm following conversations among my queer friends. One way I attempt to overcome this is by engaging the creative works and scholarship of people in different communities from mine. It's a well-worn cliché that reading is a way to build empathy and immerse yourself in the worlds of others who aren't like you. We can extend the work of empathy building beyond literature. We need to ask ourselves: Are we watching the experimental film directed by an undocumented migrant from Malawi? Are we reading the sonnet written by a poor woman from Soweto? Are we listening to the dance album produced by the differently abled man from Harare? Are we watching the one-woman play written by a trans woman from Brixton? Are we interested in hearing, and *feeling our way through,* the language-worlds inhabited by those different from us?

More than this, more than simply appreciating coded silences, we must appreciate *why* they've come to exist in the very first place and

---

ii 'Can I have some water?' [Zulu].

iii 'Top dog' in isiZulu. The word was made famous among white South Africans by the late South African kwaito star Mandoza, whose song 'Nkalakatha' was a crossover hit in the 2000s.

fight against this. Without this, we're only reinforcing the very silence that we're asking each other to break.

•

We need to pay attention to the ways in which we can use our imaginations to hear the silence. For me, as a young Black woman writer who has sought to write about the early life of my late grandmother, with precious few records of that time, I have been particularly inspired by the ways Black women writers have used fiction and the imagination to overcome great historical silences in the face of great historical trauma.

South Africa's history contains silences where the voices of its enslaved people should have figured. As slaves were for the most part denied literacy, let alone access to the printing press, there was seemingly no chance for them to develop a literary voice, a written voice, a record for future generations. The repression of the slave voice has contributed to the creation of a South African history that is a 'master's history' in which slavery and emancipation in the nineteenth-century Cape Colony were undramatic and inconsequential. In the absence of accounts from the mouths of South Africa's enslaved, we are left to interrogate our collective memory and ask: *What stays unheard by force of repression? What stays unsaid by force of resistance?*

To answer these silences, Toni Morrison's concept of 're-memory' invites us to 'journey to a site to see what remains were left behind and to reconstruct the world that these remains imply' in order to re-humanise those who have been 'disremembered and unaccounted for'.[7]

Rayda Jacobs's *The Slave Book* and Yvette Christiansë's *Unconfessed* are two such novels that recover and re-memory the 'dis-remembered' past of the Cape Colony, through an imaginative revisiting of the fragments of this history. *The Slave Book*, which takes its title from the register that stipulated the codes controlling enslaved people at the Cape of Good Hope, is set against the backdrop of the 1834 abolition of slavery and the subsequent four-year period of forced apprenticeship for the emancipated. The novel excavates the years preceding the emancipation, through the narrative of Salamah, his wife Noria, and her daughters Sangora and Somiela. Sangora and Somiela are separated from Noria when they are sold to the De Villiers family at a slave auction. At the heart of the story is the love affair between Somiela, who is of mixed heritage, and the foreman Harman Kloot, a white *vryburger* (free man) who is later revealed also to be of mixed ancestry. Through this union, Jacobs destabilises racial and sexual boundaries central to the slavocratic society in which sexual abuse was as routine a weapon of control as the whip and chain.

Yvette Christiansë's *Unconfessed* centres the silences at the heart of the life of the historical figure Sila van den Kaap, a slave woman who was incarcerated for the *kindermoord*, child murder, of her nine-year-old son, Baro. Her life is spared because she was pregnant. Sila is later sent to Robben Island to serve an extended sentence of 14 years, after which her fate is unknown. The fact of her having taken her son's life is unquestioned, but whether this constitutes a crime is contested.

'I could not say as they wanted me to say,' says Sila. Throughout the novel, she refuses to confess to the crime for which she has been tried. Christiansë then dedicates the narrative to re-memorying an enslaved woman who uses the act of *kindermoord* to enact motherhood by controlling the circumstances of her child's life to protect him from the pain of enslavement. Towards the end of the novel, Sila laments:

[t]he daughters and sons of my generations will say, we are not people, we are things ... And I will be weeping in my grave ... hungering after other people's children, for my children will be running behind me, forgotten too as their children's children, those rocks who were once people, smash and smash some terrible future into shape.[8]

Together, *The Slave Book* and *Unconfessed* offer a haunting, poignant poetics that foregrounds language, voice and presence in order to re-memory the silences of enslaved women. In the face of great historical silences, Black women's imaginative works are wreaths lain on the graves of ancestors so that they may not weep: so that they know, we, the daughters and sons of their generations say: we are *not* things, we are *people*.

•

For me, it has been Black women writing about women silenced by history that's taught me the delicate art of storying the silence without speaking over it. The generations of women I spent time with as I tried to reimagine my late paternal grandmother's early life have helped me understand: *silence need not represent a dead end, but rather, a beginning.*

•

After that initial night in my surviving grandmother's bedroom, I decided to put my questions away and just focus on *being* with her.

Before then, I'd never really spent much time alone with Mbuya. Language was often a barrier. As I work to reclaim my mother tongue, Shona, I'm struck by the fact that the word kunzwa not only means 'to hear'; it also means 'to feel', 'to understand'. I thought about hearing as feeling and understanding as the silences between my grandmother and I became an opportunity for pause, for deep introspection, deep imagination and hard work at creating a new language between us – one of feeling and understanding. When I least expected it – perhaps in the middle of tending to her flowers or walking to church – Mbuya shared things with me I hadn't even *thought* to ask about.

It was only through this space, a space created by a respect for my grandmother's silences, that I was finally able to *hear* her.

3.
Remaking

CHAPTER 17

Thinking Through Transnational Feminist Solidarities

Leigh-Ann Naidoo

One of the most pressing questions for the work towards radical change and resistance is how to build solidarity locally and globally, across difference. The question of solidarity haunts me because there is power in numbers and yet building large movements across issues, time and space is so difficult. As we have repeatedly seen, mass resistance forces people in power to listen to our demands and can produce the kinds of change we want. It is therefore important, in addition to defending our progressive movements from external attacks, to address how we negotiate solidarity within our movements, knowing that unequal power relations can and are often reproduced in the very spaces of resistance we create to redistribute that power. The inability to deal with how power operates through us and our relations with one another results in us – often with the best of intentions – doing harm to one another and to the possibility of solidarity.

My experience of movements has included witnessing many moments of solidarity. What defined these moments for me was how activists relinquished their relative privilege and personal position in order to place themselves in political communion with others.

My earliest recollection of such moments is of my father, Derrick Naidoo, who over his lifetime has committed acts of class suicide to live and work among working-class and poor people who did not have the educational and class privileges that he did. In 1981, he survived a 40-day hunger strike in prison aimed at raising international awareness of South African students who were tortured and imprisoned with him for their anti-apartheid politics. His anti-racist and anti-capitalist beliefs provided me with a model for tying one's fate to others in political acts that oblige one to relinquish privilege and face extreme risks. I continue to be inspired and humbled by the many acts of bravery and sacrifice that I witnessed during the fight against apartheid. The vast majority of them were not memorialised, but are remembered in the personal stories of so many black South Africans.

Here, I reflect on ideas about solidarity, struggle and current challenges for radicalism that emerged afresh during my experience on the Women's Boat to Gaza (WBG), on which I sailed in September 2016. WBG was created, in my estimation, as an act of transnational feminist solidarity with the women of Gaza and Palestine. South African participation in the WBG was organised through the Palestine Solidarity Alliance, and the invitation to put my name forward as a possible participant came during the massive student uprisings at South African universities in 2015/16. #FeesMustFall and #RhodesMustFall were among the most important protests since the end of apartheid, and my active participation in them as a postgraduate student, as well as my history of activism as a queer Olympic beach volleyball player, had caught the attention of the WBG organisers.

Challenges for feminist solidarity

The Gaza Strip is home to around 1.8 million Palestinians who have been living under siege since 2007. The land, air and sea blockade has created what many have described as a huge open-air prison. In addition to being occupied and isolated, Gaza is also under constant threat of military attack from the Israeli Occupation Forces (IOF). Palestine and South Africa have a historic relationship that dates back to the formal beginnings of both Israel and apartheid in 1948. Over the last 50 years, the Palestinian liberation movement and the anti-apartheid movement have forged a solidarity that has persisted in the post-apartheid period in South Africa, despite the active support of Zionism by organisations and individuals both inside and outside of the state.

Much has also been said about the similarities between South African apartheid and what has become known as Israeli apartheid. The violence and suppression of the indigenous people by settlers is an obvious similarity, as is the extreme segregation along with the inequality that it produces. I have participated in protests in support of Palestine since I was a young child. Because of this, and because of a commitment to responding to calls for solidarity and support against (neo-)colonialism and injustice, I was open to the idea of joining a protest that would highlight the continued struggle faced in Occupied Palestine and particularly in Gaza.

For the first time in the history of freedom flotillas, a boat made up of 13 women from around the world would cross the Mediterranean Sea in an attempt to reach the shores of occupied Gaza. In so doing, we would attempt to break the ongoing and devastating blockade of Gaza by taking a message of international solidarity. I had many questions about the mission's politics. I was wary of the kinds of political work to which the category 'woman' was being deployed. At one level, the WBG would be a story of women's achievements and sacrifice during a solidarity mission and would bring media attention to the particular experiences of women in Gaza, which are often under-reported. At another level, the all-women mission appealed both explicitly and implicitly to an associated idea of peace in the face of militarism, traditionally associated with masculinity. I was uncomfortable with this gendered stereotype of peace and militancy and especially of how the WBG might be construed as a mission of womanly peace in opposition to Israeli militarism. I stepped onto the boat imagining that the mission would entail the participants' animated engagement with questions of power, gender, feminism, peace, resistance and, above all, the work of solidarity.

All of the activist women on the boat were involved in various struggles in their home countries, and some were involved in international ones. I was sure there would be a range of ideas and positions that would be debated and worked through amongst us. Although it was very interesting and important for me to hear about the work of the different women on the boat, what was not part of our conversation was our different political and social positions, our relationship to solidarity work and a discussion about how we constituted our collective mission. Overall, the mission was a remarkable political education for me. It allowed me to experience the

Figure 17.1. WBG Messina Departure group, 2016. Photograph by Sandra Barrilaro – Rumbo a Gaza.

satisfaction of an extraordinary transnational mission, and to learn about struggles from Aotearoa to Algeria. But it also taught me how deeply power relations are embedded even in our movements and missions, and how much more attention we need to pay to how we come together, and how we move together.

On the boat: The face of feminist solidarity

I left Johannesburg in September 2016 to join the WBG in Italy. Consumed by thoughts of what was transpiring at universities in South Africa, I spent five days in Messina meeting with participants and organisers from around the world to prepare for the last leg of the boat trip to Gaza. We set sail from Messina on the morning of 27 September 2016, excited, scared, and aware that, at the beginning of our nine-day sail to Gaza over very rough waters, seasickness would be the first challenge for us all to overcome.

Each of us came with a multitude of different experiences which, along with the global systems of power that structure all of our lives, should have presented us with fertile opportunities outside of the confines of our own local or regional concerns to engage each other collectively. We were in the unsettling but potentially productive situation of being away from our direct national struggles and networks. The highlights of the boat trip for me were the individual conversations I managed to have with other participants in getting to know them, their contexts and activism. I had the realisation that there were so many ongoing battles across the world. As we went further across the Mediterranean, we were also in satellite communication with organisations and people in Gaza who were preparing to meet us at the beach. As we counted down the miles, we started believing that we would make it. Our hopes were pinned on reaching the shores of Gaza without being intercepted by the IOF. We were a small boat and had made it known that we carried no supplies, weapons or materials other than our own sparse food and clothing. In the last few days of our voyage, our boat captain and our selected boat leader gathered us together for a discussion that would allow us to prepare for what would be the final day at sea. We were to discuss two eventualities. First, the more dangerous one, which would see us boarded by the IOF to prevent us from breaking the blockade. Second, the possibility of reaching the Gaza coast, one of the most structurally violent places in the world.

At the onset, the conversation went well. We were in agreement about what would happen should we be intercepted. We discussed and agreed to cede our voices to our boat captain, who would be the negotiator when the IOF made radio contact. She was knowledgeable and had dealt with radio communication between ship captains before. We also agreed on the same with our boat leader, who would be the only one to communicate with the soldiers if they boarded our boat physically. Again, she was the team member with the most military experience, being a retired US army colonel, and was calm under pressure, having been on previous flotilla missions. We would be acting as a team and had agreed to the selected leadership in the event of capture. Our leaders would present to the Israeli soldiers our message of peace and non-violence to clarify that we had no weapons or materials other than our solidarity with Gaza. Individual participants could only speak for themselves again when they returned to their home countries to recount the mission to local media, telling either of their experience of engaging with Gazans or the experience of capture, imprisonment and deportation.

What did not go as easily was the discussion about what would happen if we were to land in Gaza. The conversation started to heat up when it was proposed that the nature of our mission was one of spreading peace. I remember being uncomfortable with the idea that we would make landfall speaking only one message when we engaged the women of Gaza. I raised my concern: surely we couldn't arrive in Gaza to present a single narrative of why we were there and were lending our support to Palestine? How could we get off the boat to engage with the women we would meet and declare that we were there in the name of peaceful, non-violent resistance? Would this not be patronising to the Palestinian resistance movement? How would they react to us taking a predetermined position that peace and non-violence was the only legitimate form of struggle to engage in?

I urged for engagement not from a singular position of supporting non-violent action, but from a dialogue about how we might be able to engage the ongoing struggles for Palestinian freedom. I wanted to ask critical questions about the relevance of different forms of struggle against extremely violent forms of oppression. Ours, I argued on the boat, was not a mission to convince Gazans of the merits of non-violent resistance but to show solidarity with *their* experiences and political priorities.

The conversation broke down very quickly. The two elders on the boat were international peace activists, one having spent years working in the military and seeing the devastating effects of military violence, the other a pacifist and (I discovered after the mission) an anti-abortion advocate. Some of us on the boat had lived through historical struggles for freedom that involved the strategic use of violence against brutal regimes and were not convinced that violence against an illegitimate regime was unprincipled. We all spoke from our personal experiences of violence and struggle, but our capacity to listen to each other's views was strained and ragged. In particular, the question of peace and non-violence as universally applicable caused a lot of friction and was not at all settled in the group.

What became problematic from my perspective was not the diversity of experience and positions in relation to violence and the possibilities of non-violent resistance, but the rigidity of the stance that some adopted, which had the effect of silencing others. The conversation played out along familiar lines: the more privileged women on board were advocates of non-violence, while those of us from the Global South did not hold such a straightforward position. I observed that the privileged and mostly white women from the Global North were unwilling to recognise how the context of a deeply unequal (and structurally violent) world, in terms of raced, classed, geographic, and gendered inequality and exploitation, might provide a shifting reading of strategy in relation to the forms that resistance might take.

The breakdown of the conversation made me realise that the form of solidarity we were practising was not one that pushed us to understand one another's positions and contexts and to grapple with the discomfort of recognising what our differences implied in practice. When the very real differences between us surfaced, it did not allow us to exercise political rigour to deal with those differences. Nor did it ask us to think about those differences in relation to the particular needs of Palestinian women. Rather, the conversation ended with a more privileged woman from the Global North (probably the most powerful in terms of social position and expertise) criticising our lack of 'team spirit'. She implied that we had embarked on the mission under false pretences and that the insistence on acknowledging and contending with diverse views was not politically productive or necessary, but in fact destructive to the mission. It was made clear that the dominant definition of being a good member of the transnational collective meant conforming to a single view of what protest should entail. Additionally, it was the right of privileged members of the mission to define activist goals and methods. If there were multiple views held by the majority white women on the boat, this was made explicit not in the collective discussion but rather through individual conversation later or after the mission.

Perhaps it was too much to ask us to have these kinds of weighty political discussions on a small boat far from land, pushing through storms and broken rigging. Perhaps the only version of solidarity that

Figure 17.2. IOF approach the WBG in Zodiac boats, 35 miles from Gaza, 2016. Photograph by Sandra Barrilaro – Rumbo a Gaza.

could be practised was one that conceded to a clear premise and held a single line. But it was difficult not to feel the power dynamics on the boat and the creeping sense that something was wrong, and that an opportunity had been missed. This sense was to be dramatically confirmed after we were intercepted by Israeli soldiers just a day before we were due to reach the shores of Gaza.

Prison: The myth of women's universal experiences

Of the 13 women who set sail to break the illegal Israeli occupation of the Gaza Strip, 11 were kidnapped in international waters and imprisoned. Two journalists from Al Jazeera, who had documented the journey through daily packaged episodes and numerous live feeds from the WBG, had signed papers which meant they were immediately deported back to their country of residence, where they could continue their reporting from the outside. The 11 of us who were imprisoned were taken to Ashdod Port, which was transformed into a military camp for processing. Then we were transported separately to Givon Prison. This process included officers from the Israeli navy, military, prison service and police. We were questioned individually by immigration officers and a number of strip-searches were conducted. A scene unfolded in the prison the next day that was startling. We were all taken out of our cells in the morning and put in an open courtyard. But we were not all afforded the right to sit on the wooden benches in the open air. Three of us were locked in a cage on one side of the courtyard, while the remaining eight sat talking on the benches. They were meeting their consular representatives and our shared lawyers to discuss the conditions of our capture and imprisonment and to negotiate our release. I realised that all of the white and Northern women were sitting on the benches. In the cage sat three of us, all broadly defined as black, two of us in hijab, two from the African continent. Looking out, I felt the same sense of wariness that I had felt in the conversation on the boat.

It is hard to know exactly why we three were caged while our eight comrades were allowed to walk about. On some level it might be as simple as we three had no one coming to visit us during the scheduled consular visit, because our governments did not have cosy relationships with Israel. But as the three of us sat in a four-by-four-metre holding cell in the courtyard of the prison, I remember my shock at being separated and treated differently from my comrades. Although I understood the inequalities that are always present between nationality and race, etc., my will to have acts of solidarity reduce those inequalities was still strong. The experience of being confined to this hierarchy against my most fervent aspirations of a solidarity mission was disappointing. Maybe it would have been more palatable if we were taken out of view from the rest of our group. But the cage functioned as the perfect viewing deck for me to see more clearly how power played out even in the context of a collective action meant to unite women from a dozen countries. While we shared the same boat and sea conditions, it was clear that we were in fact not on the same mission. Nor were we treated as equal participants. The experience in the courtyard complemented the difficult conversation on the boat: racial and national distinctions mattered in how decisions were made, how conversations unfolded and how care circulated.

For the two weeks leading up to our capture, we were struggling in concert against the elements of a sea voyage. Even though we had met only a week or two earlier, we quickly had to adjust to living with each other in a confined space, tackling the seasickness and sharing the many little tasks that keep a boat at sea working. The process of building a shared set of principles and ideas around our mission was not always smooth sailing, even before we stepped on board. And I was surprised at how much we were unable to explicitly discuss power and how it manifested internally, negatively affecting our mission.

I turned to the other caged women and asked if they too felt that this was a problematic way to be treated. We huddled together and felt some solace because at least we were experiencing the isolation together. Being prevented from reaching the Gaza shoreline, and being treated like terrorists by the Israeli regime, paled in comparison to being forgotten or not held in consciousness and care by our comrades. How could we as feminists register a mode of critical thinking and practice that is a condition for solidarity? Could it be that, throughout the mission and beyond, an important part of the work was to consider more critically the daily engagements and experiences of resistance and solidarity? Should we have acknowledged that through this struggle there would also inadvertently be experiences of discrimination, oppression or dehumanisation of some members?

At our request, our lawyer attempted to have us released so that we could join the rest of our group, but the prison guard brushed off his request without any explanation. One or maybe two of the uncaged women from our mission came over to us to see what was happening. It seemed they felt uncomfortable about the situation, but not enough to insist that our confinement end. The possibility of joining us in the cage did not seem to enter the minds of our comrades. And yet it seemed from the inside of the cage that the very least condition for a collective mission once captured was to hold the tension between having one vision and one voice, while also agreeing on how to work across difference together. Our different bodies, origins and contexts, as well as those of the Palestinians we were supporting, had to be contended with if we were to arrive at something that we might call critical solidarity. What does it take to consciously commit oneself in action and consequence to a position different from or outside of one's own experience, privilege, desire and social position? Could this be the most difficult yet important aspect of solidarity?

Towards a conclusion

The question of how to express critical solidarity with Palestine took shape for me in the context of the two key incidents I have discussed: the conversation on the boat among the women, and our treatment by both the Israeli military and the women with whom we had believed we shared political ideals. These experiences led me to a series of questions. Who decides strategy when planning an action across national (or any other) contexts? Who sets the terms for an act of solidarity? How do we understand the principles of what constitutes a solidaristic effort? During the mission, would there have been less or no difficulty if the participants on the boat had similar experiences or were socially positioned more closely to each other? What is the relationship between solidarity and interest? Is it solidarity when you, for example, are marching with fellow workers for your own benefit? Or does solidarity have to involve some sort of act of sacrifice? Solidarity seems to be premised on the capacity to move beyond oneself, and to think about working not only for your own interest but for those of others; or at least being able to read something of your own experience into the experience of someone else. Does this translation across experience imply that solidarity is a greatly varied and complex act of communication and relation? Perhaps the more distant your own experience is from the experience of those to whom solidarity is expressed, the more translation work has to be done. Also, the more distant your experience, especially in terms of privilege, the more critically aware you have to be about *how* you do the work of moving beyond your own experience.

It seems it is precisely a knowledge of the intersecting and always evolving identities that shapes one's capacity to be in relationships with others, and which contextualises the possibility of showing solidarity and empathy for others' positions. This solidarity would require the development of a practice of moving oneself into another position, not with appropriation or force, but in order to decentre the self, to find technologies for correspondence across difference. If this careful practice is not at the centre of solidarity work, then it can devolve into something else quite quickly.

What this reveals for me is that there is a relationship between proximity and distance that enables solidarity. There is something about the hook of experience as well as the importance of difference that makes solidarity so necessary and yet so difficult. Because if you are just in the experience, then you can't express real solidarity because you don't do it beyond yourself. There is something about solidarity that implies distance, that implies the capacity to transcend one's own direct experience, in order to be with other people. There is also something about the terrain of experience that you have lived through which possibly creates a different sensitivity to what the practice of solidarity looks like. If you don't have some capacity to recognise how diversity of experience and opportunity have shaped firstly your own life and then other people's lives, you are likely to reproduce your privileged experience. And this inevitably will impact those whom you have chosen to act in concert with.

The simplest way for me to keep thinking through solidarity is to continue to act in solidarity with those who have a different and less privileged position from mine and therefore different life experiences. In this way I practise a form of auto-critique, and in so doing contribute to a more complex practice of fighting oppressive power, while at the same time fighting it internally in our resistance processes and movements. I do this not alone but with other comrades of collectives, movements, organisations and campaigns.

Instead of concluding with a rehearsal of the arguments of this chapter, I end with a set of suggestions that might help us to confront the work of building critical solidarity in our times.

An agenda for critical solidarity

1. Recognising, through an analysis of the structures of power and how they work through us all, who is 'the last' and putting them first or centring their experiences and voices when figuring out tactics and strategy.

2. Considering the possibility of solidarity as being able to recognise one's positionality and the privilege/s it affords – precisely this knowledge (of intersectionality and the complexity of identity) affords the possibility of empathy and therefore solidarity.

3. Understanding sacrifice as an essential part of solidarity work.

4. Building solidarity as a collective rather than individual project.

5. Creating reflective space to critically think through, alone and with others, individual and group experiences of the solidarity work being done.

6. Devoting time to 'translation work' between individual experiences and other people's experiences (especially if one is privileged). Put differently, figuring out how to do the work of going beyond a single experience.

7. Recognising the importance of and valuing difference as a fundamental material which allows for stretching what is possible away from simply one individual's experience and from the status quo.

8. Admitting at the start that one will make mistakes because of the learning process, and that these mistakes are probably going to hurt, alienate or anger someone.

9. Being willing to work on repair and make sure that repair is not only apologising but also being vulnerable through changed action and more collective work.

10. Acknowledging the indivisibility of struggles – that there is never a space where one can be outside of necessary ongoing critique and struggle. It is important to rest and recover but there is always a call to return to a condition of struggle.

11. Granting that the world is changed in one realm by thinking and writing radically, but that this is not enough.

CHAPTER 18

The Music of My Orgasm

Makhosazana Xaba

My Mama was a teacher of what was once called domestic science. She had qualified as a teacher with this specialisation at Lovedale College in the then Cape Province, after completing her matric at Inanda Girls' Seminary in the 1940s. Her name was Glenrose Nomvula Mbatha. Born in 1929, she died in 2011.

My Mama's Mama (Gogo) died when Mama was only eight years old. Mama told me a story about my Gogo's death that has stayed with me over the years. After the funeral, Mama's father, Alban Hamilton S. Mbatha, also a teacher, whom we called Mkhulu, sat all four of his daughters down and told them: I promise never to get married until you are all grown up and capable of looking after yourselves. They were living in a homestead in Magogo, not far from Nquthu, in the province then known as Natal. Their grandmother also looked after them for some years, until my Mkhulu decided to leave South Africa in 1942, as the rumours of that time were that the National Party would, soon enough, take over completely. He moved his family to Hlatikhulu, Swaziland, and he honoured his word.

The reason I have never forgotten this story is because of *how* Mama told it, and she told it a good few times. Her smile covered her whole face and pride shone through like stars in the night sky. My Mkhulu's message was loud and unequivocal. He went against the often-accepted societal norm of men replacing wives before their bones were exposed in their graves.

I have also never forgotten this story because most of what Mama told me about her father suggested to me that Mkhulu was a feminist, especially in his beliefs about equality between women and men, as well as how he chose to take full responsibility for his children after his wife's death. He did not rush to find a woman to mother his four girls. I have often wondered, because I never asked, which specific lessons Mama learned from Mkhulu and which ones she learned from her Gogo before they emigrated to Swaziland.

There are many lessons about freedoms, sexual autonomy, women's rights and reproductive independence that I learned from Mama over the years. I share some of them below, specifically the ones that laid firm foundations for my own feminism, which has been firmly grounded in a belief that women can and must claim their independent bodily and sexual freedoms in societies that deny us the rights to claim and own these freedoms. Mama planted the seeds of my embodied feminist knowledge where we grew up, a small rural area called Ndaleni.

I believe in the power of personal experiences and the lessons they offer. This chapter draws lessons from experiences during my childhood and youth in order to connect these to my feminist practice; in particular, the choices I made to work in the field of women's health that nurtures a holistic understanding of women's bodily and political well-being. I am in complete agreement with Patricia McFadden, who argues that '[t]he mining of our personal experiences as political narratives that speak to realities beyond our experiences as individual women is a critical feminist resource and analytical tool'.[1] McFadden further argues: 'By drawing strength and vision from long-standing traditions of feminist resistance against patriarchal sexual hegemony and heteronormative intolerance, we can embrace women's erotic power as a political resource in transforming our various social spaces and ourselves.'[2]

The stories that follow are a collective example of how some women of a generation before mine – my Mama was no exception, I believe – handled the education of girls, how they went against the grain of culture that sought to control the bodies and minds of girls and women. And how they were feminists long before the word became commonplace in South Africa. Through these stories I offer an argument for experiential feminism grounded in knowledge about bodily and sexual freedoms and claiming them.

Waiting for baby brother

The last-born in our family, our baby brother, was born in 1964, when I was in my second year of primary school. I have no recollection of the day I first knew about Mama being pregnant. I just remember that I felt as if I was waiting forever for this baby to arrive. Mama let me touch her abdomen and kept telling me he was growing bigger and bigger and how he was going to come out of her body. He was born on 22 June, which meant that he and Mama shared a birthdate. I remember arriving at school very late on the morning after his birth, and announcing to my teacher that I had been spending time with him. He was born at night, at home. A well-known midwife – Mama kaMfundo as we knew her – assisted Mama during my brother's birth.

From that day I started to notice just how little other girls knew about where babies come from. I had great fun whenever the subject came up (which was rare) in telling them that girls have a special hole for babies located between the urine hole and faeces hole. I was at an age at which I believed that my Mama knew everything, so I shared the information with gusto, although I was never sure how to deal with the shock and disbelief I received each time I told the story. I could not understand why it was necessary to hide the facts of pregnancy and birth either. I was to learn that even in high school, some classmates were still unsure about these facts of biology.

A lesson in a kitchen

We were in the kitchen, my two sisters and Mama, attending to various tasks while our father sat reading a newspaper at the second table near the window, when our little brother, the last-born, who was playing on the floor, asked Mama where babies came from. It must have been winter for all of us to have been gathered in the kitchen. Mama answered in a matter-of-fact way. Babies come out of women's bodies through a third hole that men don't have. She went on to explain that the bodies of girls and boys are created differently. She explained to my brother about his urine hole and his faeces hole. She added that a baby grows in *izisu ezidalelwe bona*[i] for nine months, and comes out when old enough. Baby brother seemed satisfied with this answer. He did not probe further. Direct speech and accurate information, I thought. But isn't he too young to hear this? I asked in my head. No one else in the kitchen spoke.

While eavesdropping

Around the same period as the explanation about the various holes, I overheard a conversation between Mama and her friend, another schoolteacher, about an event that had shocked the school. Mama was walking her out of our home after a visit. The path leading from the back door to the gate meandered past the storeroom – a rectangular mud structure housing gardening tools and miscellaneous things that could not be kept in the main house. With two windows at the front, facing the path, and one side window, it was easy to overhear the conversations of passers-by.

On this day, this teacher and Mama were discussing a story that had unfolded at the teacher training college where our father taught. A student had thrown her newly born infant into the pit toilet. The infant had apparently been heard crying, which was when

---

i Stomachs made especially for them.

school management was alerted; but by the time it was rescued, it had died. Mama and her friend kept going over the details and saying how shameful it was for the school and *umphakathi*, the community, that this student had to do this. They would take a few steps, then stop and go over the details again.

What fascinated me about that conversation was Mama's repeated conclusion: *'Lafa elihle kakhulu'* (directly translated, 'The beautiful and best world has died'). It's an expression used when people bemoan the changes in societal values, ethics and morals. Not once did Mama and her friend blame the student. Instead, they talked about how communities of old would never have led the student to this desperate act, because a community member would have offered to raise the baby or the women would have helped her to have an abortion early on. The student clearly realised that her child would be without another parent, as it was reported that the student had refused to share who had made her pregnant. What I concluded from this conversation was that Mama and her friend thought the student had been let down by society, not that she had done something wrong. They were on her side. This was my introduction to the idea that a woman can choose between abortion or giving a child away. It is an idea and a gift that I received through eavesdropping. Knowing what I know today about parenting, I am willing to bet that Mama had seen me in the storeroom and was content with me hearing about this incident. It was, after all, a learning opportunity.

The book that started it all

I was 12 years old in 1969 when Mama gave me a book that taught me how to masturbate. This was the first non-fiction book in English that I read. While I found the anatomy drawings interesting, including those showing how a penis enters a vagina, it was the section on how to masturbate that became my takeaway from that book, whose title I no longer remember. What I do remember is Mama saying to me: '*Odadewenu basebancane ukuthi bangazi okukulencwadi, nawe ungabafundeli*' (Your sisters are too young to learn about the contents of this book, don't even read it to them).

The book was difficult to read. I did not understand many of the words in it. So I used one of the dictionaries that Mama kept in one of the kitchen drawers. Her instructions had been very clear: never come to me for a definition of a word if you have not first looked it up in the dictionary. She was only available for further and detailed explanations of words, not the basics that the dictionaries covered. When I finally finished the book and offered it back to Mama, she said I should keep it because there were details I might want to return to. Return I did, to the clitoris and what to do with it in order to reach an orgasm. I read this on innumerable occasions. There was only one challenge: privacy! I shared a bedroom and a bed with siblings, and there was never much time to be completely alone so I could practise what I had learned.

In this book, the word 'game' was used to describe masturbation: a game everyone can play alone, with their own body. This description was liberating for me because I was already aware that I did not like the competitiveness of many games, including the Monopoly that we played as a family on cold winter days and rainy summer days (I always opted to be the banker). I found excuses for not playing card games as well, and at school I selected who I played with carefully because the enthusiastic competitors were well known. Reading was a game I enjoyed, but it was not always easy, and I needed a book for it. With masturbation, I needed no one and nothing else – just my own body. It was not until boarding school that I finally experimented with this game, and in time I learned how to pleasure myself to ecstasy.

Masturbation gave me many gifts: free, solitary, self-controlled and self-led pleasure. It gave me thrills I did not have to pay for. It gave me individual joy I did not have to share with anyone. It gave me private ecstasy I did not have to explain to anyone. I could win with myself, for myself. It taught me the value of experimentation. It taught me self-control and gave me self-reliance; I made the decisions about when and how I would indulge. I gave myself permission, and once I was done and content, I reported to no one. It opened my ears to the music of my orgasms, and I learned how to play this music in varying tunes and rhythms. I knew how to pick the notes, lead myself in my music, and choose how high to go each time.

The physiological release of masturbation had its benefits, but in time the significance of this retreated to the background. It was the existential gifts I received – control being the most important – that I valued the most: the way they translated seamlessly into other areas of my life. In her essay 'Uses of the Erotic', Audre Lorde argues that 'the erotic offers a well of replenishing and provocative force to the woman who does not fear its revelation, nor succumb to the belief that sensation is enough'.[3]

As a teenager, I learned the truth of Lorde's words long before I came across the word feminism, long before I came across her writings. This is one of the ways in which body-grounded experiences of women are indeed universal. Decades later, as I read Patricia McFadden's 'Sexual Pleasure as Feminist Choice', I was pleasantly surprised by the deep resonance I heard in this:

> For me, becoming a feminist has always been about the joy of being free; of owning the pleasure that comes from constantly growing through engagement and enquiry, and knowing that I have the ability to give pleasure at many levels of human interaction – intellectually, socially, intimately, physically, and sexually and to receive it as a precious gift. It is the joy of freedom that makes it so empowering.[4]

I began using the gifts of masturbation when making decisions about many things in my life. And this became a pattern of my life. Today I can say, and this is when a cliché is welcome – 'without any fear of contradiction' – that masturbation was foundational to my feminism.

The body and blood

The year following my reading on masturbation, Mama told me about menstruation. It was an ordinary Saturday afternoon, close to the end of my final year in primary school. Outside I was playing *amagendi*[ii] with my sisters, and I was losing to my younger sister when I heard Mama call my name. I promptly stood up and went into the house. I was surprised to find her in our bedroom, sitting on my sisters' bed. She invited me to sit next to her and started talking right away.

She began with what had become an exciting topic of family conversation for me: going away to boarding school the following year, 1971. The summary of what she said translated to: 'If by the time you leave home for boarding school your first period has not come, it will definitely arrive when you are there, so I need you to know what to expect and be ready.' I remembered reading about blood from my 'masturbation book' and how unimportant that section had seemed to me. Mama explained that the blood would arrive once every month, showed me sanitary pads, and told me that I should keep them somewhere safe. She explained the relationship between menstruation, sex and pregnancy. This time when she spoke about sex, she used a more emphatic tone: *'Ungake ulinge uvumele namuphi umfana afake ugwayi wakhe kunana wakho ngoba uzokhulelwa.*[5] *Akufanele ukhulelwe ungakaqedi ukufunda.'* Clarity! 'Never ever let any boy put his penis into your vagina because you will get pregnant. You should not get pregnant before you finish schooling.'

Mama's words made complete sense to me; I was not going to allow any boy to put his penis inside my vagina. I did not understand why she needed to be so emphatic about it – as if there was a chance I would disagree. I did not like school, but being smart and getting good grades made it tolerable. She said that she would keep the

---

ii A game often played by girls while sitting on the ground. The aim is to accumulate as many stones as possible as they take turns moving the stones in and out of a circle.

packet of sanitary pads safe, and I should ask for them when I saw blood come out of my third hole. If not, then she would hand them over to me when I left for boarding school at the start of the following year. And she did.

Playing families and same-sex lovers

Arriving at boarding school in 1971 gave me another crucial experience: that 'playing families' also included 'playing same-sex lovers'. The game had been common in primary school, but my experience of it was that it was limited to families. There were many play-lovers in the girls' boarding houses when I arrived at Pholela High School. But it was clear to me and all of those observing that some of these play-play lovers were much more serious; this love was not a game for them.

I was a keen watcher. They kissed around corners of buildings in the dark, after study period, and inside the dormitories before lights out. Some of them even shared beds, and their movements under the covers left very little to the imagination. With my understanding of masturbation, this made complete sense to me.

Interestingly, no one ever spoke badly of this. No one was punished for it, in a school where we were punished for walking on the green lawn. Our transgressions were called out in public in the dining hall on Saturday mornings after breakfast. Not once in those three years did I hear of lovers being punished for kissing and sharing a bed. Nor did I hear students condemn the lovers either. In fact, we followed their stories and took sides when break-ups happened. I silently wished someone could ask me to be their play-play lover. No one did.

Here is a curious observation. Girls and boys were monitored during weekdays: they were allowed to stand and talk on the lawns between classrooms, in view of everyone. They never kissed. It was during the weekends, behind soccer-watching crowds, under the trees, that

I saw them kiss, hug and embrace. This meant that, to me, the play-play same-sex kissing game was more visible than the opposite-sex kissing game.[6] In my first year at boarding school I was introduced to same-sex love, lesbian love to be specific, as a natural phenomenon of life. It was only decades later that I heard stories of trauma from lesbians whose families went as far as disowning them.

It was in boarding school that I started hearing traumatic stories of menarche. Many girls talked about how no one had told them about menstruation, and how they found it a menacing experience because they associated blood with injury and death.

Infanticide at a tea farm on the hill

It may have been during my first or second year of holidays from boarding school when Mama told me the story of how a young woman at the tea farm on the hill had drowned her newborn infant in a bucketful of water. Again, she never blamed this young woman, who, I learned from Mama, had been *undabizekwayo*[iii] in our area. She told me that she needed to tell me this story as a reminder of the significance of choosing school and staying with it until I finished matric.

Gratitude in the kitchen

At the end of my matric year, even before we got our results, Mama instructed me to sit down in the kitchen one day. She began this conversation with the words: 'Thank you for finishing school. Everyone in this community told me that you would have a child before you had a matric certificate.' I can see the paint of pride on her face each time I remember this story. She handed over a piece of paper on which she had drawn a map of Richmond and the part

iii Loosely translated as 'making headline news'.

of town that had a contraception clinic. She showed it to me and said, 'When you feel ready to go there, just let me know.' When Mama talked about contraception, she called it by its English name, contraception. She did not use the words 'family planning'. That was not only important to me, it was liberating. By now, I had made up my mind that I would never get married nor have children.

I do not know why I never asked Mama what took her so long to talk about contraception. That is the conversation I thought she should have had with me when she told me about menstruation. I would like to think that she did this because she knew that sexual self-pleasure would delay my need, desire and curiosity about having sex with a boy. But then maybe she was just holding on to some vague hope that I would indeed never have sex with a boy.

This brief, serious, one-on-one mother-daughter conversation on contraception was the last building block of my feminist foundation. I had learned to pleasure myself sexually before I had my first menstrual period, before I learned about contraception, before I kissed anyone. I could speak about sex, sexual pleasure, pregnancy, birth, contraception and abortion in the same tone I used for talking about water, food, sport, school and the weather – because Mama made it so. None of this information on sex, sexual pleasure, pregnancy, birth and abortion was taught at school, in my time. Not once. Not even in high school. Mama made it possible for me to live as a feminist in so far as I knew about my body and had control over it, long before I came across the word feminism and read about it, and long before I made choices about work, activism and relationships.

Having revisited what I call the seeds of my feminism and how they are grounded in my body, I now move to the choices I made as an adult that allowed these seeds to bear feminist fruits. I share a few examples of these choices, and wish at this point to acknowledge and thank the many women I worked with at the ANC Women's Section office in Lusaka and back in Johannesburg, those at the Women's Health Project and at Ipas. I feel honoured to have been a part of feminist work that became building blocks for my later feminist praxis. A collective praxis underpinned most of the work we did, most of the time. While some of the feminist fruits of our collective work in the 1990s and early 2000s have rotted away and now live underground like corpses, some have continued to sprout, bearing even more fruits.

Abortion support for women

In 1977, I was in my first year as a student nurse at Edendale Nursing College in Pietermaritzburg, when one of my classmates asked me to accompany her to visit a doctor because she needed to 'get rid of this'. I agreed. When the doctor was done, he told me to come into the surgery and explained to me how I needed to support my friend. She had no complications. We were relieved. This abortion support story was the first of many that found me in my life, and I understood why: women found my matter-of-fact speech on these issues comforting and affirming.

There are many in-between anecdotes I could share, but the experience that confirmed for me the choice-based nature of abortion was when I was working in a ward called 3B2, where women who had complications from so-called backstreet abortions were nursed. Many had severe infections, and many died because they had come to hospital too late. Watching and talking – with those who could – made me realise that women are prepared to risk death if they do not want a pregnancy. They *will* make that choice.

Our Bodies, Ourselves: The book of my feminist affirmations

In the late 1980s, I worked as a broadcaster for Radio Freedom, a station for the ANC in Lusaka, Zambia. My favourite programme was one on book reviews, which I curated. The first half of the hour-long culture programme on Sunday afternoons was on music.

During the second half, I had the pleasure of reading, reviewing and talking about books. The preparations for my section involved reading at least three books each week so I could select one to review on Sunday. It was while I was in the ANC-run library that I came across *Our Bodies, Ourselves: A Book by and for Women*, published by The Boston Women's Health Book Collective in 1971.

This book changed my intellectual thinking in many ways. Firstly, it affirmed everything I had learned from Mama. It demonstrated a way of being for women where my nursing training had failed dismally. In *Our Bodies, Ourselves*, I read women's articulations of feminist perspectives on health that I wish I had learned about during training. In *Our Bodies, Ourselves*, women were taking control of their lives, using their personal experiences to write and envision a world '. . . made whole by their presence'.[7] Most importantly, this book underlined for me the fact that although the problematic nature of nursing training was an international phenomenon, it could be changed through feminist practices. From this book I remember reading:

> Relationships with men in this society have a built-in power imbalance, and few of us who have explored the possibilities of relationships between women would choose again *to start with that handicap* [my emphasis].[8]

A fact that is not often talked about in our current political climate is that women of the ANC Women's Section in exile infused the draft constitution for a future South Africa, which the ANC had put together, with its feminist perspectives. To give just one example, it was from the lawyer and comrade Brigitte Mabandla that I first heard that freedom of sexual orientation ought to be inserted into the Constitution and the Bill of Rights. While my readings from *Our Bodies, Ourselves* were confirming the international nature of same-sex attraction and intimacy, the conversations we had as women within the ANC motivated for the inclusion of sex/gender and sexual orientation as specific grounds against which people should not be discriminated in a democratic South Africa.

Back in South Africa in October 1990, when the first Gay Pride March took place in Hillbrow, my job that day was to participate in the march so I could report back to my comrades in the office on Monday. I worked as a journalist for the ANC Women's Section Task Force, as we called ourselves then. I walked from my flat in Hillbrow to the starting point of the march, listened to the speeches, walked, took notes; and all the time, the images of girls kissing against walls after the evening study periods back at school flashed through my mind. Magical memory flashes dotted the kaleidoscopic images of that historic march on the streets of Johannesburg.

On body-centred feminist practice

The work I did from 1991 to 2003 at the Women's Health Project (WHP) and Ipas made logical sense to me career-wise. It made even more sense from my feminist and political perspectives. It was while working at the WHP that I fully appreciated the value of Mama's straightforward talk and clarity about the anatomy and physiology of the body. At the WHP I listened to innumerable tragic stories from women about how absence of information and misinformation about how their bodies worked had led not only to confusion, shame, embarrassment and trauma, but also to what they recognised, in retrospect, were bad decisions. These bad decisions may have seemed trite at the time but, for some women, had irreversible, negative and lifelong consequences. One constant and glaring piece of misinformation was that it was impossible to get pregnant through first intercourse. Numerous women told stories of choosing to carry their pregnancy through even though it had not been planned. And many spoke about the conflictual and guilt-ridden motherhood they experienced as they had not been ready for pregnancy. Numerous women shared stories of how they had allowed themselves to 'give their men sex' even when they did not feel like it, because they had accepted society's teaching that that's what girlfriends and wives ought to do.

The most memorable story was told to me by a woman during one of the gender and health training workshops I co-facilitated with Emelda Boikanyo. A woman who had been married for a long time and had children – I will call her Limakatso – told us the story of how when she had her first orgasm, she left her husband asleep in bed and went to the kitchen to be on her own. She wondered what had just happened to her, thinking she might have been bewitched, shocked that her body was capable of giving her so much ecstasy; pleasure so inexplicable she didn't even know how to describe it to us. No one, she said emphatically, had ever mentioned to her that there was a thing like that, an orgasm. So there she was, totally confused instead of celebrating. How many Limakatsos are still out there in the world?

It is this story that motivated me to introduce the topic of masturbation during our training sessions. These workshops often ran for three to five days. If there was someone, and often it was more than half the group, who had not masturbated, I gave them hotel homework, and they reported on it the next day. It was also mind-blowing to find out just how many women had never used a mirror to look at their genitalia.[9] Is it possible to be a feminist who doesn't know anything about their body?

The history of the WHP and the work it did still needs systematic and dedicated archiving. Starting with the groundbreaking Women's Health Conference of 1994, to the *South African Women's Health Handbook* published in 1996, to the numerous training materials we developed and published, as well as the monthly newsletter which circulated in South Africa and internationally: all this material resulted in many policies being implemented by government. This included the extraordinary victory that led to the enactment of the Choice of Termination of Pregnancy Act, No. 92 of 1996 (CTOP Act). The nationwide spread of accessible information on women's bodies, their sexual and reproductive health and rights to the grassroots level represented significant feminist strides for the period, when most activists were committed to working towards changes based on the Constitution and the Bill of Rights. Without the lessons from Mama, I doubt I would have made the choice to work at the WHP, let alone stay for nine years and three months!

Training midwives for abortion services

My decision in 2000 to take on a job as the first country director of Ipas, an international NGO headquartered in Chapel Hill, North Carolina, was made matter-of-factly. This was the job that was to make possible the implementation of the CTOP Act of 1996. It was a natural career progression. Midwives needed to be trained on a massive scale to do manual vacuum aspirations of foetuses in order for abortion services to be accessible within the public health sector. The numerous challenges – protests, debates and court cases – that surrounded the formulation and subsequent implementation of the CTOP Act are material for a stand-alone book. Here was a moment in South African history when the most highly contested feminist topic – abortion – was at the centre of public discourse; and Mama's concept of women having choices over their own bodies solidified within me, effortlessly.

Writing and feminism

Reading saved my life. Clichéd as this is, it is true for me. Even as reading was saving my life during my late teens and early 20s, I had neither plans nor dreams to become a writer, let alone facilitate the writing of others. This poem came to me many decades later:

These hands
now caress the keyboard,
fondle pens

that massage papers,

weaning fear,

weaving words,

wishing with every fingerprint

that this relationship

will last forever.[10]

It has been over a decade since my first poetry collection, *These Hands*, was published, and this final stanza speaks of the current tool of my feminist praxis, writing. But it is the facilitation of the writing of others I wish to approach as I end this chapter. Why? Because therein lies the essence of my collective approach to feminism. I have found indescribable satisfaction in facilitating the creative work of aspirant writers and those who just want to tell their stories without necessarily aiming to become professional writers.

The three anthologies that I worked on with Karen Martin – *Queer Africa: New and Collected Fiction*; *Queer Africa 2: New Stories*; and *Queer Africa: Selected Stories* – are predominantly filled with work from aspirational writers and some established writers. *Proudly Malawian: Life Stories from Lesbian and Gender-Nonconforming Individuals* and *Like the Untouchable Wind: An Anthology of Poems* are the result of writing workshops with individuals who just wanted to tell their life stories, and were excited to be guided through the process. These two collaborative projects were responses to silencing and downright discrimination against lesbians in Malawi and Zimbabwe. Designing writing exercises, facilitating the writing during the workshops, and later working on the drafts produced with individuals via email resulted in feminist book projects that were not only groundbreaking in their approach, but also affirming of intersectional queer and feminist activism.

The most recent anthology I've worked on, *Our Words, Our Worlds: Writing on Black South African Women Poets, 2000–2018*, while unapologetically feminist, also focuses on poetry, a genre often viewed as marginal and obscure and, for the capitalist world, commercially unviable. However, it is this genre that allows individual acts by poets and demonstrates their contribution to literary history. *Our Words, Our Worlds* tells the story of the seismic shift that transformed South African national culture through poetry, becoming the first of its kind to explore the history and impact of poetry by Black women, in their own voices. It straddles disciplines: literary theory, feminism, history of the book and politics while using literary critique, personal essays and interviews as genres of telling. In her introduction, Gabeba Baderoon asserts that this book 'is a result of a mind that has asked what freedom looks like for Black women writers'.[11]

These books are examples of a commitment to a feminist agenda that has led to projects previously unheard of in our worlds. They are my latest addition to my growing feminist praxis: acts of seeding, watering and nurturing new fruits to add to the feminist fruit salad. Through this work, the background music of body-centredness has played incessantly, continuing to ground my praxis.

In closing

Mama made sure in the way she raised me that I did not start my life with a handicap. The body-centredness of information I internalised during childhood and my teenage years grounded the way in which I understood and navigated the world. Moving from the body to intellectual, political and emotional levels of human engagement and interaction could not be anything but feminist. I have Mama – Glenrose Nomvula Mbatha – to thank for that; and I have a suspicion that she has her father, my Mkhulu – Alban Hamilton S. Mbatha – to thank for her feminist ideals.

CHAPTER 19

Bringing Water to Krotoa's Gardens: Decolonisation as Direct Action

Yvette Abrahams

Friends, let's talk, laugh a little and shed a tear
or two over tea/See those crumbs over
there/it's enough dough to bake a cake
to serve a different reality today.[1]

Colonialism could be so overwhelmingly patriarchal. Jan van Riebeeck no doubt did not see the irony when he observed, in his diary entry for 28 and 29 April 1656:

Fine sunshine, wind variable; a lot of carrots put into the ground, and a morgen of ground sown with wheat. The rainy season having commenced the time has arrived to prepare the empty plots and new acres, and fill them with European seeds; work zealously commenced.[2]

From the indigenous point of view, his actions seemed ludicrous. In the vicinity of the clay-and-wood fort his troops had built, the ground, already filled with local plants providing a wide variety of food, medicine and cosmetics, was cleared, dug up, and replanted with 'European seed', which regularly keeled over in the wind or dried out in our hot dry summers. With indigenous plants, the autumn was traditionally a season of harvest, where the clans gathered much before their annual migration north and eastwards. In Van Riebeeck's diary, it is a season of scarcity and hard work, recovering from drought and ploughing new ground for sowing. A better metaphor for how colonialism created the violence of poverty from abundance cannot be imagined.

As a farmer practising indigenous knowledge systems, I have begun to see more and more starkly how absurd European farming is, simply from doing its opposite. Apart from an initial deep-trenching, made necessary by the fact that this land has been exploited for 367 years and does not possess an atom of humus in it, this earth is never dug. Instead I layer wood, manure, grass and any other organic matter I can get on the earth. Plants are allowed to die in place; any food taken from the garden is replaced by an equivalent amount of compost. There is a very friendly coffee shop down the road which gives me coffee grounds for my worm farms. I fetch it when I shop for groceries, so lots of nutrients are provided for zero additional carbon. I also compost family green waste, once again bringing buckets home from town as I pass by on my visits. I brew effective micro-organisms to replace the microbial ecology destroyed by centuries of patriarchy, and watch the plants beginning to sing a natural mystic.

Much of my farming consists of the technique called 'chop and drop' made famous by permaculture, where plants specifically grown for their vigour and the substances they bio-accumulate are cut regularly and placed around the roots of crops. This keeps the soil cool, increases its water-holding capacity, and breaks down, gradually enriching soil life. In this way I decolonise this land one square metre at a time. It is a slow process. I have been busy for 13 years and it might take another five before I can call this garden mature, fruitful and, in spirit, something like the garden Van Riebeeck dug up and burned. Sometimes, in areas which have been worked intensely, I can walk and feel the ground spring under my feet, touching the thick duff slowly created. Then I know what it is to walk like a free person. A deep ancestral feeling in the soles of my feet lets me know I have achieved something worthwhile with my life. To restore one hectare of land to its decolonised state is the highest life purpose I can imagine.

This place is not paradise, far from it. It is just an average African smallholding of one hectare, kept going by off-farm income diversification. Like millions of migrant labourers, I have travelled far at times to earn the money required to restore this land back to health. It is the labour of my hands and brain that restores what colonialism destroyed, not reparations.

This place began when, after 13 years of researching these plants from within higher education institutions, I grew tired of reading about them. I desired to touch them, feel them, hold them in my hands, and make the salves and ointments I had read about. I bought this land and spent another 13 years educating myself on how to rebuild ecosystems. In order to generate income, I started a small business making handmade soap and body products based on KhoeSan traditions. I have continued the work of understanding colonialism in a deeper way by producing its opposite. The more I made soap, the more I understood how the industrial use of petrochemicals in cosmetics after the Second World War, like so many other processes arising out of the need to make money off research investments, was harmful to our bodies. We have gone from feeling health as a natural state to a variety of itches, sores, lesions and breakouts that I see every day in my business. I sometimes wonder how much it weakens the feminist movement that so much of our energy is devoted to enduring or healing from illness. It is all coming out now, as the first generation who has bathed from babyhood in these substances and are now in ageing, ailing bodies. In an effort to render ourselves 'hygienic', we douse our bodies in substances that cause cancer and a multitude of skin diseases.[3] We buy cars and emit carbon as we transport ourselves to shops where we can buy these things with money earned while suffering the ravages of a colonial education system and workplace. We get depressed when we find ourselves sustaining the system in order to earn this money. As if, in Gabeba Baderoon's words, Black women have bought into the colonial 'formulation of inherent deviance and infinite reparability'.[4] Baderoon makes this point in a different context, in relation to the evolution of the prison-industrial complex in South Africa; still, it rings true when one observes the pains we undergo in order to render ourselves assimilable. I have no intention of exempting myself from this general conclusion. In fact, even phrasing it is the result of years of hard work. I learn all this in undoing it, in growing herbs on the farm, making cosmetics in the solar cooker, and using them on my skin. Centimetre by centimetre my body begins to feel decolonised, brain cell by brain cell I begin to appreciate just how deeply I have been colonised. I am much struck by Desiree Lewis's observation that

> analysis, strategising and goal-setting around violence have become the subject of feminists' rigorous questioning . . . They point out the inherently authoritarian, violent or flawed context in which legal and other regulating and public protecting or opinion-making mechanisms (including the media) operate.
>
> I have been struck by the courage of feminists recently raising these concerns. I find them courageous because they speak out at a time when – it often seems to me – being 'seen-to-be- feminist' is equal to *not* asking challenging questions about how power works in intersectional, self-identity-making, contextually-specific and relational ways.[5]

Of course, if we don't ask how power operates in relation to the personal and most private spaces of our bodies, then we become incapable of asking how it manifests in those same spaces. So instead of being outraged at the notion that our movement has reached the point where one can appear to be a feminist without challenging power in every minute detail, I act. For me, it is no use being conscious of the harm petrochemicals do to women without making an effort to be present with alternatives, especially at a time when the soap business is vastly expanding its direct sales to the public. So, I call the city council and ask for a spot to sell my handmade organic soaps, made with local plants, directly to the public at the Company's Gardens – these very same gardens which Van Riebeeck colonised. It seems appropriate: the ground zero of colonialism, so to speak. The official I speak to tells me that I can send in an application, but it is unlikely to be processed soon, because the informal (South African–speak for illegal) traders who are already there will receive first preference. That being the case, it seems to me urgent to immediately become an informal trader myself. I pick a nice spot right behind Parliament and start business.

In KhoeSan culture every !nau (transition) requires that you be led by somebody who has been there before. As I sit in the Gardens, I can feel Krotoa's spirit still roaming there. She was a 'servant' in the house of Van Riebeeck and was, amongst many other things, the first Khoe-speaking woman to learn Dutch. As Krotoa began the first steps of transition which would end in our complete colonisation – that level where we oppress ourselves – it seems apposite that she guides me through this turning of the wheel, because it occurs to me that I am actually decolonising. In my culture land cannot be owned, all the land is Godde's and one only holds it in trust for future generations. But in a non-possessive sense, the metre of land that my stall occupies is mine. I pay no white man for it. The wheel turns upwards. It is a tremendous spiritual experience.

Somewhere around this time, I finally begin to read Sarah Malotane Henkeman's courageous work. It dismantles the last vestiges of colonialism in my mind because it helps me see how much I have been complicit in my own oppression. Her field is peace research, and what floors me completely is her description of invisible or structural violence. It is an apt concept through which to explore the damage women have done to their bodies through their use of synthetic chemicals. Not in the abstract, but in intimate daily detail as women begin to pass the stall and show me various bodily mutilations which up to now they had thought were inborn or inescapable. It is incredible how large a role skin plays in our perception of ourselves.

What blew my head apart was the way Henkeman demonstrates our level of complicity in the creation of structural violence. She argues that middle-class denial plays a large role in upholding those structures which subject us to a constant matrix of violence from which the occasional rape or murder emerges. She forces us to take a broader, deeper, wider, longer look at the factors that normalise violence in our society:

> When we say . . . that we want to disrupt denial about invisible/visible violence and the trauma it generates, we mean that we want to expose the links between past and present political, social and economic arrangements that shape individual lives . . . even if we lock up every single individual who commits violent acts today, the system will continue to produce violent individuals who will take out their impotent rage on those closest to them, and the most vulnerable in society.[6]

This is something which all feminists seeking to end gender-based violence might do well to consider. Beyond that, feminists, especially middle-class ones, must consider their role in building those structures of violence. Henkeman's study of social development workers in Cape Town enabled her to develop a typology of the denial we all seem to be living in to a greater or lesser degree. In her research, she interviewed peace practitioners who all seemed to be aware of colonialism as structural violence, but who then manage to do nothing about it through various sophisticated methods of denial. To them, structural violence exists in the abstract, but not in the concrete. They have the knowledge, but they choose not to apply it. One can speak of colonialism in the same way. You can recognise the structures at play in colonialism but not recognise it in the everyday acts of living, the things that we choose to inflict on our bodies. For example, how applying aluminium to one's underarms as deodorant is a risk viewed as justifiable. Even though one could develop Alzheimer's, the pressure not to smell of sweat and appear hygienic is stronger.

Practitioners would also choose the 'We know, but . . .' option – namely, where knowledge exists in theory but not in practice. Henkeman calls this 'trained blindness', where '[a]spects of professional training leads to filtering out of information that is inconsistent with the criminal law definition of violence that holds only the individual responsible'.[7] So we might be aware that weed-killer products can cause cancer. Yet, we do not collectively organise against local government spraying toxic chemicals on our sidewalks. We might walk right past the municipal worker spraying the chemical, most likely to be its first victim, on our way to the supermarket to buy organic food.

Henkeman lists many other forms of denial, but perhaps most relevant for my purposes here is the one she names 'knowing and not-acting'. She writes about how some practitioners revealed that they were 'overwhelmed by the "too huge" challenges presented by structural violence, so they do not include it' in the way they work.[8] This is something I observed in parts of the feminist movement for years, where it often takes the shape of choosing a form of resistance that is bound to be ineffective. We could demand, for instance, longer jail sentences for rapists, a measure that

- is based on the philosophical assumptions that a patriarchal state is going to care about protecting us and that pushing it to do so represents the best use of our energies;

- reinforces notions of Black men as inherently violent and enslaves them to the prison-industrial complex; and
- does absolutely nothing about the structural violence Black women are subjected to on a daily basis, which renders them more vulnerable to more violence: poverty, inferiority/ superiority complexes, racism, homophobia, etc.

In this way, people can be comfortable in their activism without challenging patriarchy in meaningful ways. Structures of violence remain unaddressed while we all walk home from the rallies and speeches feeling that we have 'done something'. Whether this is about protecting class privilege or simply a deep-seated fear of the unknown, I know not. All I know is that I now question every proposed event I am invited to, in order to understand whether it addresses structural, qualitative change, or is a way to make us feel better while we continue to enjoy middle-class privilege.

I am not saying that individual actions do not make a difference. What I am saying is that one can choose to act against the system, or to treat the individual as if they were the problem. I am not saying that we should not take individual responsibility for our actions. What Henkeman has taught me is that this principle extends to the ways in which we each uphold the system through denial.

Be warned, once the eyes are open it is impossible to close them again. I discovered that I had for years been blind to the system because if I had to be aware of the depth of my oppression, I would not have been able to live. To see the violence of the system with clear eyes is a soul-searing experience that taxes my strength to the utmost. Because it is everywhere and all the time, in the earthworms and micro-organisms that are missing in our ecosystem, and in the herbicides which are killing bees. I could produce a long list of the 'feminists' who would never dream of purchasing or using a single bar of my home-made soap, yet blithely spend a small fortune on soap and cosmetics that are commercially produced and bear big brand names.

On an intellectual level they can make the connections between global multinationals founded in colonialism, but can't practise the way we are taking back what patriarchy stole one bar of soap at a time. Or I could talk about the violence I have seen feminists do to themselves and each other in the movement, because the concept of hierarchy itself seems to be something to which we remain inescapably wedded. It is easier to write papers on decolonisation than to act. Is it easier to praise each other for our fine words than to ask, 'What are we doing?'

I do not mean to set up an opposition between words and deeds or individual versus collective actions. In a womanist frame, the answer to 'either/or' is usually 'both'. What I am drawing attention to is the way we use these seeming opposites to avoid accomplishing effective change. It is a problematic issue I have dealt with for a long time in relation to climate change. I fly when I do off-farm income diversification work. I used to plant a tree or two for every flight but soon ran out of space. Now I work on increasing levels of humus in the soil – but can undo a month's work in one transatlantic flight.

The farm truck takes diesel for a reason, and I look forward to producing biodiesel for it in time. But I look at my house, trying to imagine it plastic-free, and get weak. It is going to take at least a decade. The notion of disrupting denial helped me see the feeling of weakness for what it was. Reducing carbon emissions is something we can all do. Should there be no functioning ecosystem for the next generation of feminists, we are all complicit. Yes, the ultimate cause is a white supremacist heteropatriarchal capitalist system that uses the earth as if her resources were not finite. Yet we are the proximate causes through our enslavement to the system. It is here that the opportunity for new forms of activism must arise, measures which accomplish system change one act at a time.

I myself could not have read Henkeman's work with compassion if I had not been land-occupying at the time. I still experience long periods of denial. It is, after all, the way I have lived and been expensively trained to do so my whole life. Denial is a comfort zone that enables me to survive oppression.

After much prayer and communion on this topic, I start quietly laying mulch and pouring micro-organisms on the strip of soil behind our stall. I greet the plants and explain that soon we shall be an active ecosystem again. I start bringing a bowl of water to Krotoa's Gardens. The water in the one and only public toilet got switched off in 2019 during the drought in Cape Town, and every city council amenity replaced running taps with hand sanitiser that is pure petrochemical evil in a bottle. A feature of my soap stall is open pots of ointment which anybody can test. After a few days, homeless people and sex workers started stopping off, complaining of a pimple here, an itch there, a lesion in some other place. As time went by, they became more courageous in helping themselves. These are the people who were deprived of water when the taps were closed. How they drink, I know not. For me, decolonisation has become the very act of filling a drum from my rainwater tank and carting it into the city centre where my stall stands. I find myself becoming more and more adept at communicating non-verbally. Here is the water of life. Be welcome.

Living a Radical African Feminist Life: A Journey to Sufficiency Through Contemporarity

Patricia McFadden

Every now and then, as the result of a personal encounter that has brought me tremendous joy or sadness, or as the outcome of an intense struggle with some patriarchal institution or socio-cultural force, I find myself at a conjuncture in my feminist consciousness and lived reality.* I realise that I am in a new place in my creative imagination and social circumstances. This sense of consciousness is what I understand as being at the cutting edge, consciously positioned in the shift as it occurs around one and within oneself. Over the years, I have learned to stop and take a careful, curious look inside my feminist self and acknowledge that I am growing intellectually and politically. I take time to scrutinise the material and political terrains which encompass each particular moment. Learning to recognise the flutter of change inside one is always very rewarding in thinking and pleasuring terms.

---

* This chapter is republished by permission of the copyright holder, and the present publisher, Duke University Press. www.dukeupress.edu. This chapter first appeared as Patricia McFadden, 'Contemporarity: Sufficiency in a Radical African Feminist Life', in *Meridians* 17, no. 2 (2018): 415–431.

It is this sense of consciousness which is a key element in my notion of *becoming* contemporary – of imagining and shaping the identity and political content of 'Contemporarity', which is the pulse of current African feminist theorising and activism.[1] Over the past decade, as a response to the inadequacy of feminism as a universal politics of women's resistance to patriarchal repression, and because of the seepage of nationalist ideology into feminist discourses on the continent, I have begun searching for an alternative feminist sensibility within the African context.

Initially, I started with a critique of liberal declarations and practices of citizenship, which keep the majority of women outside the ambit of laws and protections that are supposed to be universal entitlements. The realisation that women would have to reinvent the notion and practice of citizenship was a spark that set me on a new journey towards thinking about how African women must achieve Contemporarity. The notion of the contemporary is run through by debates of modernity and Westernism on the one hand. On the other is the inevitable backlash this elicits among African nationalists, those passionately searching for the authentic African male identity, which lies at the heart of nationalism and neo-colonialism.

While I am aware of some of the lively, extensive debates around the notions and practices of nationalism, nationhood, third world feminism, and transnational feminism beyond the terrains of the West, Aniko Imre's definition of nationalism lies closest to my own critical theoretical stance towards this male-defined ideology and practice:

It has been well established that the *we* of nationalism implies a homosocial form of male bonding that includes women only symbolically, most prominently in the trope of the mother . . . nationalist discourses are especially eager to reassert the 'natural' division of labour between the sexes and to relegate women to traditional reproductive roles.[2]

However, being critical of nationalism and citizenship did not translate into a new and different consciousness. I needed to reimagine a different concept of rights, dignity and, eventually, wellness and sufficiency, and how this can translate into real changes in our lives. Contemporarity is not conceived as the opposite of the modern or the Western. It is about finding the innovative feminist energies and sensibilities that will enable each of us to live the new politics of this moment in African time. Therefore, I found the notion of spatial intimacy both fascinating and illuminating in terms of my own positioning at the interface of new consciousness and radical living. I felt a visceral intellectual familiarity with Nthabiseng Motsemme's reading of 'violence and place', which helped me lean more closely towards the yearning for new spaces of intellectual feminist discourse and solidarity.[3] Such radical thinking about the interactions of black women with colonial and neo-colonial infrastructures of patriarchal power, privilege and dominance can enable new creative conceptual terrains. Thinking like this opens up possibilities of different explanations of hegemonic masculinist supremacy and practice.

Sometimes I become aware of the shift in my intellectual and organic feelings about a particular issue with which I have battled for as long as I have had a feminist consciousness. Take, for example, the vexatious persistence and escalation of hetero-impunity and violation against mainly women of all ages. For many years in my activist writing and engagement with this expression of patriarchal supremacy, I felt the injustice of sexual impunity viscerally – in my core. My responses were largely reflective of an essentialist existentialism of outrage, accompanied by a sense of helplessness about how effectively to respond to this enormously destructive phenomenon. More recently, however, I have realised that my responses to incidents of heteropatriarchal violation – recounted daily in the media – have become habitual. One expects to hear about it with each news bulletin. It becomes the norm within one's feminist listening. One still feels the outrage, particularly when the incident is especially egregious, and one is overwhelmed by a sense of deep sorrow. But the seeming inevitability of women being violated creates a learned response, which translates into a tendency to 'lean sideways' so as to let the information pass by as the day moves on.

No doubt within women's organisations, which work to find adequate political responses to patriarchal violation, the struggle to protect women and demand accountability from the State and its representatives is an everyday challenge. However, not all radical women operate within the context of organisations and formal political structures. Here I reflect on my own internal political stagnation and moments of growth as a feminist who has stepped back from the established sites of nationalist gendered women's movements/organisations.

The initial inkling that a gap had developed between my radical sensibilities regarding patriarchal violation and actively finding ways to resist such violation came while attending tribunals on women's narrations of hurt and grief about what they had experienced. I felt uneasy about being part of what seemed to be a kind of voyeurism that fed on women's pain, in spite of the insistence by other feminists that women should be able to expose violations within safe spaces that are created by, and for, women. This initial sense of dis-ease has persisted, propelling me to examine its roots within my own experiences as a gendered woman growing up in a deeply patriarchally feudal society in Eswatini. Upon reflection on the events that have wounded me, as well as the adoption of a radically critical feminist perspective on hetero-violation, I felt a shift in my own consciousness about violation, impunity and supremacy. Making the personal political in an actively subjective manner, which nurtures my political consciousness and sense of protectiveness, signalled the enduring relevance of core feminist mantras and principles.

By returning to these core notions of feminist theorising about patriarchal power and privilege, I realised that, for example, publishing incidents of sexual violation had become a business prop for many newspapers. It keeps the circulation numbers up and provides a perverse form of voyeuristic entertainment for the public, who seem to have become inured to the horrors of brutality that little girls and older women endure, largely in working-class communities.

The sense of collective helplessness about how to solve the problem of violence hangs heavily between a moralistic outrage and the urgent need for a critical understanding of patriarchy as a brutal and dehumanising system. Feminists know that bemoaning the loss of culture or the impact of Westernisation will not answer fundamental questions regarding impunity and misogyny. Critical thinking about the interfaces between heteropatriarchal supremacy and impunity, as well as the rampant plunder and mauling of any female body, will have to be imagined and located within key discursive and activist sites across the African continent. As Pumla Dineo Gqola succinctly put it during an interview:

I think we need to collectively re-invest in the value of critical thinking. It's not just nationally that there is a general consumerist, lazy, dumbing down and conformist culture. It is global, so we need to be quite mindful of this even as we cultivate critical thinking as valuable at the local level.[4]

Increasing male activism around issues of violation seems to indicate a long overdue response on the part of men who are beginning to reimagine their masculinities and identities as black men. However, a large section of this activism is being influenced by sensibilities of shame and moral indictment driven by the twin right-wing forces of the Initiatives of Change organisation (formerly the Moral Re-Armament Movement) and Christian fundamentalism. These reactionary energies create a sense of 'male exceptionalism' rather than leading to the kinds of political clarity and consciousness which are required to resolve the challenges presented by patriarchal supremacy and men's sexual privilege.

One of the most effective mechanisms that patriarchy deploys against femaleness is the claim that our creativity, imaginations, and sensibilities of freedom and pleasure are taboo and must be suppressed. From girlhood, we are taught and we learn obedience. We learn how to suppress our uniqueness as girls and women and to dress it up in all sorts of excuses and performances, so that we eventually become the un-imagining custodians and gatekeepers of patriarchal privilege and power:

> If women are in many ways socialized into submissiveness from the earliest age by rape and the threat of rape, whole peoples can be trained to intellectual passivity through invasive systems of knowledge.[5]

I believe that we never lose our instinct to be free. Every time I draw on my childhood refusals to be engineered into a conforming girl, I resuscitate an instinct which continues to infuse my entire feminist political consciousness with rebelliousness. Within the often overwhelming existence of being a woman in heteropatriarchal societies everywhere, performing radical actions daily to remain outside the quagmire of patriarchal conformity becomes a necessary tactic of human autonomy and feminist resistance.

As feminists, we know this narrative well and many of us resent the historical fact that we were taught how to become patriarchalised women. We experience patriarchy's constraints and suppressions each day in intimate and public encounters, yet to a great extent we still allow this reality to define our lives. This collusive stance remains a major challenge for all women. Unlearning is a difficult and daunting task. So many women catch a glimpse of the possibilities of crafting new identities for themselves that are based on a sense of freedom from the control of men. But often, at some point during their lifetimes, they revert to being 'good and decent' women, and, sometimes, it seems that they are relieved at having returned to the fold of patriarchal solace and the rewards of being acceptable. The fear of being unaccepted and, therefore, inauthentic functions as another leveller of women's political imaginations. All African women are still expected to aspire to be good mothers, wives, daughters, sisters and grandmothers. If they cannot be totally self-sacrificing, then at least they should perform the parody of being women in the African cultural sense.

I continue to be challenged by these repressive forces, and to struggle, often alone, to retrieve my instincts of freedom and well-being. In so doing I have come to understand that being free of patriarchy in new ways is essential to my dignity as a woman. I cannot experience pleasure as an intellectual and creative force without crafting and living a life of feminist dignity. Generally, I think that the compromise with African feudo-patriarchy remains the most critical challenge and impediment to the freedom and dignity of black women. However, in this context, I will not be speaking to women generally, because I understand that indulging in the generalities of woman-ness is another noose around the necks of radical women.

What I am referring to as a compromise with feudal patriarchy in the African context – and beyond, in the wider diaspora – is a conceptual and political essentialism that we have inherited from nationalism. It is baggage that has distracted us from the critical work that we owe to ourselves. When women are free, our communities and societies benefit too. At the same time, it is a deeply entrenched marker of learned patriarchy to need to save everyone as though our lives depended on it, which they do not. Thinking, speaking and undertaking activism in terms of large, all-encompassing programmes is not only dangerously idealistic – after all, women are differentiated by class, race, gender, age, social location, ability, sexual identity, etc. – but it is also deeply nationalistic and reactionary. This is the ideological bridle that male nationalists have kept fastened to our political vocality and language. Imagining original, autonomously radical political forms and discourses while positioning our politics as wide-open platforms onto which everyone is welcomed feeds the altruism and self-abnegation that is an enduring hallmark of reactionary nationalist ideology. One can get caught up in the traps that nationalist ideology sets for us, through the construction of female politics as an extension of men's interests and privilege.

Just the realisation that the time for a different kind of feminism has arrived, one which puts the individual black woman at the centre of its epistemology and lived aesthetic, creates a deep rupture with the intimate hold that nationalism has had over black feminist politics and activism. The ripple effects of our lived freedoms and dignity should not be a consequence from which we take incidental pleasure. It should be a deliberate act of self-nurturing. In appraising my journey to a radical sensibility, two main sources of propulsion seem to stand out. First, stepping away from the nationalist African women's movement a decade ago was an important gesture of self-rescue. Second, redefining retrieval as a reclamation of my black female sexual and bodily integrity enabled a life of dignity and wellness.

Retrieving the feminist imagination

Before I stepped away, I started to notice that much of the thinking and activist language which feminists were using was in reality defined and controlled by gender activists who had mainstreamed feminist concepts but stripped them of their radical political content and meaning. For example, GBV (gender-based violence) has systematically and insistently replaced concepts of heteropatriarchal violence, domestic violence or sexual violence, let alone the more powerful notions of patriarchal impunity and violation in discussions regarding the integrity of women's bodies. GBV is an outcome of the softer, less discomforting, conservative discourses of gender mainstreaming, which comes out of the technocratic vocabulary of the UN and other global status quo structures. What is politically astounding is the ease with which this new 'UN-speak' has gained hegemony in the media, within the academy, in women's organisations and across our social landscapes. The acronym has become so ubiquitous that people do not even stop to consider what it actually means in conceptual and activist terms.

This neo-liberal and reactionary linguistic technology is both conceptually limited and theoretically ineffectual. It has systematically shut down the debates and passions which had driven women's radical demands on the State and the UN system, transforming most women intellectuals into gender activists. Women's bodily and sexual integrity have been replaced by structural and policy concerns expressed through a language that does not enable women to acquire a deeper consciousness of entitlements, rights or protections. The main protagonists of the response to violence against women and girls have become the State and the UN system, as opposed to women's organisations and radical groups. The latter have been shunted to the edges of social engagement and have been largely silenced. Language can either be an effective weapon in instilling conformity in people, especially in women, or it can serve as an open doorway to intellectual and personal freedoms. What you say, and the tone you use, can still get you killed in many societies across the world today. Language and words are, importantly, about power and access to financial and social resources. In the context of gender mainstreaming, the language one utilises indicates whether that woman can get a lucrative consultancy or not. In most instances, class and social reproduction trump any memory of radical thinking and activism against patriarchy.

Therefore, in this deeply problematic context, retrieving the powerful language and passion of feminist agency becomes a necessity for fulfilling the possibilities of new imaginaries. Personally, I refuse to use the depoliticised terminology of GBV and instead take every opportunity to speak out against its hegemony in women's conversations and debates. For African women, the persistent insertion of 'cutting/ surgery' to erase 'mutilation' in the radical language of female genital mutilation presents another such dangerous strategy to change the meaning and content of the debate, and silence the demand for bodily and sexual integrity.[6]

A radical process of retrieval is, thus, critical to imagining differently. It is by engaging in retrieval that we begin to redefine language as a feminist prerogative and initiate the new contemporary African feminism. Imbuing the notion of retrieval with a deliberately feminist sense of ownership and agency is also an intimate conceptual act. It enables one to instigate alternative theoretical, activist and existential trajectories, using the possibilities of this crucial moment in the neo-colonial conjuncture to redirect our lives. I say this deliberately because I know that such shifts in consciousness and personal reality come seldom during one's life. The personal opportunities that women have created through struggles against patriarchy – as feudalism, capitalism, settler and other colonialisms, and their practically and ideologically exploitative infrastructures – will be lost if we do not anticipate the future in new ways. What tomorrow becomes depends on how we perceive it and what we do to define and live it differently.

Stepping away to lean forward

In thinking about the challenges that face us as feminists now, I have found that the gesture of stepping back – in a personal and conceptual sense – enables one to understand more clearly the dominant hegemonies and their impacts on feminism. In clarifying the definition of the State in neo-imperial and neo-colonial terms, M. Jacqui Alexander argues:

> While differently located, both neo-imperial state formations (those advanced capitalist states that are the dominant partners in the global 'order') and neo-colonial state formations (those that emerged from the colonial 'order' as the forfeiters to nationalist claims to sovereignty and autonomy) are central to our understandings of the production of hegemonies.[7]

This implies the need to adopt a very critical conceptual and activist stance in relation to nationalism, the State, and towards black men. For me, taking a step back from the subjectivities and surveillances of nationalism and gendered nationalist conservatism was essential in reimagining what being contemporary, African and feminist could mean.

Many black women of my generation found their voices and political sensibilities through the resistance against white colonial patriarchy. We brought our resentment of African feudal and colonial patriarchal oppression to the broad platforms which male nationalists had created and crafted for their own masculinist political agendas. In the course of struggle, we learned to adapt and adjust our political imaginaries to the larger project of independence for all Africans. Unfortunately, we retained the ideological infrastructures of nationalist politics and its compromises with black feudo-patriarchy, as a means of reiterating our black femininity and Africanness, which remained deeply conservative and politically reactionary.

In this context, many women activists and scholars learned how to manipulate the opportunities which the neo-colonial moment presented through the organisations that comprised what was called the African Women's Movement. This site became a deeply contested and often brutal terrain. The radical agencies of feminists were conveniently applauded when it suited the agendas of the donors and the gender activists, or were vilified and driven out, often through homophobic malice, outright lies and malignant rumour-mongering.[8] This signalled the profound ideological and structural crisis of women's collusive relationships with feudo-patriarchal state occupants at the national and continental levels. The upward mobility of a small clique of black women who fought ferociously to retain their middle-class status and the material wealth associated with gendered mainstreaming is one of the most significant expressions of the demise of gendered nationalist organising. Most of those who fought against radical ideas in women's organisations have become well-paid functionaries in global state structures and donor-driven initiatives. For the majority of African women, however, life has remained basically what it has always been – precarious, vulnerable and unjust.

Once again, the lesson learned is a clearer understanding of nationalism as a masculinist ideology and identity, and its translation into black ruling-class power within and outside the State. The more important illumination from this experience is realising the necessity of returning to the source – a feminist consciousness that is unencumbered by the conservative instincts and acquisitiveness of nationalism.[9] As a collective ideology and mobilising strategy, nationalism never professed to being the means for black women's freedoms. Feminists imbued nationalism with a radicalism which it did not possess or aspire to, and we have paid a high price for that idealism in not having built our own feminist organisations or conceptualising an African feminism that is able to take us beyond the nationalist moment.

Alternative lived practice

For the past decade, I have hidden away on one of the world's oldest mountains, living precariously in a tiny house crammed full of my clutter – the stuff of my life – as I sought to find myself in newly radical and invigorating ways. Thinking back, I intuit that my first steps towards Contemporarity began with my sense of dis-ease about the tensions within the African Women's Movement. Issues around LGBTQI people, sexuality, and pleasure, particularly in relation to a critical articulation of violation and the impact of HIV/ AIDS on women's sexuality, and heteronormative conformity were a catalyst for my departure. These four issues were particularly vexatious and, eventually, led to my expulsion from Zimbabwe and me being labelled a slut.[10] Raising the necessity of recognising lesbian feminism and the political relevance of LGBTQI struggles drew the ire of many reactionaries who had taken political cover under the broad umbrella of the African Women's Movement. The value of lessons to be drawn from the struggles of the many groups of human beings who strive for dignity and rights in ways that are similar to those of women across all class and other divides was lost on them.

Stepping away from the sites of gendered nationalism signalled my personal retrospective on who I had become. It signified the conscious construction of myself; redefinition in personal terms (how I live in my middle-aged body), in theoretical terms (thinking about what it means to become contemporary), in political terms (interrogating my relationships with the infrastructures of political and state power), and in activist terms (how I would live my daily life in radically transformational ways). These became the signposts of my journey towards a contemporary identity which I would craft at all levels.

Theoretically, I have found that by approaching notions such as citizenship, for example, with a critically feminist gaze transforms the entire discourse into a dynamic debate about women's personhood, entitlements, consciousness, rights, and the critical policy issues of accessibility and protection. The idea of citizenship becomes a very specific political process for African women to reach beyond the normative and conservative identities that we are imbued with by the neo-colonial state. For centuries, we have been located outside the most minimal recognitions of African personhood through colonial racist discourses and policies which have colluded with long-entrenched feudal African notions and practices. The struggles of all politically and socio-culturally excluded constituencies for an inclusive notion and practice of citizenship are crucial to the formulation of, and demand for, a different kind of national belonging.[11]

During the colonial period, black men could imagine themselves becoming citizens in liberal, albeit limited, ways. Black women could not. In her critique of culture, religion and tradition, and their impact on women's sexuality in Nigeria, Charmaine Pereira argues:

> The balance of power at any one time shapes which group is excluded, marginalized, or exploited in the process. Understanding the context is thus crucial for discerning which spheres of activism may be invigorated by analytical as well as imaginative exploration of the conceptual dimensions involved and which strategies to adopt.[12]

In exploring the possibilities of Contemporarity, each one of us as feminists reinvigorates her relationship with radical concepts, their essential meanings and the paths these notions have travelled over the past century.

I have chosen to be a vegan and to live as an ecological feminist and herbal healer as the means of locating myself in a revolutionary landscape, wherein I can reconfigure the core feminist principles of bodily, sexual and spiritual integrity, wellness and wholeness. This radical location enables me to use the distance I have created between myself and gendered nationalists to scrutinise and interrogate their collusive tactics and strategies, as well as to craft new imaginaries of feminist freedom.

On a daily basis, I have learned to translate what I feel and intuit in the field as I coax new seeds into life and maturity so that I can feed my body and nurture my soul from the wholeness and bounty that nature so graciously bequeaths us. From this generosity I have recognised that integrity is the core of nature's power. As women, we become invincible the moment we embrace our connection to this natural source, and translate our sense of integrity into political and ethical discourses and activism. Integrity infuses our demands and efforts for lives of dignity with an authenticity that cannot be denied. When we are born, we arrive with all the forms of integrity that are inalienable to the human experience of life. They are our heritage, and it is these sensibilities which undergird the politics and ethics of feminism as an ideology, an identity and a way of living.

Locating myself as closely as possible to nature's power of life and generosity, I observed that the quality and the quantities of the crops I am growing increased with every season, despite being grown on the very same amount of land. With care and deep respect, I have carefully sought and begun to find the point of balance between the earth's nurturing capacities and my own abilities to live simply, quietly and wholesomely. This translates into sufficiency – the ability to feed and nurture ourselves, to have ENOUGH – through a balanced relationship with the earth and other living ecosystems. The conceptual feminist challenge that awaits me is how to translate what are still largely feelings and instincts about the intersectionality between the integrity, strength and inherent fairness of the living world with the ideas, desires, dreams and imaginaries that drive women's freedoms.

Beyond my personal experiences as I live a life that is attentive to the earth and its bounty of boundless spiritual, nurturing and aesthetic gifts, I have also been able to initiate new relationships with some of my neighbours on the mountain. Over the past few years, I have supported and encouraged a neighbour who lives very precariously. She and her partner are living with HIV/AIDS, their son is in a wheelchair with Down's syndrome, and the only income they have is a measly, unpredictable social grant received twice a year, which barely suffices. One day, I suggested to my neighbour that we clean out a little patch of land adjacent to her two-roomed house, and rebuild the land so that she could grow some food. We spent a week removing the broken bottles, tins and rubber, and slowly we brought in the manure, the compost, the seeds and the love. It was magical. Today she looks forward to the rainy season, when she can put the seedlings down, and the joy on her face when she has a successful crop is irreplaceable. The family is able to live off that little piece of land for several months a year.

This initiative changed our relationship in several ways. She, a working-class woman with minimal education, and I, a 'worldly traveller', have been able to build a bridge of solidarity between us based on a sense of integrity and self-exploration. We share knowledge about seed preservation, and she often teaches me about indigenous greens that have come back on that land, changing my own attitudes towards weeds and their immeasurable value to health and healing. She has a little corner of some of the basic herbs needed to control flu, pain, stomach upsets, etc. We have become new women in ways that neither of us imagined.

In terms of class solidarities, this relationship has enabled me to reject the prejudices that are inbuilt in the dynamics of class and social status. Initially, we had to work our way through much of the baggage that constructs us as black women in a feudal, patriarchal monarchy. We had to find a language with which to share this knowledge that has changed our lives. I watched her slowly let go of the fear that accompanies interactions between differently classed women. I also found a sense of ease with her abilities to transform her life without me directing the process. It was a slow, caring and rewarding journey. Now we discuss global warming and its impact on our smallholder farming (we grow mainly indigenous and drought-resistant crops) and what changes we will have to make in the next season. She is becoming more autonomous – to the ire of the locals who have more money than she does – and her sense of freedom has convinced me that such initiatives must form the core of the new contemporary African feminism.

Conclusion

Choosing to locate myself in the process of growing organic food as the source of my new consciousness and experience of freedom has also increased the depth of my respect for healing and the use of medicinal herbs. I grow them around me and use them for my own needs and to support my neighbours and friends within my community – in a society where allopathic medicine has a dominant presence and systematically ridicules herbs even as the State claims to respect indigenous knowledge systems and practices.

This relocation into a site which has its challenges and joys provides me with bursts of insight and energy for contemplating what it means to live radically and to be engaged in resistance to this particular moment of neo-colonial hegemony and blatant capitalist over-consumption. Undoubtedly, there are many sites of reinvigoration that each of us can relocate to, ideologically and physically. The larger challenge remains how to bring new ideas, energies, agencies and shifts in consciousness to the process through which African feminists can motivate and embrace the notion and practice of Contemporarity by crafting, articulating and living an alternative future.

Speaking from my vegan/eco-feminist location, it is clear that the appropriation of new ideas around herbal healing and organic production, which in many ways have remained the bedrock of subsistence agriculture for most rural African women, is becoming an urgent political matter affecting the livelihoods of most African people.[13] It is these clarities from my lived experiences which have convinced me that the dialectical relationship between theory and praxis remains crucial in the articulation of a contemporary African feminism, and that Contemporarity is both revolutionary and essential to the making of new realities and life-scapes for us on the continent and beyond.

Notes

Introduction: Being Black and Feminist

1   *Chambers Thesaurus*, 5th edition (Bengal: Allied Publishers, 2015), 990.
2   Patricia Hill Collins, 'Black Feminist Thought in the Matrix of Domination', in *Black Feminist Thought: Knowledge, Consciousness, and the Politics of Empowerment* (Boston: Unwin Hyman, 1990), 25.
3   Bessie Head, *A Woman Alone: Autobiographical Writings*, edited by Craig MacKenzie (Oxford: Heinemann, 1990), 63.
4   Stuart Hall, 'Cultural Identity and Diaspora', in *Identity: Community, Culture, Difference*, edited by Jonathan Rutherford (London: Lawrence and Wishart, 1990), 223–235.
5   Jasbir Puar, *Terrorist Assemblages: Homonationalism in Queer Times* (Durham: Duke University Press, 2007), 213.
6   Anna Bogic,'Theory in Perpetual Motion and Translation: Assemblage and Intersectionality in Feminist Studies', *Atlantis* 38, no. 1 (2017): 146.
7   Chandra Mohanty, '"Under Western Eyes" Revisited: Feminist Solidarity Through Anticapitalist Struggles', *Signs: Journal of Women in Culture and Society* 28, no. 2 (2003): 499–535.

Chapter 1: Winnie Mandela and the Archive: Reflections on Feminist Biography

1   Shireen Hassim, 'Not Just Nelson's Wife: Winnie Madikizela-Mandela, Violence and Radicalism in South Africa', *Journal of Southern African Studies* 44, no. 5 (2018): 895–912, DOI: 10.1080/03057070.2018.1514566; and Shireen Hassim, 'The Impossible Contract: The Political and Private Marriage of Nelson and Winnie Mandela', *Journal of Southern African Studies* 45, no. 6 (2019): 1151–1171, DOI: 10.1080/03057070.2019.1697137.
2   Mondli Makhanya, 'We Must Not Want to Be Winnie', *City Press*, 4 September 2018, https://city-press.news24.com/News/mondli-makhanya-we-must-not-want-to-be-winnie-20180409.
3   Nico Gous, 'Winnie Disobeyed Orders from ANC Leadership to Disband Football Club: Mbeki', *Sunday Times*, 3 April 2018, https://www.timeslive.co.za/politics/2018-04-03-winnie-disobeyed-orders-from-anc-leadership-to-disband-football-club-mbeki/.
4   Ed Cropley, '"Mother" Then "Mugger" of the Nation', *Sydney Morning Herald*, 3 April 2018, https://www.smh.com.au/world/africa/winnie-mandela-obituary-mother-then-mugger-of-new-south-africa-20180403-p4z7gh.html.

5   Barbara Caine, 'Feminist Biography and Feminist History', *Women's History Review* 3, no. 2 (1994): 250.
6   Gerda Lerner, 'Placing Women in History: A 1975 Perspective', in *Liberating Women's History*, edited by Berenice A. Carroll (Urbana: University of Illinois Press, 1986), 6.
7   Lerner, 'Placing Women in History', 8.
8   Nelson Mandela, *The Prison Letters of Nelson Mandela* (New York: Liveright Publishing, 2018).
9   Saidiya Hartman, *Wayward Lives, Beautiful Experiments: Intimate Histories of Riotous Black Girls, Troublesome Women and Queer Radicals* (London: Serpent's Tail Press, 2019), xv.

Chapter 2: Representing Sara Baartman in the New Millennium

1   Shose Kessi. 'Of Black Pain, Animal Rights and the Politics of the Belly', *Mail & Guardian Thought Leader*, 25 September 2015, https://thoughtleader.co.za/blackacademiccaucus/2015/09/25/of-black-pain-animal-rights-and-the-politics-of-the-belly/.
2   Kwame Anthony Appiah, *The Ethics of Identity* (Princeton: Princeton University Press, 2005), 124. (Here he refers to John Tomasi, 'Kymlicka, Liberalism, and Respect for Cultural Minorities', *Ethics* 105, no. 3 (1995): 590.)
3   The watercolour painting was produced in 2011 and is connected to performative work in which the artist uses an alter ego named after her mother.
4   Yvette Abrahams, 'Colonialism, Dysfunction and Dysjuncture: The Historiography of Sarah Baartman', PhD thesis, University of Cape Town, 2000.
5   Diana Ferrus, 'I've Come to Take You Home', in *I've Come to Take you Home* by Diana Ferrus (Kuils River: Diana Ferrus Publishers, 2011), 15.
6   Zoë Wicomb, *David's Story* (New York: Feminist Press, 2002), 135.
7   Rosemarie Buikema, 'The Arena of Imaginings: Sarah Bartmann and the Ethics of Representation', in *Doing Gender in Media, Art and Culture*, edited by Rosemarie Buikema and Iris van der Tuin (London: Routledge, 2009), 70–85.
8   Debra Walker King, *African Americans and the Culture of Pain* (Charlottesville: University of Virginia Press, 2008), 52.
9   Njabulo Ndebele, 'They Are Burning Memory', 10th Annual Helen Joseph Lecture, 2016, https://www.njabulondebele.co.za/2016/09/they-are-burning-memory/.
10 Willie Bester quoted in 'Sarah Baartman Sculptor Speaks Out Against Art Censorship', *Daily Maverick*, 5 June 2017, https://www.dailymaverick.co.za/article/2017-06-05-groundup-sarah-baartman-sculptor-speaks-out-against-art-censorship/#gsc.tab=0.

Chapter 3: a playful but also very serious love letter to gabrielle goliath

1   Phillippa Yaa de Villiers, 'Lasso', in *The Everyday Wife* by Phillippa Yaa de Villiers (Cape Town: Modjaji Books, 2010), 13.
2   Myesha Jenkins, 'Transformation', in *We Are . . . A Poetry Anthology*, compiled and edited by Natalia Molebatsi (Johannesburg: Penguin Books, 2008), 28.
3   Natalia Molebatsi, 'she, my story', in *Come as You Are: Poems for Four Strings* by Natalia Molebatsi and Simone Serafini (Piemonte: NOTA).

4   Napo Masheane, 'a room between my legs', in *We Are . . . A Poetry Anthology*, compiled and edited by Natalia Molebatsi (Johannesburg: Penguin Books, 2008), 52.
5   Napo Masheane, 'when it rains', in *Fat Songs for My Girlfriends* by Napo Masheane (Johannesburg: Village Gossip Productions, 2011), 28.

Chapter 4: Teaching Black, Teaching Gender, Teaching Feminism

1   Rogério Junqueira, 'Pedagogy of the Closet: Heterosexism and Gender Surveillance on Brazilian Everyday School Life', *Annual Review of Critical Psychology* 11 (2014): 173–188.

Chapter 5: Querying the Queer

1   Quoted in Natalie Oswin, 'Producing Homonormativity in Neoliberal South Africa: Recognition, Redistribution, and the Equality Project', *Signs: Journal of Women in Culture and Society* 32, no. 3 (2007): 649–669.
2   I choose to render the first-person personal pronoun as the small letter i in keeping with my other languages (Khoekhoegowab, Kinyarwanda, Afrikaans) and with other European languages, such as Dutch, French, etc. As is the convention, i use capital I at the beginning of a sentence.
3   Professor Kimberlé Crenshaw coined the term 'intersectionality' in a 1989 academic paper: https://www.racialequitytools.org/resourcefiles/mapping-margins.pdf. However, i need to emphasise that in South Africa (and probably elsewhere) women's structures were acutely aware of this. In 1913, the Association of Native and Coloured Women went to Parliament to protest against passes being instituted for African women. So, there was also cross race/class solidarity. The United Women's Organisation in 1981 had as part of policy fighting 'against the triple oppression of women: as black, working class and women'. As our structures grew, this developed into a cognisance of other axes of oppression: location, abilities, languages, albinism, etc.
4   The Cape Flats is a region outside metropolitan Cape Town to which Coloured residents were moved after being evicted from their homes under apartheid legislation.
5   Shaun Viljoen, *Richard Rive: A Partial Biography* (Johannesburg: Wits University Press, 2013), 11.
6   Maureen Isaacson, 'Sally Gross: The Fight for Intersex People Loses a Giant', *Daily Maverick*, 25 February 2014, https://www.dailymaverick.co.za/article/2014-02-25-sally-gross-the-fight-for-gender-equality-loses-a-giant.
7   Stephen Coan, 'The Journey from Selwyn to Sally', *The Witness*, 28 August 2009, https://www.news24.com/The-journey-from-Selwyn-to-Sally.
8   Stephen Coan, 'The Journey from Selwyn to Sally', *Natal Witness*, 25 February 2000, https://isna.org/pdf/gross1.pdf.

Chapter 6: South African Feminists in Search of the Sacred

1   Mary Daly, *Beyond God the Father: Towards a Philosophy for Women's Liberation* (Boston: Beacon Press, 1985), 146.
2   Daly, *Beyond God the Father*, xix.
3   Nancy Frankenberry, 'Feminist Philosophy of Religion', in *The Stanford Encyclopedia of Philosophy Online* (Summer 2018), edited by Edward N. Zalta (Stanford: Stanford University Press, 2018).

4 amina wadud, 'Can One Critique Cancel All Previous Efforts?', *Journal of Feminist Studies in Religion* 32, no. 2 (2016): 134.

5 amina wadud, 'The Ethics of Tawhid and Qiwamah', in *Men in Charge: Rethinking Authority in Muslim Legal Tradition*, edited by Ziba Mir-Hosseini, Mulki Al-Sharmani and Jana Rumminger (London: One World Press, 2015), 258.

6 Omaima Abou-Bakr, 'Interpretive Legacy of Qiwamah', in *Men in Charge: Rethinking Authority in Muslim Legal Tradition*, edited by Ziba Mir-Hosseini, Mulki Al-Sharmani and Jana Rumminger (London: One World Press, 2015), 61.

7 YaSiin Rahmaan, 'Feminist Edges of Muslim Feminist Readings of the Qur'an', *Journal of Feminist Studies in Religion* 32, no. 2 (2016): 146.

8 Rahmaan, 'Feminist edges', 146.

9 Sa'diyya Shaikh, *Sufi Narratives of Intimacy: Ibn 'Arabī, Gender and Sexuality* (Chapel Hill: University of North Carolina Press, 2012), 161.

10 Shaikh, *Sufi Narratives*, 175.

11 Shaikh, *Sufi Narratives*, 202.

12 Oyeronke Olajubu, *Women in the Yoruba Religious Sphere* (Albany: State University of New York Press, 2003).

13 Elizabeth Prevost, *The Communion of Women: Missions and Gender in Colonial Africa and the British Metropole* (Oxford: Oxford University Press, 2010), 1.

14 Kwok Pui Lan, *Postcolonial Imagination and Feminist Theology* (Louisville: Westminster John Knox Press, 2005), 224.

15 Pui Lan, *Postcolonial Imagination*, 79.

16 Pui Lan, *Postcolonial Imagination*, 79.

17 Pui Lan, *Postcolonial Imagination*, 81–85.

18 Musa Dube, 'Readings of Semoya: Batswana Women's Interpretations of Matt. 15: 21–28', *Semeia* 73 (1996): 112–115.

19 Pui Lan, *Postcolonial Imagination*, 83–84.

20 Mercy Amba Oduyoye, *Introducing African Women's Theology* (Sheffield: Sheffield Academic Press, 2001).

21 Nokuzola Mndende, 'From Underground Praxis to Recognized Religion: Challenges Facing African Religions', in *Religion and Politics in South Africa: From Apartheid to Democracy Volume 1*, edited by Wolfram Weisse and Abdulkader Tayob (Munich: Waxmann, 1999).

22 Nkunzi Nkabinde and Ruth Morgan, '"This Has Happened Since Ancient Times . . . It's Something That You Are Born With": Ancestral Wives Among Same-Sex Sangomas in South Africa', *Agenda* 20, no. 67 (2006): 9–19; Nkunzi Zandile Nkabinde, *Black Bull, Ancestors and Me: My Life as a Lesbian Sangoma* (Auckland Park: Fanele, 2008).

Chapter 7: 'Who Do You Think You Are to Speak to Me Like That?'

1 I believe the concept of 'Coloured', though it was and remains official, is a contested, administrative category, as argued by Zimitri Erasmus in her book *Race Otherwise: Forging a New Humanism for South Africa* (Johannesburg: Wits University Press, 2017). The capitalisation references a meaning that is thus context specific.

2 jackï job, '*The Kiss* (an excerpt)', 2003, YouTube video, https://www.youtube.com/watch?v=LWg6TpkCjvA.

Chapter 8: Refining Islamic Feminisms: Gender, Subjectivity and the Divine Feminine

1 South African Muslim liberation theology as it emerged in that historical moment is traced in an important work by Farid Esack, *Qur'an Liberation and Pluralism: An Islamic Perspective of Interreligious Solidarity Against Oppression* (Oxford: Oneworld, 1997).

2 The influence of Muslim anti-apartheid activism on our approach to gender justice was a broader political trend that developed in South Africa in the period between the mid-'80s and mid-'90s.

3 Denise Ackermann, *After the Locusts: Letters from a Landscape of Faith* (Cape Town: David Philip Publishers, 2003), 47.

4 amina wadud, *Qur'an and Woman: Rereading the Sacred Text from a Woman's Perspective* (Kuala Lumpur: Penerbit Fajar Bakti Sdn. Bhd, 1992).

5 With the exception of China, where there is a history of exclusively female mosques with women in positions of religious leadership, there were few if any mosques at all with women playing leadership roles at that time.

6 This sermon has been published in amina wadud's subsequent book *Inside the Gender Jihad: Women's Reform in Islam* (Oxford: Oneworld, 2006), 158–162.

7 Cited in Sa'diyya Shaikh, *Sufi Narratives of Intimacy: Ibn 'Arabī, Gender and Sexuality* (Chapel Hill: University of North Carolina Press, 2012; Cape Town: UCT Press, 2013), 129.

8 Surah Baqara, verse 156. See http://tanzil.net/#2:156.

9 Cited in Ralph Austin, 'The Feminine Dimensions of Ibn 'Arabī's Thought', *Journal of the Muhyiddin Ibn 'Arabī Society* 2 (1984): 8–9.

10 Ibn 'Arabi, Muhyi al-Din, *al-Futuhat al-Makkiya* (Cairo: N.p., 1911), Vol. 6: 445.

11 *Uwaysi* relationships are a developed trope in Islamic thought. The term refers to inspirational relationships and mysterious/mystical connections with a teacher whom one might not have met physically or who is not physically present, possibly also involving relations across time. The term originated in the long-distance relationship of devotion between the Yemeni Uways al-Qarani (d.657) with the Prophet Muhammad, whom he never met in person.

12 See also Ebrahim Moosa, *Ghāzalī and the Poetics of Imagination* (Durham: University of North Carolina Press, 2005), 38–40.

Chapter 10: Conversations about Photography with Keorapetse Mosimane, Thania Petersen and Tshepiso Mazibuko

1 Ariella Azoulay, *Civil Imagination: A Political Ontology of Photography,* translated by Louise Bethlehem (London: Verso, 2012), 52–53.

2 Both these photographs are now part of the permanent collections of the Iziko Museums of South Africa. *Androgenia – a beautiful boy* was collected in 2005 and *B(e)aring our Load* in 2019.

3 In addition to being part of the permanent collections of the Iziko Museums of South Africa, the two photographs by Mosimane also form part of the Market Photo Workshop archives.

4 Petersen donated part of the *I am Royal* series to the Iziko Museums of South Africa in 2018.

Chapter 11: What We Make to Unmake: The Imagination in Feminist Struggles

1   bell hooks, 'Eating the Other: Desire and Resistance', in *Black Looks: Race and Representation* (Boston: South End Press,1992), 310.
2   Yewande Omotoso, *The Woman Next Door* (London: Chatto and Windus, 2016), 32 (my emphasis).
3   bell hooks, *Art on My Mind: Visual Politics* (New York: New Press, 1995), 11.
4   Wanda Sykes, 'White People Are Looking', HBO, streamed live on 16 January 2018, YouTube video, https://www.youtube.com/watch?v=ENrqOq219Oo.

Chapter 12: Breathing Under Water

1   M. Jacqui Alexander, *Pedagogies of Crossing: Meditations on Feminism, Sexual Politics, and the Sacred* (Durham: Duke University Press, 2005), 1.
2   Vangile Gantsho, 'untitled', in *red cotton* (Tshwane: Impepho press, 2018), 9.
3   Koleka Putuma, 'SUICIDE', in *Collective Amnesia* (Cape Town: uHhlanga Press, 2017), 73.
4   Christina Sharpe, *In the Wake: On Blackness and Being* (Durham: Duke University Press, 2016), 10–11.
5   Lisa Lowe, *The Intimacies of Four Continents* (Durham: Duke University Press, 2015).
6   Lowe, *The Intimacies*, 18.
7   Vangile Gantsho, 'schizophrenia', in *red cotton* (Tshwane: Impepho press, 2018), 26, emphasis in the original.
8   Gillian Stead Eilersen, *Bessie Head: Thunder Behind Her Ears* (Cape Town: David Philip Publishers, 1995), 131.
9   Eilersen, *Bessie Head*, 143.
10 Eilersen, *Bessie Head*, 144.
11 Trinh T. Minh-ha, *Lovecidal: Walking with the Disappeared* (Durham: Duke University Press, 2016), 5.
12 Minh-ha, *Lovecidal*, 7, emphasis in the original.
13 Minh-ha, *Lovecidal*, 8.
14 Gabeba Baderoon, 'The History of Intimacy', in *The History of Intimacy: Poems* (Cape Town: Kwela Books, 2018), 66.
15 Sindiswa Busuku-Mathese, 'The Father, The Mother, The Girl at the table with lights', in *Loud and Yellow Laughter* (Johannesburg: Botsotso, 2016), 27.
16 Busisiwe Mahlangu, 'Magic Wonder', in *Surviving Loss* (Tshwane: Impepho press, 2018), 47.
17 Vangile Gantsho, 'untitled', in *red cotton* (Tshwane: Impepho Press, 2018), 2.
18 Lauren Berlant, *Cruel Optimism* (Durham: Duke University Press, 2011), 145.
19 Busisiwe Mahlangu, 'rescue', in *Surviving Loss* (Tshwane: Impepho Press, 2018), 28.
20 Sara Ahmed, *Willful Subjects* (Durham: Duke University Press, 2014), 1.
21 Sara Ahmed, *Living a Feminist Life* (Durham: Duke University Press, 2017), 25.
22 Ahmed, *Living a Feminist Life*, 26.
23 Vangile Gantsho, 'small girl', in *red cotton* (Tshwane: Impepho Press, 2018), 11.
24 Vangile Gantsho, 'I'm standing in the middle of the road', in *red cotton* (Tshwane: Impepho Press, 2018), 3

25 Putuma, 'Twenty-one Ways of Leaving, in *Collective Amnesia* (Cape Town: uHlanga Press, 2017), 45.

26 Gantsho, 'small girl', 11.

27 Vangile Gantsho, 'breathing under water', in *red cotton* (Tshwane: Impepho Press, 2018), 13

28 Danai S. Mupotsa, 'untitled', in *feeling and ugly* (Tshwane: Impepho Press, 2018), 4.

29 Audre Lorde, 'Inheritance – His', in *The Collected Poems of Audre Lorde* (New York: W.W. Norton, 1997), 437.

30 Baderoon, 'The Word' in *The History of Intimacy: Poems* (Cape Town: Kwela Books, 2018), 56.

31 Busuku-Mathese, 'Mother's Lyric', in *Loud and Yellow Laughter* (Johannesburg: Botsotso, 2016), 34.

32 Busuku-Mathese, 'Mother's Lyric', 34.

33 Alexander, *Pedagogies*, 298.

34 Alexander, *Pedagogies*, 298

35 Gantsho, 'breathing under water', 13.

Chapter 14: Echoes of Miriam Tlali

1 Pamela Ryan, 'Black Womxn Do Not Have Time to Dream: The Politics of Time and Space', *Tulsa Studies in Womxn's Literature* 11, no. 1 (1992): 95.

2 Margaret Lenta, 'Two Womxn and Their Territories: Sheila Roberts and Miriam Tlali', *Tulsa Studies in Womxn's Literature* 11, no. 1 (1992): 103.

3 I use the term 'white feminism' to signify a strand of feminism that centres the lived experience and particular forms of oppression experienced by white womxn, ignoring the salience of race in structuring womxn's lives and often marginalising or dismissing the experiences of black womxn and womxn of colour.

4 Miriam Tlali, *Between Two Worlds* (Ontario: Broadview Press, 2004).

5 Miriam Tlali, *Muriel at Metropolitan* (Johannesburg: Ravan Press, 1975).

6 Chikwenye Okonjo Ogunyemi, 'Womxnism: The Dynamics of the Contemporary Black Female Novel in English', *Signs: Journal of Women in Culture and Society* 11, no. 1 (1985): 68.

7 Pravin Ram, 'The Mobilisation of Womxn: The Black Womxn's Federation 1975–1977: With particular reference to Natal', MA diss., University of Natal, 1992.

8 Ram, 'The Mobilisation of Womxn', 44.

9 Ram, 'The Mobilisation of Womxn', 44.

10 Miriam Tlali, *Soweto Stories* (London: Pandora Press, 1989), 37.

11 Tlali, *Soweto Stories*, 41.

12 Tlali, *Soweto Stories*, 42.

13 Zoë Wicomb, 'To Hear the Variety of Discourses', in *South African Feminisms: Writing, Theory and Criticism, 1990–1994*, edited by Margaret J. Daymond (New York and London: Garland Publishing, 1996), 51.

14 Miriam Tlali, Letter to the author, 11 March 2011.

15 Tlali, Letter.

16 Tlali, Letter.

17 Tlali, Letter.

18 Tlali, Letter.

19 Tlali, Letter.

20 Simidele Dosekun, 'Defending Feminism in Africa', *Postamble* 3, no. 1 (2007): 46.

21 Wanelisa Xaba, 'Challenging Fanon: A Black Radical Feminist Perspective on Violence and the Fees Must Fall Movement', *Agenda* 31, no. 3–4 (2017): 96.

22 Mbali Matandela, 'Rhodes Must Fall: How Black Womxn Claimed Their Place', *Mail and Guardian*, 30 March 2015, https://mg.co.za/article/2015-03-30-rhodes-must-fall-how-black-women-claimed-their-place/.

23 Mbali Matandela, 'Redefining Black Consciousness and Resistance: The Intersection of Black Consciousness and Black Feminist Thought', *Agenda* 31, no. 3–4 (2017): 11.

24 Tlali, *Soweto Stories*, 41.

Chapter 15: My Two Husbands

1 Wangari Maathai, *Unbowed: A Memoir* (New York: Anchor Books, 2008), 146.

2 Toni Morrison, *The Bluest Eye* (New York: Vintage, 2007), 82–84.

3 Morrison, *The Bluest Eye*, 82–84.

4 Shannon Hengen and Ashley Thomson, *Margaret Atwood: A Reference Guide, 1988–2005* (Lanham: Scarecrow Press, 2007), 20.

5 Elizabeth Freeman, *Time Binds: Queer Temporalities, Queer Histories* (Durham and London: Duke University Press, 2007), 3–12.

Chapter 16: Hearing the Silence

1 Joyce Chen, 'Lupita Nyong'o on Sharing Her Weinstein Story: My Silence Felt Uncomfortable', *Rolling Stone*, 25 January 2018, https://www.rollingstone.com/culture/culture-news/lupita-nyongo-on-sharing-her-weinstein-story-my-silence-felt-uncomfortable-203169/.

2 Gabeba Baderoon, *Regarding Muslims: From Slavery to Post-apartheid* (Johannesburg: Wits University Press, 2014), p. 84.

3 Stuart Oldman, 'Salma Hayek Says Harvey Weinstein Only Responded to Her and Lupita Nyong'o's Harassment Claims Because Women of Color Are Easier to Discredit', *Variety*, 13 May 2018, https://variety.com/2018/film/news/salma-hayek-says-harvey-weinstein-only-responded-to-her-and-lupita-nyongos-harassment-claims-because-women-of-color-are-easier-to-discredit-1202808828/.

4 Daniel Kreps, 'Chance the Rapper: "Making a Song With R. Kelly Was a Mistake"', *Rolling Stone*, 5 January 2019, https://www.rollingstone.com/music/music-news/chance-the-rapper-r-kelly-mistake-775431/.

5 See comments from one of the accused in Mel Frykberg, 'Ghanaian Professor Threatens to Sue BBC over Sex for Grades Allegation', *IOL*, 9 October 2019, https://www.iol.co.za/news/africa/ghanaian-professor-threatens-to-sue-bbc-over-sex-for-grades-allegation-34442718.

6 Sindi van Zyl (@sindivanzyl), 2017, 'Sindi van Zyl Twitter post', Twitter, 15 November 2017, 9:44 p.m., https://twitter.com/sindivanzyl/status/930989829013295105?s=20.

7 Toni Morrison, 'The Site of Memory', in *What Moves at the Margin: Selected Nonfiction*, edited by Carolyn C. Denard (Jackson: University Press of Mississippi, 2008).

8 Yvette Christiansë, *Unconfessed* (New York: Other Press, 2006).

Chapter 18: The Music of My Orgasm

1 Patricia McFadden, 'Sexual Pleasure as Feminist Choice', *Feminist Africa* 2 (2003): 8.

2 McFadden, 'Sexual Pleasure', 2.

3 Audre Lorde, 'Uses of the Erotic: The Erotic as Power', in *Sister Outsider: Essays and Speeches by Audre Lorde* (Berkeley: Crossing Press, 1984), 53–58.

4   McFadden, 'Sexual Pleasure', 57.

5   *Ukukhulelwa*: The direct translation for this word is 'to have someone grow up for you'. What is implied here is that something is growing from inside of you. I have always found this linguistically fascinating because instead of the commonly used English expression 'to fall pregnant', the emphasis is on the thing/person that grows and not the woman who has fallen pregnant. It's the same with the phrase 'falling in love'; I have often been curious about the historical background to these expressions because of their obvious absence of agency.

6   It was only in 1976 that television came to South Africa; before that, I had never seen people kiss on screen. So the first time I saw people kiss romantically was at Pholela High School. I came from a kissing family, but the brief touching of lips was the only kind of kiss I had ever seen. I was curious. I stood and watched each time an opportunity presented itself. What happened to their tongues? And the saliva? I had no way of understanding why this deep kissing seemed so integral to being lovers. Truth be told, deep kissing looked disgusting to me. I found the idea of having someone else's saliva in my mouth the opposite of romantic.

7   Gabeba Baderoon, 'Introduction', in *Our Words, Our Worlds: Writing on Black South African Women Poets, 2000–2018*, edited by Makhosazana Xaba (Pietermartizburg: University of KwaZulu-Natal Press, 2019), 5.

8   The Boston Women's Health Book Collective, 'In Amerika They Call Us Dykes', in *Our Bodies, Ourselves: A Book by and for Women* (New York: Simon and Schuster, 1979), 81.

9   In 1994, I wrote a short piece, published in *Agenda: A Journal about Women and Gender*, on isiZulu words used for the vulva (vagina, clitoris, inner and outer labia). It was based on interviews I had conducted and built on research I had undertaken using 16 dictionaries. I concluded that these words fall into four categories: derogatory, reflecting male possession and gratification, euphemistic and vague.

10 Makhosazana Xaba, 'These Hands', in *These Hands* (Elim: Timbila Poetry Project, 2005), 12i.

11 Baderoon, 'Introduction', 5.

Chapter 19: Bringing Water to Krotoa's Gardens: Decolonisation as Direct Action

1   Yvette Abrahams, 'Untitled', in Poet on Watch, *Sageburner: Simple Pleasures* (Austin: Freeverse Publishing, 2012), 83.

2   H.C.V. Leibbrandt, *Precis of the Archives of the Cape of Good Hope: Letters Despatched, 1656–1658* (Cape Town: W.A. Richards and Sons, 1897).

3   Sam Levin and Patrick Greenfield, 'Monsanto Ordered to Pay $289m as Jury Rules Weedkiller Caused Man's Cancer', *The Guardian*, 10 August 2018, https://www.theguardian.com/business/2018/aug/10/monsanto-trial-cancer-dewayne-johnson-ruling.

4   Gabeba Baderoon, 'The Creation of Black Criminality in South Africa', *Africa Is a Country*, 16 December 2018, https://africasacountry.com/2018/12/the-creation-of-black-criminality-in-south-africa.

5   Desiree Lewis, 'Violence Against Women and the Politics of Feminism', *Amandla Magazine* 60, no. 28 (November 2018), http://aidc.org.za/violence-women-politics-feminism/.

6   Sarah Malotane Henkeman, ed., *Disrupting Denial: Analysing Narratives of Invisible/ Visible Violence and Trauma* (Cape Town: New Adventure Publishing, 2018).
7   Henkeman, *Disrupting Denial*, 35.
8   Henkeman, *Disrupting Denial*, 37.

Chapter 20: Living a Radical African Feminist Life: A Journey to Sufficiency Through Contemporarity

1   'Contemporarity' is a term I coined in Patricia McFadden, *Meridians* 17, no. 2 (2018): 415–431.
2   Aniko Imre, 'Lesbian Nationalism', *Signs: Journal of Women in Culture and Society* 33, no. 2 (2008): 255.
3   Nthabiseng Motsemme, 'The Mute Always Speak: On Women's Silences at the Truth and Reconciliation Commission', *Current Sociology* 52, no. 5 (2004): 909–932.
4   Pumla D. Gqola, 'Moving Beyond Patriarchy', *MindMap-SA*, 22 February 2012, https://mindmapsa.wordpress.com/2012/02/22/pumla-gqola-moving-beyond-patriarchy/.
5   Susan Griffin, *The Eros of Everyday Life: Essays on Ecology, Gender and Society* (New York: Anchor Books, 1996), 93.
6   Awa Thiam, *Black Sisters, Speak Out: Feminism and Oppression in Black Africa* (London: Pluto Press, 1986).
7   M. Jacqui Alexander, *Pedagogies of Crossing: Meditations on Feminism, Sexual Politics, Meditation, and the Sacred* (Durham: Duke University Press, 2005), 4.
8   Some supposedly progressive black men who claim to be feminists derisively referred to these contestations as personal fights, exposing their own inability to acknowledge that women can, and do, engage in political contestation and struggles over ideology and power.
9   Amílcar Cabral, *Return to the Source: Selected Speeches of Amílcar Cabral* (New York: Monthly Review Press, 1973).
10 In a public conversation among a group of women, two 'sisters' confronted me about my sexual behaviour, implying that I was promiscuous and that I had an uncontrollable urge to have sex all the time. In Southern Africa, there is a deep undercurrent of learned racial bigotry, which constructs mixed-race women, like me, as sexually compulsive. Writing on sexuality and pleasure has tended to surface these prejudices in apparently unintended ways.
11 M. Jacqui Alexander, 'Not Just (Any) Body Can Be a Citizen: The Politics of Law, Sexuality and Postcoloniality in Trinidad and Tobago and the Bahamas', *Feminist Review* 48 (Autumn 1994): 5–23.
12 Charmaine Pereira, 'Setting Agendas for Feminist Thought and Practice in Nigeria', *Signs: Journal of Women in Culture and Society* 34, no. 2 (2009): 264.
13 The invasion by genetically modified organisms (GMOs) of the African countryside, as well as the push for title deeds in respect of communal land ownership, is the new onslaught aimed at further commodifying African rural societies and African biodiversity.

Contributors

Yvette Abrahams holds a PhD in economic history from the University of Cape Town. She has consulted for government and various NGOs on issues relating to gender equality in policy and practice, while publishing widely both locally and internationally on gender equality, queer theory, climate change as well as the history of First Nations South Africans. She served as Commissioner for Gender Equality, heading their programmes on poverty, energy and climate change. She also worked as an Advisor to Project 90 by 2030, an NGO which focuses on food security, energy, and promoting renewable energy and energy efficiency entrepreneurship in the context of climate change. She served as Commissioner on the University of Cape Town's Institutional Reconciliation and Truth Commission. Today she runs a small business making organic carbon-neutral soaps and body products on her smallholding east of Cape Town. Her blog is www.khoelife.com.

While she was a PhD student in literature, **Gabeba Baderoon** took an extramural class in writing poetry, an experience of simultaneously being a beginner and deeply practised that has reverberated in her life since. She has now authored four poetry collections: *The Dream in the Next Body, The Museum of Ordinary Life, A Hundred Silences* and, most recently, *The History of Intimacy*. She also writes as an academic and scholar on slavery, sexuality and Islam in her critically acclaimed book *Regarding Muslims: From Slavery to Post-apartheid*. She has edited several collections by women poets and is a member of the board of the African Poetry Book Fund, which has published over 60 collections of poetry by writers from the continent. Baderoon co-directs the African Feminist Initiative at Pennsylvania State University, where she is an Associate Professor of Women's, Gender and Sexuality Studies and African Studies. In addition, she is an Extraordinary Professor of English at Stellenbosch University and a Fellow of the Stellenbosch Institute for Advanced Study (STIAS).

Barbara Boswell is a feminist literary scholar with an interest in Black diasporic women's writing, Black South African women's literature, and queer theory. She has a PhD in gender and women's studies and has taught South African literature, feminist theory, and representations of race and gender at universities in the USA and South Africa. She is also the author of *Grace: A Novel*.

Panashe Chigumadzi is an essayist, editor and fiction writer whose work seeks to redefine the meanings of black and African thought through critical engagements with post-apartheid identity formation and the post-colonial dynamic of race, gender, class, religion, spirituality and nationality. Her debut novel, *Sweet Medicine*, won the 2016 K. Sello Duiker Literary Award. Her second book, *These Bones Will Rise Again*, is a reflection on the late Robert Mugabe's military deposement through the spirits of anti-colonial heroine Mbuya Nehanda and her late grandmother Mbuya Lilian Chigumadzi, and was shortlisted for the 2019 Alan Paton Award for Non-fiction. Chigumadzi was the founding editor of *Vanguard Magazine*, a platform for young black women coming of age in post-apartheid South Africa. Her work has featured in periodicals including *The Guardian, Chimurenga, Africa Is a Country, Transition, Washington Post, New York Times* and *Die Zeit*.

gertrude fester-wicomb has been active in anti-apartheid politics since she was a teenager, focusing on both women's and national liberation. Born in Cape Town, she participated in the Women's National Coalition, which advocated for a gender-sensitive Constitution, and founded the Women's Education and Artistic Voice Expression, a feminist writing collective which generated self-published anthologies and encouraged young black women's writing. She actively encourages inter-generational work, and the oppression of women and marginalised groups has been a central theme in her fiction and non-fiction writing. Her prison play, *The Spirit Cannot Be Caged,* composed in her head during solitary confinement as a prisoner under apartheid, was performed at the Fourth Women's United Nations Conference in Beijing. After 1994 she served as a Member of Parliament and a Commissioner for Gender Equality. She has taught at Rutgers University in the USA and the University of Rwanda. She is currently an Honorary Professor at the University of Cape Town.

Pumla Dineo Gqola is an award-winning feminist author and Research Professor at Nelson Mandela University. Her books include *What is Slavery to Me? Postcolonial/Slave Memory in Post-apartheid South Africa; Rape: A South African Nightmare*; and *Reflecting Rogue: Inside the Mind of a Feminist.*

Mary Hames is involved in formal teaching in two faculties at South African institutions of higher learning. Yet, she is convinced that more inclusive and holistic teaching is taking place outside the formal classroom. Years of experiential learning and teaching about feminism, critical race studies, sexuality, sexual orientation, gender and gender identity to generations of students outside the classroom have seen her students taking up important positions in student leadership and beyond. Teaching critical consciousness and social justice in a safe and supportive environment through creative arts, debates, writing and reading has unlocked a myriad of inventive ways to learn and share ideas and experiences. Hames has produced multiple workshopped productions, delivered several talks and papers, and spearheaded innovative programmes in collaboration with her students. She has also published numerous articles and book chapters on these programmes and continues to reflect on the praxis of creative feminist pedagogy.

jackï job was born in Cape Town, South Africa, and began her professional journey in contemporary dance as a company member of Jazzart Dance Theatre. Following her resignation in 1994, she launched her independent performance career and has since conceived, directed, choreographed and performed more than 70 full-length works, and produced interdisciplinary collaborations on various platforms globally. She lived in Japan from 2003 to 2011 and forged an eclectic creative network across various artistic disciplines and academic institutions. From 2014 to 2017, she served as director and choreographer of Cape Town Opera's *African Angels*, which performed in prestigious opera theatres in Europe. Currently, she lectures in the Centre for Theatre, Dance and Performance Studies at the University of Cape Town. Her vision and philosophy is to find expansive and creative ways to explore notions of identity beyond privileging the human.

Desiree Lewis has published on the politics of South African and global feminism from a black perspective since the early 1990s. Her recent work focuses on neo-liberalism in relation to feminism, as well as feminism and food as material culture. The author of *Living on a Horizon: Bessie Head and the Politics of Imagining*, she has guest-edited special issues of feminist journals including *Feminist Africa* and *Agenda*, and has served on the editorial boards of *Australian Feminist Studies* and *Feminist Africa* as well as other interdisciplinary journals. Lewis began her teaching and writing career as a literary scholar, but now teaches, writes and thinks in transdisciplinary ways that involve seeking to reanimate knowledge-making in the academy. As a feminist academic and intellectual activist, she is passionate about radical knowledge-making and creative expression that transcends academic and generic conventions.

Ingrid Masondo is the curator of photography and new media at the Iziko South African National Gallery in Cape Town. Her involvement with the arts, culture and heritage sectors spans more than two decades at a variety of institutions. She has held various positions, including archivist at the Mayibuye Archives; projects and curriculum manager at the Market Photo Workshop; researcher, photo editor and member of the editorial team at *Chimurenga Chronic*; and curator at Badilisha Poetry Radio.

Zethu Matebeni is fascinated by women and their feminist energies. Perhaps this explains why she wrote and published her doctoral thesis on black lesbians, weaving together feminism, queerness, gender identity and space. She co-produced and co-directed the documentary film *Breaking Out of the Box: Stories of Black Lesbians in South Africa*. An Associate Professor of Sociology at the University of the Western Cape, Matebeni spends most of her time writing and rewriting queer theory for everyday use. Her edited books include *Reclaiming Afrikan: Queer Perspectives on Sexual and Gender Identities* and co-edited volumes *Queer in Africa: LGBTQI Identities, Citizenship and Activism* and *Beyond the Mountain: Queer Life in 'Africa's Gay Capital'*. Matebeni's creative work is deeply engaged with the fulfilment of young lesbians' desire to be black, young, queer, at home and pursuing freedom.

Patricia McFadden is a radical feminist, born in Africa, who currently resides on a mountain in the eastern part of Eswatini (formerly Swaziland). She has been a vegan for three decades and in recent times has begun to translate the experiences and insights she harvests from working as an organic farmer – growing food for her own table – into her feminist ideas, energies and writing. She has positioned herself at the nexus of producing for life in ethical and self-loving ways and writing for life through a return to the source of feminist intellectual ideas and agency. Freedom, autonomy, integrity and dignity are central to her recalibration of core feminist notions and her search for the roots of feminist creativity and critical knowledge production in this contemporary moment.

Sisonke Msimang writes about justice, accountability and power in South Africa and beyond. Her work aims to deepen public conversations about democracy and belonging in an accessible and meaningful way. Sisonke's essays and opinion pieces have appeared in a range of publications including *Africa Is a Country*, *New York Times*, *The Guardian*, *Washington Post*, *Newsweek* and *Al Jazeera*. Sisonke is a Fellow at the Wits Institute of Social and Economic Research (WiSER) and has held fellowships at Yale University, the Aspen Institute and the

Bellagio Center of the Rockefeller Foundation. She is the author of two books: *Always Another Country: A Memoir of Exile and Home* and *The Resurrection of Winnie Mandela*.

Harare-born poet and academic **Danai S. Mupotsa** is a Senior Lecturer in African literature at the University of the Witwatersrand, Johannesburg. She specialises in gender and sexualities, black intellectual traditions and histories, intimacy and affect, and feminist pedagogies. She is a member of the editorial collective of *Agenda*, sits on the editorial board of the Brill series in youth cultures and serves on the executive board of the International Girlhood Studies Association. In 2018, she published her first collection of poetry, *feeling and ugly*.

Grace A. Musila serves as an Associate Professor in the Department of African Literature at the University of the Witwatersrand, Johannesburg. Her teaching and research centres on Eastern and Southern African literatures and popular cultures. She is the editor of *Wangari Maathai's Registers of Freedom*, author of *A Death Retold in Truth and Rumour: Kenya, Britain and the Julie Ward Murder* and co-editor of *Rethinking Eastern African Intellectual Landscapes*. She is partial to ideas, and the freedoms ideas afford or impede, especially in women's lives.

Leigh-Ann Naidoo is an educator and activist concerned with the ways in which pedagogy can be used in ongoing struggles for the redistribution of power and resources in South Africa and beyond. She comes from a family of educators and activists who were involved in the struggle against apartheid and capitalism. She draws strength from the histories of the Unity Movement and the Black Consciousness Movement in South Africa. Leigh-Ann currently works at the School of Education at the University of Cape Town and is completing a PhD on black student intellectuals and the complexity of entailment in the #RhodesMustFall student movement. Her research tracks the processes of the student movement, which she reads as an important experiment with new politics and subjectivities in South Africa.

Born in Barbados, **Yewande Omotoso** grew up in Nigeria and currently lives in Johannesburg, South Africa. She studied architecture and completed her master's in creative writing from the University of Cape Town. Her debut novel, *Bom Boy*, won the South African Literary Award First-Time Published Author Prize as well as being shortlisted for numerous local and international book awards. She was a 2013 Norman Mailer Fellow and a 2014 Etisalat Fellow. In 2015 she was a Miles Morland Scholar. Her second novel, *The Woman Next Door*, was shortlisted for the International Dublin Literary Award, the Aidoo-Snyder Prize, the Barry Ronge Fiction Prize and the University of Johannesburg Literary Prize.

Fatima Seedat is a Senior Lecturer in Gender Studies at the African Gender Institute, University of Cape Town, where she teaches African feminism and feminist research methods. Fatima writes and researches on law, religion and sexuality in the context of Islam. She has taught at the University of KwaZulu-Natal (UKZN) and McGill University (Canada), where she also completed her PhD in Islamic law. Her earlier career was in the NGO and government sectors locally and internationally. She is a member of the Muslim Personal Law Network, and facilitates *khula* (divorce) pronouncements.

Sa'diyya Shaikh is the author of *Sufi Narratives of Intimacy: Ibn 'Arabī, Gender and Sexuality*, which won the University of Cape Town Book Prize in 2015. An Associate Professor of Religious Studies at UCT, her study of Islam began with an abiding interest in existential questions and their connections to issues of social justice. Shaikh has co-edited two feminist collections, *Theorising Gender and Islam* with Gabeba Baderoon and Nina Hoel, and *Violence Against Women in Contemporary World Religion: Roots and Cures* with Catholic theologian Dan Maguire. Her areas of research include gender-sensitive readings of *hadith* (narratives relating to the Prophet Muhammad), Qur'anic exegesis and Sufi texts, theoretical and political debates on Islam and feminism, Muslim ethics, and contemporary Muslim women's embodied, experiential and everyday modes of Islamic ethics.

Zukiswa Wanner is the author of the novels *The Madams, Behind Every Successful Man, Men of the South* and *London Cape Town Joburg*. She has also written two works of nonfiction, *Maid in SA: 30 Ways to Leave Your Madam* and *Hardly Working*. A 2020 Goethe Medallist, Wanner has authored three children's books: *Jama Loves Bananas, Refilwe* and *Africa (A True Book: The Seven Continents)*. She is founder and majority owner of the indie publishing house Paivapo. Wanner thrives on finding novel ways to make literature exciting. She is one of the founding members of ReadSA and founded and curated Artistic Encounters in Nairobi. With funding from the Goethe-Institut in sub-Saharan Africa, Wanner conceptualised and edited the AfroYA anthology *Water Birds on the Lakeshore* and, in the coronavirus era, founded and curated the monthly virtual literary festival Afrolit Sans Frontières.

Zoë Wicomb is a South African–Scottish writer of fiction and literary and cultural criticism. She was awarded the illustrious Yale Windham-Campbell Prize for fiction in 2014. Wicomb gained attention in South Africa and internationally with her first book, *You Can't Get Lost in Cape Town*, a collection of interrelated short stories. Her latest works include *Race, Nation, Translation: South African Essays* and the novels *October* and *Still Life*. She is currently Emeritus Professor at the University of Strathclyde, Scotland.

Makhosazana Xaba is currently a Research Associate at Wits Institute for Social and Economic Research (WiSER) working on a biography of Helen Nontando Jabavu, one of South Africa's foundational writers. She is an anthologist, short story writer and poet who has published three collections of poetry: *These Hands, Tongues of Their Mothers* and *The Alkalinity of Bottled Water. Running and Other Stories* was a joint winner of the Nadine Gordimer Short Story Award in 2014. Prior to becoming a professional writer, Xaba worked in the field of women's health and published extensively in this area, developing training materials on reproductive and sexual health and rights, including co-writing *Health Workers for Change*, a training manual used internationally. The expansive multi-genre range of Xaba's writing is reflected in her contribution to feminist knowledge production founded on collective, collaborative and inclusive practices.

Permission Credits

Chapter 3

Extract of 'Lasso' by Phillipa Yaa de Villiers, in Phillipa Yaa de Villiers, *The Everyday Wife* (Cape Town: Modjaji Books, 2010), p. 13. © Phillipa Yaa de Villiers

Extract of 'Transformation' by Myesha Jenkins, in *We Are . . . A Poetry Anthology*, compiled and edited by Natalia Melobatsi (Johannesburg: Penguin Books, 2008), p. 28. © Myesha Jenkins

Extract of 'she, my story' by Natalia Molebatsi, in Natalia Molebatsi and Simone Serafini, *Come as You Are: Poems for Four Strings* (Piemonte: NOTA). © Natalia Molebatsi

Extract of 'a room between my legs' by Napo Masheane, in *We Are . . . A Poetry Anthology*, compiled and edited by Natalia Molebatsi (Johannesburg: Penguin Books, 2008), p. 52. © Napo Masheane

Extract of 'when it rains' by Napo Masheane, in Napo Masheane, *Fat Songs for My Girlfriends* (Johannesburg: Village Gossip Productions, 2011), p. 28. © Napo Masheane

Chapter 4

Figure 4.1 Graphic design by Carol Burmeister

Chapter 7

Figure 7.1 *Of Dreams and Dragons,* 2017. © Cedric Leherle
Figure 7.2 *Love Is . . . ,* 2012. © Cedric Leherle
Figure 7.3 *The Kiss,* 2004. © Cedric Leherle
Figure 7.4 *This Side Up,* 2003. © Cedric Leherle

Chapter 10

Figure 10.1 *Erasure 2*, 2017. © Thania Petersen

Figure 10.2 *Androgenia – a beautiful boy*, 2004. © Keorapetse Mosimane

Figure 10.3 *Mazibuko family, Thokoza*, 2016, from the series *Gone and There*. © Tshepiso Mazibuko

Figure 10.4 *Erasure 1*, 2017. © Thania Petersen

Figure 10.5 *B(e)aring our Load*, 2004. © Keorapetse Mosimane

Figure 10.6 *Neo le Katleho*, 2016, from the series *Gone and There*. © Tshepiso Mazibuko

Figure 10.7 *Erasure 3*, 2017. © Thania Petersen

Chapter 12

Extract of 'untitled' by Vangile Gantsho, in Vangile Gantsho, *red cotton* (Tshwane: Impepho Press, 2018), p. 9. © Vangile Gantsho

Extract of 'SUICIDE' by Koleka Putuma, in Koleka Putuma, *Collective Amnesia* (Cape Town: uHlanga Press, 2017), p. 73. © Koleka Putuma, uHlanga Press, 2017

Extract of 'schizophenia' by Vangile Gantsho, in Vangile Gantsho, *red cotton* (Tshwane: Impepho Press, 2018), p. 26. © Vangile Gantsho

Extract of 'The History of Intimacy' by Gabeba Baderoon, in Gabeba Baderoon, *The History of Intimacy: Poems* (Cape Town: Kwela Books, 2018), p. 66. © Gabeba Baderoon; reproduced with permission of Kwela, an imprint of NB Publishers

Extract of 'The Father, The Mother, The Girl at the table with lights' by Sindiswa Busuku-Mathese, in Sindiswa Busuku-Mathese, *Loud and Yellow Laughter* (Johannesburg: Botsotso, 2016), p. 27. © Sindiswa Busuku-Mathese

Extract of 'Magic Wonder' by Busisiwe Mahlangu, in Busisiwe Mahlangu, *Surviving Loss* (Tshwane: Impepho Press, 2018), p. 47. © Busisiwe Mahlangu

Extract of 'untitled' by Vangile Gantsho, in Vangile Gantsho, *red cotton* (Tshwane: Impepho Press, 2018), p. 2. © Vangile Gantsho

Extract of 'rescue' by Busisiwe Mahlangu, in Busisiwe Mahlangu, *Surviving Loss* (Tshwane: Impepho Press, 2018), p. 28. © Busisiwe Mahlangu

Extract of 'small girl' by Vangile Gantsho, in Vangile Gantsho, *red cotton* (Tshwane: Impepho Press, 2018), p. 11. © Vangile Gantsho

Extract of 'I'm standing in the middle of the road' by Vangile Gantsho, in Vangile Gantsho, *red cotton* (Tshwane: Impepho Press, 2018), p. 3. © Vangile Gantsho

Extract of 'Twenty-one Ways of Leaving' by Koleka Putuma, in Koleka Putuma, *Collective Amnesia* (Cape Town: uHlanga Press, 2017), p. 45. © Koleka Putuma, uHlanga Press, 2017

Extract of 'small girl' by Vangile Gantsho, in Vangile Gantsho, *red cotton* (Tshwane: Impepho Press, 2018), p. 11. © Vangile Gantsho

Extract of 'breathing under water' by Vangile Gantsho, in Vangile Gantsho, *red cotton* (Tshwane: Impepho Press, 2018), p. 13. © Vangile Gantsho

Extract of 'untitled' by Danai S. Mupotsa, in Danai S. Mupotsa, *feeling and ugly* (Tshwane: Impepho Press, 2018), p. 4. © Danai S. Mupotsa

Extract of 'Inheritance – His'. Copyright © 1993 by Audre Lorde, from THE COLLECTED POEMS OF AUDRE LORDE by Audre Lorde. Used by permission of W.W. Norton & Company, Inc.

Extract of 'The Word' by Gabeba Baderoon, in Gabeba Baderoon, *The History of Intimacy: Poems* (Cape Town: Kwela Books, 2018), p. 56. © Gabeba Baderoon, reproduced with permission of Kwela, an imprint of NB Publishers

Extracts of 'Mother's Lyric' by Sindiswa Busuku-Mathese, in Sindiswa Busuku-Mathese, *Loud and Yellow Laughter* (Johannesburg: Botsoso, 2016), p. 34. © Sindiswa Busuku-Mathese

Extract of 'breathing under water' by Vangile Gantsho, in Vangile Gantsho, *red cotton* (Tshwane: Impepho Press, 2018), p. 13. © Vangile Gantsho

Chapter 16

A version of this essay was delivered as part of Panashe Chigumadzi's 2019 TEDxEuston talk, also entitled 'Hearing the Silence'. Panashe Chigumadzi | Hearing the Silence | TEDxEuston 2019

Chapter 17

Figure 17.2 WBG Messina Departure group, 2016. © Sandra Barrilaro – Rumbo a Gaza

Figure 17.2 IOF approach the WBG in Zodiac boats, 35 miles from Gaza, 2016. © Sandra Barrilaro – Rumbo a Gaza

Chapter 18

Extract of 'These Hands' by Makhosazana Xaba, in Makhosazana Xaba, *These Hands* (Elim: Timbila Poetry Project, 2005), p. 12i. © Makhosazana Xaba

Chapter 19

Extract of 'Untitled' by Yvette Abrahams, in Poet on Watch, *Sageburner: Simple Pleasures* (Austin, Texas: Freeverse Publishing, 2012), p. 83. © Yvette Abrahams

Chapter 20

Patricia McFadden, 'Contemporarity: Sufficiency in a Radical African Feminist Life', in *Meridians* 17, no. 2 (2018), 415–431. © 2018 Smith College. All rights reserved. Republished by permission of the copyright holder, and the present publisher, Duke University Press. www.dukepress.edu

Index

Printed in the USA
CPSIA information can be obtained
at www.ICGtesting.com
LVHW092007181223
766777LV00003B/317